Learning English for
Academic Purposes

Second Edition

LISTENING AND SPEAKING

DR. KEN BEATTY

D0207135

PEARSON

Montréal

Managing Editor
Patricia Hynes

Project Editor
Linda Barton

Proofreaders
Mairi MacKinnon
Brian Parsons

Coordinator, Rights and Permissions
Pierre Richard Bernier

Art Director
Hélène Cousineau

Graphic Design Coordinator
Lyse LeBlanc

Book and Cover Design
Frédérique Bouvier

Book Layout
Interscript

Dedication

To all teachers who share the passion of Plutarch's words:
"*The mind is not a vessel to be filled but a fire to be kindled.*"
And, for a life of ideas, inspiration and love, to my wife, Ann,
and my sons, Nathan and Spencer.

Audio Text Credits

Chapter 1, p. 7 "Tai Chi: A Healthy Exercise for All Ages" © Flying Squirrel Media.

Chapter 2, p. 35 "Where Did I Put … My Memory?" © Morag Loves Company.

Chapter 3, p. 47 "Stealth Social Marketing" © Canadian Broadcasting Corporation.

Chapter 4, p. 71 "Self-Promotion for Introverts" © CBS Interactive Inc.

Chapter 5, p. 92 "Fostering Innovation" © Canadian Broadcasting Corporation.

Chapter 6, p. 105 "Eradication of Smallpox" © WHO. p. 114 "A Better Way to Treat Malaria" © Médecins Sans Frontières.

Chapter 7, p. 132 "Getting Comfortable Taking Innovation Risks" © Phil McKinney & Techtrend Group LLC.

Chapter 8, p. 152 "The 100-Mile Diet" © Don Genova and Pacific Palate Enterprises.

© ÉDITIONS DU RENOUVEAU PÉDAGOGIQUE INC. (ERPI), 2012
ERPI publishes and distributes PEARSON ELT products in Canada.

5757 Cypihot Street
Saint-Laurent, Québec H4S 1R3
CANADA
Telephone: 1 800 263-3678
Fax: 1 866 334-0448
infoesl@pearsonerpi.com
http://pearsonelt.ca

Registration of copyright – Bibliothèque et Archives nationales du Québec, 2012
Registration of copyright – Library and Archives Canada, 2012

Printed in Canada   123456789   HLN 16 15 14 13 12
ISBN 978-2-7613-4583-5   134583 ABCD   OF10

INTRODUCTION

Learning English for Academic Purposes (LEAP) recognizes that traditional English programs do not always supply students with the thinking and language skills they need for college or university. *LEAP: Listening and Speaking* takes a cross-curricular approach, focusing on the development of critical-thinking skills while giving students opportunities to explore content from a range of subject areas.

Students who use *LEAP: Listening and Speaking* will listen to texts from a range of university disciplines and engage in discussions on open-ended questions. In each chapter, students are exposed to a variety of listening genres and different perspectives as they work toward individual or group assignments requiring structured presentations and debates. Along the way, students build their comprehension of concepts and vocabulary, including selections from the Academic Word List. Each chapter also features an opportunity to conduct research and to apply learning using different graphical tools, such as maps, mind maps, timelines and a variety of charts.

In an ever-changing world, students need critical-thinking and interaction skills. They need to know how to engage in active listening, understand the subtext of the messages they hear and fashion their own responses using informative, compelling and persuasive language in formal and informal settings. *LEAP: Listening and Speaking* provides students with opportunities to do all this and more, through thought-provoking listenings and tasks.

ACKNOWLEDGEMENTS

Any book of this scope requires the help of many heroes—teachers who give their time and ideas to help shape the materials that they and others will use. My thanks to Irene Kosmas, Humber College; Janice G. T. Penner, Douglas College; Marlene Toews Janzen, University of Ottawa; Julia MacDonald, Brock University; Jean Nielsen, Seneca College; Jeremy Hawbaker, University of Manitoba; François Desaulniers, L'Université du Québec à Montréal; and Ana-Marija Petrunic, University of Calgary. Thanks also to my creative and vigilant editors, Patricia Hynes and Linda Barton, and the whole Pearson ELT Canada team. And finally, my very great thanks to Julia Williams, who wrote the first edition of *LEAP* and the companion volume to this book, *LEAP: Reading and Writing*.

HIGHLIGHTS

The **overview** outlines the chapter features and expectations.

The **Gearing Up** section elicits existing knowledge by asking students to think critically about the chapter topic.

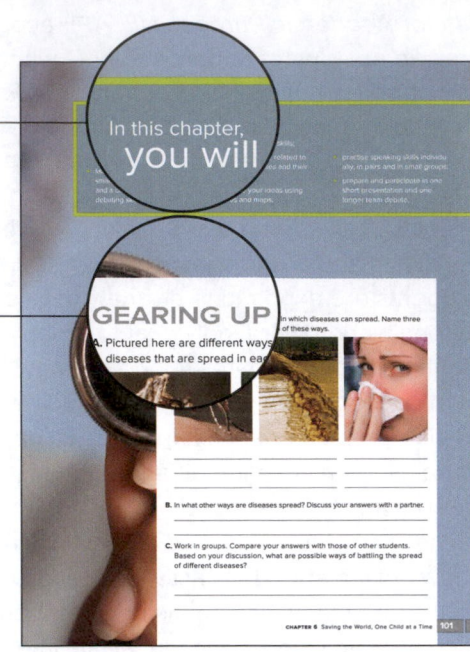

Each chapter contains three **listening** passages, offering different perspectives on an issue. Student dialogues in Listening 3 ground students in the application of the ideas to the final presentation or debate.

Before You Listen activities elicit students' prior knowledge of a subject and stimulate interest.

While You Listen activities engage students in a variety of active listening strategies, including note-taking.

After You Listen activities give students an opportunity to reflect on personal or larger issues related to what they have heard.

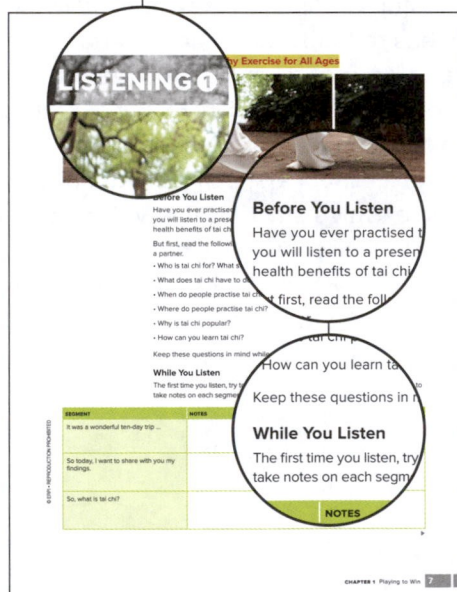

The **Warm-Up Assignment** helps students prepare a short presentation featuring different skills and presentation aids.

Vocabulary Build sections aid comprehension and develop awareness of key vocabulary on the Academic Word List. There are two sections per chapter, with many key words reinforced in Listening 3.

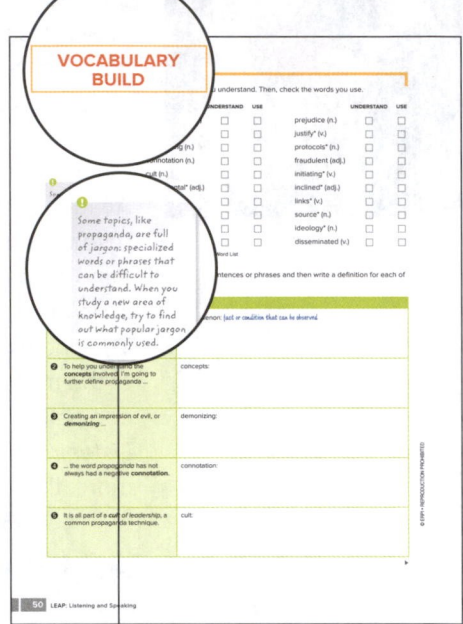

Sidebars clarify and enliven learning.

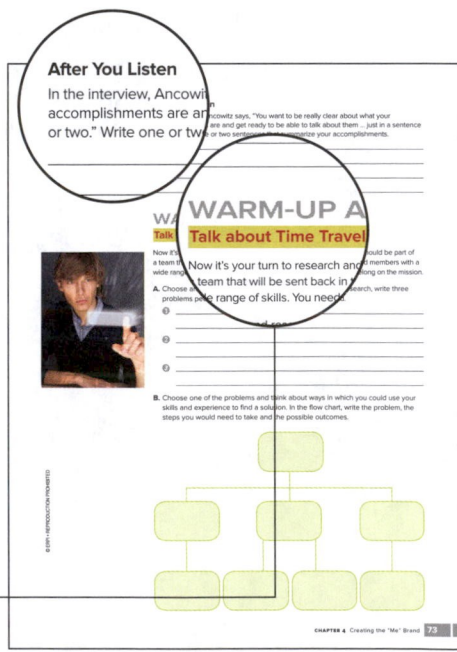

Focus on Listening prepares students to examine and interpret different graphical tools when they listen to presentations. It covers maps, mind maps, timelines and a variety of charts.

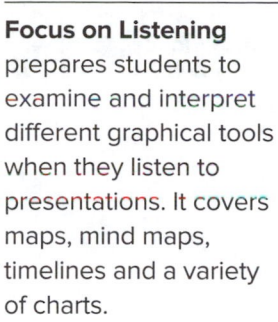
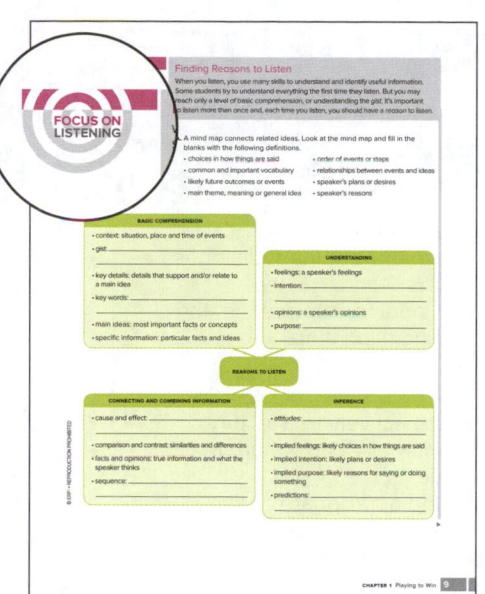

Focus on Speaking builds students' confidence by exploring common speaking and presentation strategies.

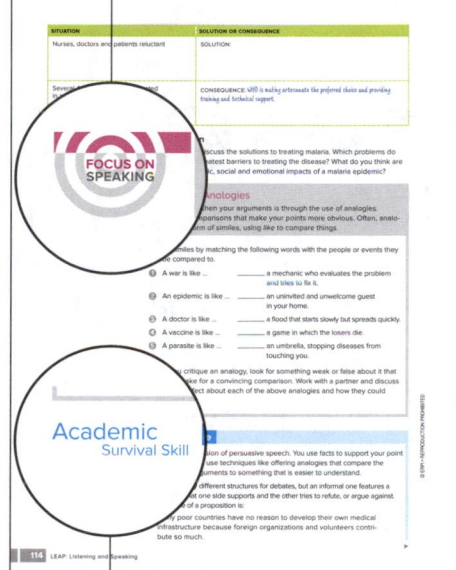

The **Final Assignment** integrates everything students have learned in the chapter and provides an opportunity to apply it in a researched and structured presentation or debate.

Academic Survival Skills help students learn effective research, documentation, critical-thinking and presentation skills.

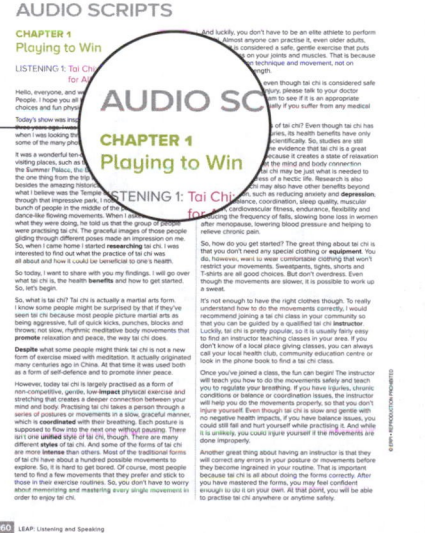

Complete **audio scripts** for all the listenings support students in linking what they hear to what they read. Vocabulary Build words are highlighted in bold.

SCOPE AND SEQUENCE

CHAPTER	LISTENING	SPEAKING
CHAPTER 1 **PLAYING TO WIN** SUBJECT AREAS: physical education, psychology, library science	• Listening actively to a podcast, a lecture and a student dialogue • Finding reasons to listen • Understanding, interpreting and explaining mind maps	• Preparing a presentation • Scripting a speech
CHAPTER 2 **LIFELONG LEARNING** SUBJECT AREAS: education, psychology, sociology	• Listening actively to a lecture, a documentary and a student dialogue • Choosing appropriate charts • Understanding, interpreting and explaining radar charts	• Talking about data • Preparing and using handouts in a presentation
CHAPTER 3 **SELLING DREAMS** SUBJECT AREAS: marketing, political science	• Listening actively to an interview, a lecture and a student dialogue • Understanding, interpreting and explaining timelines	• Changing minds through persuasive speech
CHAPTER 4 **CREATING THE "ME" BRAND** SUBJECT AREAS: marketing, psychology, history	• Listening actively to a lecture, an interview and a student dialogue • Understanding, interpreting and explaining flow charts	• Anticipating and dealing with questions during and after a presentation
CHAPTER 5 **PUTTING THE SCIENTIFIC METHOD TO WORK** SUBJECT AREAS: science, innovation, anthropology	• Listening actively to a lecture, an interview and a student dialogue • Understanding, interpreting and explaining Venn diagrams	• Referencing speeches • Using persuasive language
CHAPTER 6 **SAVING THE WORLD, ONE CHILD AT A TIME** SUBJECT AREAS: medicine, geography, sociology	• Listening actively to two podcasts and a student dialogue • Understanding, interpreting and explaining maps	• Working with analogies • Learning how to prepare for and participate in an informal debate
CHAPTER 7 **EMBRACING RISK** SUBJECT AREAS: history, psychology, sociology	• Listening actively to a lecture, a podcast and a student dialogue • Understanding, interpreting and explaining line charts	• Paraphrasing • Learning extended brainstorming techniques
CHAPTER 8 **SLOW FOOD, PLEASE!** SUBJECT AREAS: agricultural science, health and nutrition	• Listening actively to a lecture, an interview and a student dialogue • Understanding, interpreting and explaining pie charts	• Learning how to prepare for and participate in a formal debate • Creating an image in listeners' minds

WARM-UP ASSIGNMENT (SPEAKING)	FINAL ASSIGNMENT (SPEAKING)	CRITICAL THINKING
• Researching an extreme sport for a short presentation (5 min)	• Researching and creating a thesis statement for a longer presentation on a sports topic (10 min)	• Identifying critical ideas for a persuasive speech • Constructing and supporting a thesis
• Exploring exam question challenges for a short presentation featuring a radar chart (5 min)	• Researching a topic in lifelong learning for a longer presentation featuring a handout and a radar chart (10 min)	• Examining a taxonomy of thinking skills • Analyzing and prioritizing life goals
• Using propaganda techniques in a short presentation featuring a timeline (5 min)	• Researching a historical issue for a longer persuasive presentation featuring a timeline (10 min)	• Assessing messages for propaganda techniques • Constructing a problem/solution argument
• Presenting yourself in an interview as a candidate for a time-travel team (5 min)	• Researching the risks, failures and successes of a famous person for a longer presentation featuring a flow chart (10 min)	• Assessing and interpreting risk • Determining consequences of life decisions
• Researching a scientific topic for a joint presentation featuring a Venn diagram (10 min)	• Researching a scientific issue for a longer joint persuasive presentation featuring a Venn diagram (10 min)	• Applying the scientific method to a new problem • Assessing innovation • Classifying urban myths
• Researching and explaining a map of the distribution of a disease for a short presentation (5 min)	• Researching, preparing and participating in an informal debate on a medical issue, using one or more maps as evidence	• Interpreting spatial distributions of disease • Assessing methodologies in the treatment of disease
• Researching degrees of risk in everyday activities for a short presentation featuring a line chart (5 min)	• Researching a famous risk-taker for a longer presentation featuring a line chart and followed by a group brainstorming activity (10 min)	• Assessing potential risks, benefits and failures • Examining failure as a precursor to success
• Researching local food sources for a short presentation featuring a pie chart (5 min)	• Researching, preparing and participating in a formal debate on a food issue, using a pie chart as evidence	• Considering the culture of food choices • Constructing and critiquing two sides of a proposition

TABLE OF CONTENTS

CHAPTER 1 • PLAYING TO WIN 2

LISTENING 1 Tai Chi: A Healthy Exercise for All Ages (6:55 min) 7

LISTENING 2 Talking about Library Resources (9:54 min) 12

WARM-UP ASSIGNMENT Talk about an Extreme Sport 14

LISTENING 3 Signposts to a Great Speech (9:41 min) 19

FINAL ASSIGNMENT Give a Presentation 20

CHAPTER 2 • LIFELONG LEARNING 22

LISTENING 1 The Best Way to Learn (11:21 min) 27

WARM-UP ASSIGNMENT Talk about Exam Question Challenges 31

LISTENING 2 Where Did I Put ... My Memory? (9:53 min) 35

LISTENING 3 What's on Your Bucket List? (8:41 min) 38

FINAL ASSIGNMENT Give a Presentation 40

CHAPTER 3 • SELLING DREAMS 42

LISTENING 1 Stealth Social Marketing (9:28 min) 47

LISTENING 2 Understanding Propaganda (12:39 min) 53

WARM-UP ASSIGNMENT Use Propaganda Techniques to Persuade 55

LISTENING 3 A Mountain of Rice (8:51 min) 57

FINAL ASSIGNMENT Give a Persuasive Presentation 59

CHAPTER 4 • CREATING THE "ME" BRAND 60

LISTENING 1 Defining and Marketing Yourself (10:38 min) 65

LISTENING 2 Self-Promotion for Introverts (5:57 min) 71

WARM-UP ASSIGNMENT Talk about Time Travel! 73

LISTENING 3 Imagining Your Future (9:31 min) 75

FINAL ASSIGNMENT Give a Presentation 78

CHAPTER 5 • PUTTING THE SCIENTIFIC METHOD TO WORK 80

LISTENING 1 Introduction to the Scientific Method (13:13 min) 85

WARM-UP ASSIGNMENT Talk about Science 89

LISTENING 2 Fostering Innovation (10:32 min) 92

LISTENING 3 Urban Legends (10:01 min) 96

FINAL ASSIGNMENT Give a Persuasive Presentation 98

CHAPTER 6 • SAVING THE WORLD, ONE CHILD AT A TIME 100

LISTENING 1 Eradication of Smallpox (8:09 min) 105

WARM-UP ASSIGNMENT Talk about Maps 109

LISTENING 2 A Better Way to Beat Malaria (12:16 min) 114

LISTENING 3 Barriers to Solutions (9:57 min) 118

FINAL ASSIGNMENT Prepare for a Debate 120

CHAPTER 7 • EMBRACING RISK 122

LISTENING 1 Emily Carr: A Life Less Ordinary (10:43 min) 126

LISTENING 2 Getting Comfortable Taking Innovation Risks (7:08 min) 132

WARM-UP ASSIGNMENT Talk about Risk-Taking 135

LISTENING 3 First Comes Failure (10:39 min) 137

FINAL ASSIGNMENT Give a Presentation 138

CHAPTER 8 • SLOW FOOD, PLEASE! 140

LISTENING 1 Slow Food—Now! (11:44 min) 145

LISTENING 2 The 100-Mile Diet (4:52 min) 152

WARM-UP ASSIGNMENT Your 100-Mile Diet 154

LISTENING 3 Food Security (12:13 min) 156

FINAL ASSIGNMENT Participate in a Formal Debate 158

AUDIO SCRIPTS 160

PHOTO CREDITS 194

Playing to Win

Are you fit? Do you exercise or play a sport? Why or why not?

The sports and physical activities you participate in are likely to change over your lifetime. Your choices are often influenced by where you live, what family and friends enjoy or what's new, popular and fun.

People have many reasons for getting involved in different sports and activities. They might do so for social reasons, or to improve their health or simply because the sport or the activity is exciting. Often, this feeling of excitement comes with playing competitive sports or taking part in dangerous extreme sports.

In this chapter,
you will

- listen to presentations on tai chi and non-competitive and competitive sports;

- listen to a lecture on how to conduct research in preparation for a presentation;

- learn vocabulary related to sports, research and presentations;

- organize your ideas using tables, mind maps and cue cards;

- practise speaking skills individually, in pairs and in small groups;

- prepare and deliver one short and one longer presentation.

GEARING UP

A. Look at the pictures. What is going on in each one? Ask and answer *W-H* questions (*who*, *what*, *when*, *where*, *why* and *how*). Discuss your answers with a partner.

B. For each picture, choose the best answer to each question and write it in the table.

	①	②	③
WHO	two speed skaters		
WHAT			
WHEN			
WHERE			
WHY			
HOW			

C. Work in groups. Compare your answers with those of other students. Which of the sports or activities interest you? Why?

_____

_____

_____

_____

!

Reading in context
helps you understand
an unfamiliar word when
you understand the words
around it. Sometimes
you cannot guess the
exact meaning but can
understand the general
sense of the word.

A. Check the words you understand. Then, check the words you use. The part of speech is shown in parentheses next to each word.

	UNDERSTAND	USE		UNDERSTAND	USE
researching* (v.)	☐	☐	minimal* (adj.)	☐	☐
benefits* (n.)	☐	☐	focuses (v.)	☐	☐
promote (v.)	☐	☐	utilizing* (v.)	☐	☐
despite* (prep.)	☐	☐	stress (n.)	☐	☐
impact (n.)	☐	☐	depression* (n.)	☐	☐
coordinated* (v.)	☐	☐	equipment (n.)	☐	☐
unified* (adj.)	☐	☐	instructor* (n.)	☐	☐
styles (n.)	☐	☐	distractions (n.)	☐	☐
intense* (adj.)	☐	☐	overall* (adj.)	☐	☐

* Appears on the Academic Word List

B. Read the following sentences or phrases and then write a definition for each of the words in bold.

WORDS IN CONTEXT	DEFINITION
❶ So, when I came home, I started **researching** tai chi.	researching: *getting all the necessary facts and information for a new topic*
❷ I will go over what tai chi is, the health **benefits** and how to get started.	benefits:
❸ ... most people picture martial arts as being aggressive ... not slow, rhythmic meditative body movements that **promote** relaxation ...	promote:
❹ **Despite** what some people might think, tai chi is not a new form of exercise mixed with meditation.	despite:
❺ However, today tai chi is largely practised as a form of non-competitive, gentle, low-**impact** physical exercise and stretching ...	impact:
❻ Practising tai chi takes a person through a series of postures or movements ... which is **coordinated** with their breathing.	coordinated:

▶

© ERPI • REPRODUCTION PROHIBITED

WORDS IN CONTEXT	DEFINITION
7 There isn't one **unified** style of tai chi, though.	unified:
8 There are many different **styles** of tai chi.	styles:
9 And some of the forms of tai chi are more **intense** than others.	intense:
10 ... it is considered a safe, gentle exercise that puts **minimal** stress on your joints and muscles.	minimal:
11 That is because tai chi **focuses** on technique and movement, not on **utilizing** sheer strength.	focuses:
	utilizing:
12 Research is also showing that tai chi may also have other benefits beyond **stress** reduction, such as reducing anxiety and **depression** ...	stress:
	depression:
13 The great thing about tai chi is that you don't need any special clothing or **equipment**.	equipment:
14 ... I would recommend joining a tai chi class in your community so that you can be guided by a qualified tai chi **instructor**.	instructor:
15 ... find somewhere quiet so that you can practise without disturbances or **distractions**.	distractions:
16 If you do, it will help you to improve your cardiovascular fitness ... as well as decrease your stress and improve your **overall** well-being.	overall:

C. Check your definitions with a partner. If you cannot understand some words, look them up in a dictionary.

The more ways you can think about a word, the easier it is to remember!

D. When you need to learn new words, it helps if you know how they are formed. Some words are based on root words that are easier to understand. Underline the root word in each of the following.

coordinated	distractions	focuses	researching
depression	equipment	instructor	

E. Some words have more than one meaning, depending on whether they are used as a verb (an action word) or a noun (a person, place or thing). For example, look at the word *benefits*.

• You can use *benefits* as a *verb*:

Exercise **benefits** me by keeping me healthy.

• You can use *benefits* as a *noun*:

There are many **benefits** to exercise.

Write sentences using the following words, first as a verb, then as a noun.

1 research

VERB: *He will research sports at the library.*

NOUN: *She read some research about sports medicine.*

2 focus

VERB: _____

_____

NOUN: _____

_____

3 impact

VERB: _____

_____

NOUN: _____

_____

4 stress

VERB: _____

_____

NOUN: _____

_____

5 style

VERB: _____

_____

NOUN: _____

_____

Before You Listen

Have you ever practised tai chi or watched as others practised? In this section, you will listen to a presentation by Talli van Sunder, who will talk about the health benefits of tai chi.

But first, read the following questions and then discuss possible answers with a partner.

• Who is tai chi for? What sorts of people practise it?

• What does tai chi have to do with martial arts?

• When do people practise tai chi?

• Where do people practise tai chi?

• Why is tai chi popular?

• How can you learn tai chi?

Keep these questions in mind while you listen to the presentation.

While You Listen

The first time you listen, try to get the general idea, or the *gist*. Listen a second time to take notes on each segment. Listen a third time to check your notes and add details.

SEGMENT	NOTES
It was a wonderful ten-day trip ...	
So today, I want to share with you my findings.	
So, what is tai chi?	

SEGMENT	NOTES
Despite what some people might think, tai chi is not a new ...	
However, today tai chi is largely practised as a form of ...	
And luckily, you don't have to be an elite athlete to perform tai chi.	
With that being said, even though tai chi is considered safe ...	
So, what are the benefits of tai chi?	
So, how do you get started?	
It's not enough to have the right clothes, though.	
Once you've joined a class, the fun can begin!	
Another great thing about having an instructor, ...	
That is another advantage to tai chi. Unlike other forms of exercise, ...	
And don't forget, in order to reap the greatest benefits of tai chi ...	

After You Listen

Review your notes. Think about what you've written. Add other details or thoughts to your notes, such as examples that help you understand.

Finding Reasons to Listen

When you listen, you use many skills to understand and identify useful information. Some students try to understand everything the first time they listen. But you may reach only a level of basic comprehension, or understanding the *gist*. It's important to listen more than once and, each time you listen, you should have a *reason* to listen.

A. A mind map connects related ideas. Look at the mind map and fill in the blanks with the following definitions.

- choices in how things are said
- common and important vocabulary
- likely future outcomes or events
- main theme, meaning or general idea
- order of events or steps
- relationships between events and ideas
- speaker's plans or desires
- speaker's reasons

BASIC COMPREHENSION

- context: situation, place and time of events
- gist: _____
  _____
- key details: details that support and/or relate to a main idea
- key words: _____
  _____
- main ideas: most important facts or concepts
- specific information: particular facts and ideas

UNDERSTANDING

- feelings: a speaker's feelings
- intention: _____
  _____
- opinions: a speaker's opinions
- purpose: _____
  _____

REASONS TO LISTEN

CONNECTING AND COMBINING INFORMATION

- cause and effect: _____
  _____
- comparison and contrast: similarities and differences
- facts and opinions: true information and what the speaker thinks
- sequence: _____
  _____

INFERENCE

- attitudes: _____
  _____
- implied feelings: likely choices in how things are said
- implied intention: likely plans or desires
- implied purpose: likely reasons for saying or doing something
- predictions: _____
  _____

B. Look at six different situations during which people listen. What reason for listening do you have for each? Match the reason to the situation.

❶ Don't panic. Please walk quickly to the emergency exit.

❷ This one is less expensive but has more chocolate.

❸ But why did he marry a horse?

❹ Third, you need to make sure the braces around the leg are secure.

❺ It not only cuts carrots and potatoes three ways …

❻ You will meet a tall, dark stranger.

REASON FOR LISTENING

_____ listen for facts and opinions   _____ listen for sequence   _____ listen to make predictions

_____ listen for implied feelings   _____ listen for specific detail   _____ listen to compare and contrast

---

VOCABULARY BUILD

> ❗ A word like "process" is a verb with different tenses, e.g., "processed" and "processing." It is also a noun, e.g., "the writing" "process," and certain forms can function as adjectives, e.g., "processed" and "unprocessed" food. A related word, "procession," is a kind of formal walk.

A. Check the words you understand. Then, check the words you use.

	UNDERSTAND	USE		UNDERSTAND	USE
resources* (n.)	☐	☐	contradictory (adj.)	☐	☐
academic* (adj.)	☐	☐	objective (n.)	☐	☐
presentation (n.)	☐	☐	process (n.)	☐	☐
source* (n.)	☐	☐	thesis (n.)	☐	☐
unstable* (adj.)	☐	☐	journals (n.)	☐	☐

* Appears on the Academic Word List

B. Read the following sentences or phrases and then write a definition for each of the words in bold.

WORDS IN CONTEXT	DEFINITION
1 Today, I will talk about how to get information from a variety of **resources** ...	resources: *tools or supplies of assets, used to provide information*
2 ... and, most importantly, identify which ones are good **academic** sources ...	academic:
3 I understand that for your class you have to do a **presentation** on some kind of extreme sport.	presentation:
4 *Wikipedia* is a great **source**, but it's not a particularly academic one.	source:
5 It is general information, and it is also quite **unstable**.	unstable:
6 Anyone who looks up the reference after an edit might find different or even **contradictory** information.	contradictory:
7 Our **objective** is to find some basic terms we can follow up with in more academic sources.	objective:
8 In an expository essay, you could talk about the **process**, that is, how to do the particular sport.	process:
9 We call this point a **thesis** statement.	thesis:
10 The library has a wide collection of videos, computer programs and **journals**.	journals:

C. Check your definitions with a partner. If you do not understand some words, look them up in a dictionary.

D. Another way of understanding and remembering words is to look for their opposites or *antonyms*. Find the antonyms of the following key words.

KEY WORD	ANTONYM
❶ contradict	_____ informal
❷ academic	_____ product
❸ unstable	_____ agree with
❹ process	_____ stable

LISTENING ❷ — Talking about Library Resources

Before You Listen

Listen to a presentation by Joseph Cornell, a reference librarian at the Central Library. Dr. Cornell is speaking about library research resources to a group of students who have to prepare presentations on some kind of extreme sport.

But first, which of these sports do you know? Write the name under each photo. Check your answers with a partner.

1

_____ barefoot water skiing _____

2

3

4

⑤

⑥

⑦

⑧

Here is the first segment of the presentation. Read it and try to answer as many of the *W-H* questions as you can.

"Hello, and welcome to Central Library. My name is Joseph Cornell and I am a reference librarian. Today, I will talk about how to get information from a variety of resources and, most importantly, identify which ones are good academic sources, suitable for college or university research. If you have any questions, please take notes and save them until the end."

W-H QUESTIONS	ANSWER	*W-H* QUESTIONS	ANSWER
WHO	Joseph Cornell	WHERE	
WHAT		WHY	
WHEN		HOW	

While You Listen

Joseph Cornell talks about five types of presentations or essays. What is each type used for?

TYPE OF PRESENTATION/ESSAY	WHAT IS ITS PURPOSE?
DEFINITION	To explain something through a careful description
COMPARE AND CONTRAST	
EXPOSITORY	
ARGUMENTATIVE	
CAUSE AND EFFECT	

After You Listen

Here are nine extreme sports. Classify them in the table below according to whether they are air sports, land sports or water sports.

• BMX	• high wire	• snorkelling
• extreme motocross	• jet skiing	• street luge
• hang-gliding	• sandboarding	• wakeboarding

EXTREME AIR SPORTS	EXTREME LAND SPORTS	EXTREME WATER SPORTS
• gliding	• indoor climbing	• barefoot water skiing
• ski jumping	• mountain biking	• scuba diving
• skydiving	• outdoor climbing	• speed sailing
• sky surfing	• snowboarding	• surfing
• sky flying	• speed skating	• windsurfing
• _____	• _____	• _____
• _____	• _____	• _____
	• _____	• _____
	• _____	

WARM-UP ASSIGNMENT

Talk about an Extreme Sport

Now it's time to research and present a short talk on an extreme sport.

A. Choose and research one of the following sports.

- barefoot water skiing
- climbing
  (indoor or outdoor)
- extreme skiing
- gliding
- scuba diving
- sky flying
- sky surfing
- speed biking
- speed sailing
- speed skating
- surfing
- windsurfing

B. Find one source online (other than *Wikipedia*) and one source in a library about the extreme sport you chose. Note the information here.

SOURCE 1: _____

_____

SOURCE 2: _____

_____

C. Use your sources to write a definition presentation. Start by answering as many *W-H* questions as possible.

W-H QUESTIONS	ANSWER	RESOURCE	
WHO		☐ online	☐ library
WHAT		☐ online	☐ library
WHEN		☐ online	☐ library
WHERE		☐ online	☐ library
WHY		☐ online	☐ library
HOW		☐ online	☐ library

D. Prepare your presentation. Write your notes on a separate sheet of paper, using your *W-H* answers to guide you. Your presentation should last for approximately five minutes. Don't read from the page, but you may use cue cards with a few words to remind you of important points.

Preparing Your Presentation

Think about a speaker or presenter you have heard who impressed you. Why did her or his presentation stand out? What made it special?

A presentation can be divided into *content*, *structure* and *delivery*.

Content refers to what you are talking about—the main idea of your presentation.

The *structure* is how you organize your message from the introduction to the conclusion, as well as any visual aids you use, such as computer slides.

Delivery refers to how you use your voice, your body language and your overall manner—how casual or formal you are.

A. Read the following comments. Why would you *not* want to listen to these presenters? What should each have done differently? Discuss with a partner.

> What's he wearing? And look at the way he's slouching on the lectern.

> Have you seen his face? He's had his back to us during the whole presentation!

> Please tell me she's not going to read all those pages to us!

> She's so nervous; she really shouldn't be holding that paper.

> Why does he cross his arms and keep looking at the floor?

> I've never heard anyone speak so quickly! What's the rush?

B. When you prepare a presentation, you need to choose appropriate language. Writing is good for sharing *detailed information*. Speaking is good for sharing *ideas*.

When you organize the content of your presentation, identify the main idea and then use a few details or examples to illustrate and support that idea. Add explanations to make sure the audience understands the examples. Then, write key words on cue cards to help you remember the important points of your presentation.

Look at the following example.

	IMPORTANT POINTS/EXPLANATIONS	CUE CARD KEY WORDS
MAIN IDEA OR THESIS	Sports are good for your health.	aports, health
EXAMPLE	For example, running can increase the strength of your leg muscles.	running, strong legs
EXPLANATION	Your leg muscles become stronger when they are forced to do more work than usual, such as running instead of walking. These stronger muscles help you avoid injury when you have to suddenly run or otherwise strain your leg muscles.	avoid injury

C. Consider a topic related to sports. Write the main idea, an example and an explanation of that example. Then, review your important points and underline key words. Write the key words in the third column.

	IMPORTANT POINTS/EXPLANATIONS	CUE CARD KEY WORDS
MAIN IDEA OR THESIS		
EXAMPLE		
EXPLANATION		

D. On a separate sheet of paper, write three main ideas and an example with an explanation for each. Practise saying each of them using just cue cards. When you feel ready, practise them in front of a partner. Switch notes and let your partner look at what you've written to make sure you have not forgotten anything. It is okay to say more but don't forget the important points.

FOCUS ON SPEAKING

Scripting Your Speech

Writing a script for a speech is not necessarily about writing everything you will say. Rather, you need to focus on your main points so your speech sounds natural when you deliver it. Many people who seem like experts at giving speeches have actually prepared and practised carefully. For others, sounding natural comes from years of experience that have taught them to form an effective speech in their heads.

A. In the Final Assignment, you will prepare a longer presentation. Think again about the *W-H* questions and how you can apply them when scripting your speech.

Answer the following questions. Not every question will have an answer.

W-H QUESTIONS	YOUR ANSWER
WHY are you speaking? Write an objective. Why is your presentation important? Why should the audience listen to you? Are you telling them something new?	
WHO are you speaking to? Know your audience and your relationship to them. Do they think you're an expert?	
WHAT are you speaking about? Plan an introduction that gets the attention of your audience and a conclusion that asks for action and leaves a strong and lasting impression of your main idea.	
WHEN are you speaking? How much time will you have? Are you leaving time for questions?	
WHERE are you speaking? Different rooms call for different ways of presenting. Will you stand in front of a group or sit with them around a table?	
HOW will you know if your audience understands your message? Invite them to ask questions and ask them questions to learn their opinions of your presentation.	

B. Here are some phrases to help you structure the script for your presentation.

GREETING AND INTRODUCTION

"Hello, my name is … and I'd like to give you a brief presentation on …"

"In this presentation, I'd like to describe/analyze/discuss …"

Or, you might want to use a rhetorical question: "Have you ever thought about …?"

OBJECTIVE

"The purpose of this presentation is to … It is important for you because …"

ORGANIZATION

"First, I'll say something about … Then, I'll go on to talk about … Finally, I'll conclude by saying …"

MAIN POINTS

It is important to make transitions between points, to let your audience know that you are finishing one point and going on to the next point.

"Next, I'd like to turn to …"

"I've discussed … now I'd like to talk about …"

Add examples and explanations.

CONCLUSION

Never end a presentation by saying: "And that is the end of my presentation." Instead, end with a clear and final message that communicates the essence of your presentation.

"I'd like to conclude by saying …"

"To sum up, I'd like to say …"

Or, suggest an action for them to follow: "Now, it's your turn to …"

LISTENING ③ Signposts to a Great Speech

Before You Listen

Stella and Oscar are students discussing their presentations. Stella has already finished hers, but Oscar has barely begun.

Think of advice you would give someone about how to prepare a presentation. Working in a group, discuss your suggestions. Write the five best suggestions.

❶ _____

❷ _____

❸ _____

❹ _____

❺ _____

While You Listen

Listen to Stella's advice to Oscar on how to prepare an effective presentation. While you listen, list the things Oscar does wrong.

_____

_____

_____

_____

_____

_____

_____

_____

_____

After You Listen

Review Stella's advice and what Oscar does wrong. Discuss in a group. Do you or other group members make the same mistakes? Summarize the best advice.

FINAL ASSIGNMENT
Give a Presentation

Now it's your turn. Use everything you have learned in this chapter to prepare for and give a longer presentation of up to ten minutes.

A. Choose a topic related to sports or fitness and write a thesis statement that summarizes what your topic is about, as well as your point of view.

> Example: Walking is the most fun, the least expensive and a very effective form of exercise.

_____

_____

_____

B. Speak with your teacher. Ask for approval of your topic and advice on how to develop it.

C. Do your research. Find out interesting details about your topic from at least three sources.

SOURCE 1: _____

_____

SOURCE 2: _____

_____

SOURCE 3: _____

_____

D. Plan your presentation. Use the following table to write your script.

PRESENTATION STRUCTURE	NOTES
GREETING AND INTRODUCTION	
OBJECTIVE	
ORGANIZATION	
POINT 1	

PRESENTATION STRUCTURE	NOTES
• EXAMPLE	
• EXPLANATION	
POINT 2	
• EXAMPLE	
• EXPLANATION	
CONCLUSION	
QUESTIONS	
THANKS	

E. Prepare cue cards. Underline key words in your presentation notes that will help you remember what you want to say. Use as few key words as possible. It's better to forget to mention one point than to nervously read your whole speech.

F. Practise, practise, practise! Practise your presentation as many times as you can. Speak in front of a mirror until you are comfortable. Then, speak in front of friends or family members. If you are prepared, you won't be as nervous.

Good luck!

CHAPTER 2
Lifelong Learning

What are you going to do with your life? How can learning new things make that happen?

Throughout history, most people have had few opportunities to choose what they would do. If your parents were farmers, it was generally expected that you too would become a farmer. The same was true for most other occupations. These days, more and more people are able to make decisions about what they will do in life and are less and less bound by social class, traditions or local prospects.

Education, technology and opportunities to travel the world mean that you have to think about what you want in life—and how you are going to achieve it.

In this chapter, you will

- listen to a lecture on how we learn, a documentary that looks at memory and a discussion about bucket lists;

- learn vocabulary related to learning and remembering;
- organize your ideas using tables and radar charts;
- learn how to design and use handouts in a presentation;

- practise speaking skills individually, in pairs and in small groups;
- prepare and deliver one short and one longer presentation.

GEARING UP

A. Look at the different skills pictured in the table below. Think about how you might learn each one.

B. Discuss your ideas with a partner. Choose the best ways to learn each skill and write them in the table.

	BEST WAYS TO LEARN
❶	
❷	
❸	

C. Work in groups. Compare your answers with those of other students. Which skill interests you most? Which way of learning interests you? Why?

_____

_____

_____

A. Check the words you understand. Then, check the words you use.

	UNDERSTAND	USE		UNDERSTAND	USE
psychology* (n.)	☐	☐	analyzing* (v.)	☐	☐
mental* (adj.)	☐	☐	statistic* (n.)	☐	☐
evaluating* (v.)	☐	☐	encounter* (v.)	☐	☐
logical* (adj.)	☐	☐	chemical* (adj.)	☐	☐
conjecture (n.)	☐	☐	formula* (n.)	☐	☐
complex* (adj.)	☐	☐	interpret* (v.)	☐	☐
interact* (v.)	☐	☐	criterion* (n.)	☐	☐
adapted* (v.)	☐	☐	insight* (n.)	☐	☐

* Appears on the Academic Word List

B. Read the following sentences or phrases and then write a definition for each of the words in bold.

WORDS IN CONTEXT	DEFINITION
❶ In **psychology**, and most especially in educational psychology, …	psychology: *study of the mind and how it influences people's behaviour*
❷ … the **mental** processes we use in perceiving the world …	mental:
❸ … and was involved in **evaluating** examinations.	evaluating:
❹ He thought that if he could organize the questions in a **logical** way …	logical:
❺ Bloom's **conjecture** that learning is hierarchical in nature …	conjecture:
❻ … learning progresses from the simple to the **complex**.	complex:

▶

WORDS IN CONTEXT	DEFINITION
7 ... see how you understand and **interact** with knowledge ...	interact:
8 ... we now use a model **adapted** by one of his partners ...	adapted:
9 The six levels are *remembering*, *understanding*, *applying*, **analyzing**, *evaluating* and *creating*.	analyzing:
10 ... when you hear a name or a number or a **statistic** and remember it ...	statistic:
11 ... information that is more useful to us or which is built up because we **encounter** certain ideas ...	encounter:
12 ... such as a list of dates or **chemical** formulae.	chemical:
13 Most people can remember Einstein's famous **formula**, $E=MC^2$ ...	formula:
14 For that reason, *understanding* is a higher cognitive level and allows us to **interpret** ...	interpret:
15 ... often based on a **criterion** or set of standards that apply to a particular situation.	criterion:
16 ... you're likely to have **insight** into how you can make a better car.	insight:

C. Check your definitions with a partner. If you do not understand some words, look them up in a dictionary.

D. Match each of the following sciences to its field of study.

SCIENCES	FIELD OF STUDY
1 anthropology	_____ volcanoes
2 biology	_____ music
3 climatology	_____ life
4 criminology	_____ humans
5 ecology	_____ crime and criminals
6 geology	_____ Earth
7 musicology	_____ disease
8 pathology	_____ earthquakes
9 seismology	_____ climate
10 vulcanology	_____ environmental interactions

E. Many words can be modified by the addition of *-ion*, which often indicates an act, a result or a state of something. Write the meaning of each of the following words.

1 adaptation: _____

_____

2 complexion: _____

_____

3 cognition: _____

_____

4 evaluation: _____

_____

5 formulation: _____

_____

6 interaction: _____

_____

7 interpretation: _____

_____

8 memorization: _____

_____

The Best Way to Learn

Before You Listen

Have you ever wondered why some lessons seem easy to learn while others are a struggle? Have you ever thought about how you learn, or if there is a best way to learn? There are different theories on the subject, and in this section, you will listen to a lecture on how some educators approach the idea of learning.

Before you listen to the lecture, discuss these questions with a partner.

• What are some of the ways in which you have learned skills for school and for life in general?

• When facing exams, how do you prepare? What do you do to make sure you know the material?

Here is the first segment of the lecture you will listen to. Underline the words or ideas that are unfamiliar to you.

"Hello, everyone, and welcome to our first class in Educational Psychology. Today, we're going to talk about the work of Benjamin Bloom, and those who followed him, in creating the *taxonomy of cognitive objectives*. Before we begin, let's make sure we all understand the terms. A *taxonomy* is a way of classifying and organizing characteristics of and ideas about something. In biology, for instance, taxonomies group and categorize plants and animals based on similarities and differences and on relationships. In psychology, and most especially in educational psychology, Bloom's interest was with the *cognitive*—and *cognition*—both of which refer to how we learn: the mental processes we use in perceiving the world and in understanding and remembering it."

Write the words or ideas that were unfamiliar to you. Then, discuss them with your partner and work together to write definitions or explanations.

WORD/IDEA: _____

DEFINITION/EXPLANATION: _____

_____

WORD/IDEA: _____

DEFINITION/EXPLANATION: _____

_____

WORD/IDEA: _____

DEFINITION/EXPLANATION: _____

_____

WORD/IDEA: _____

DEFINITION/EXPLANATION: _____

_____

WORD/IDEA: _____

DEFINITION/EXPLANATION: _____

_____

While You Listen

Relate how you learn to the examples in the lecture. The first time you listen, try to get the general idea. Listen a second time to take notes on each of the six levels of the taxonomy. Listen a third time to check your notes and add details.

LEVELS OF THE TAXONOMY	NOTES
LEVEL 1: REMEMBERING	
LEVEL 2: UNDERSTANDING	
LEVEL 3: APPLYING	
LEVEL 4: ANALYZING	
LEVEL 5: EVALUATING	
LEVEL 6: CREATING	

After You Listen

Review your notes. Think about what you've written. Add other details or thoughts to your notes, such as examples that help you understand.

Working with Charts

Many presentations or lectures are accompanied by charts. When you listen to a presentation, it's important to evaluate the chart and anticipate the kind of information the speaker is likely to discuss. This can help you prepare for what the speaker will say and also help you determine whether you agree or disagree with what is being said.

A. Look at the different types of charts. Name each chart and write what each is used for.

❶

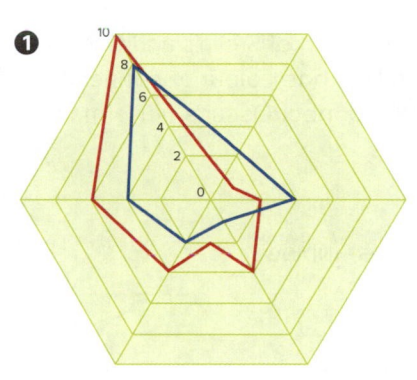

radar chart

used to compare information

_____

❷

_____

_____

_____

❸

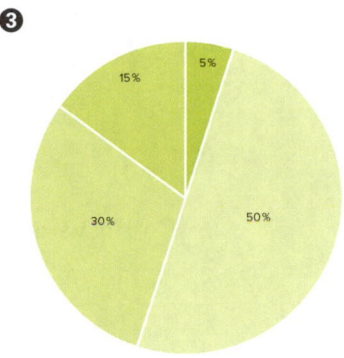

_____

_____

_____

❹

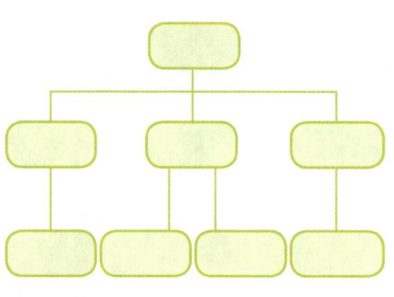

_____

_____

_____

❺

_____

_____

_____

❻

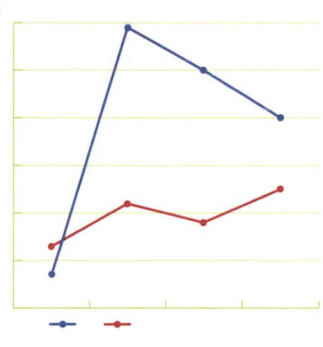

_____

_____

_____

B. A *radar chart* is a way of displaying information that makes it easier to draw comparisons.

Look at how well Stella and Oscar did on questions designed to evaluate the six levels of learning. The test they took had ten questions for each level.

Scores on General Knowledge Test

	STELLA	OSCAR
REMEMBERING	7	8
UNDERSTANDING	7	6
APPLYING	5	7
ANALYZING	9	6
EVALUATING	7	5
CREATING	6	9

C. Use the information in the table to fill in this radar chart of Stella's and Oscar's performance on the general knowledge test. Use one colour to connect Stella's performance and a different colour to connect Oscar's performance.

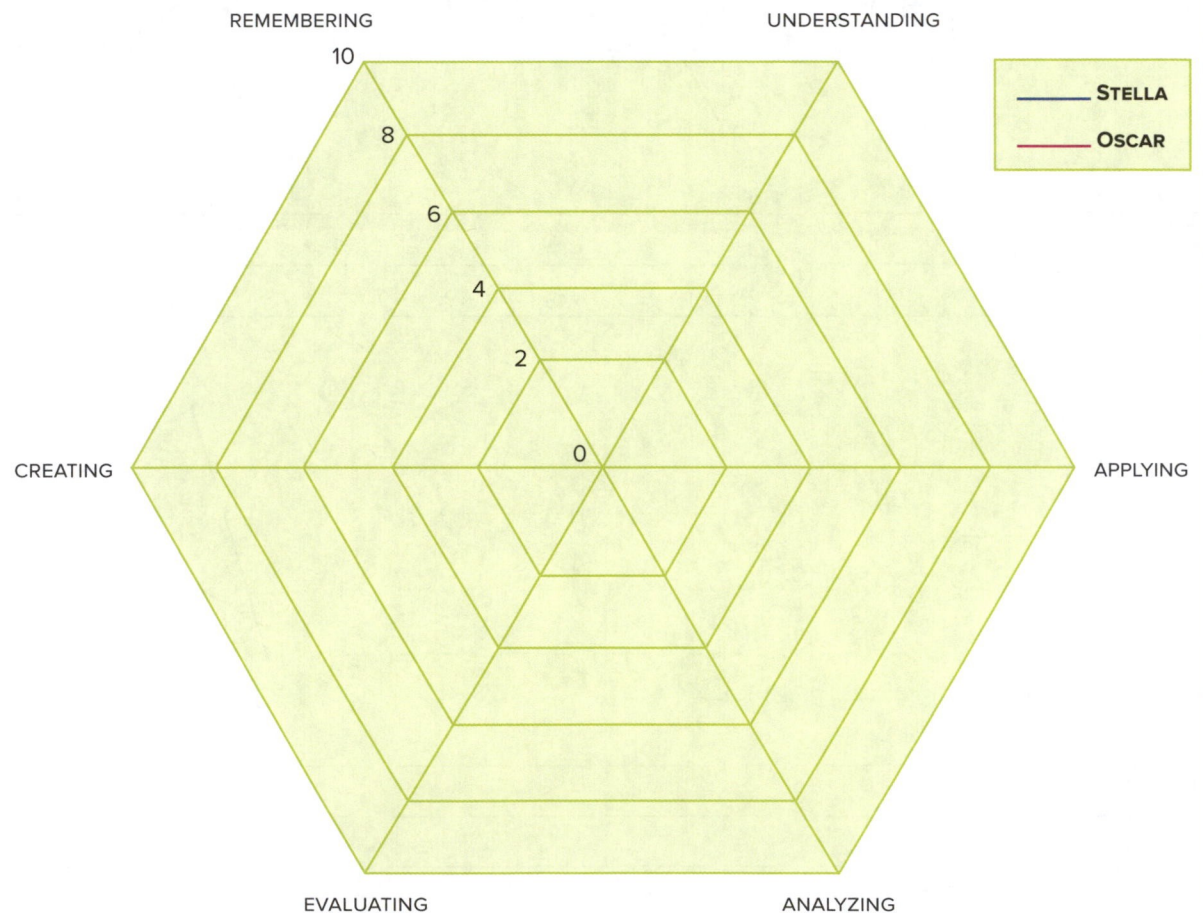

D. What other kinds of information would a radar chart be useful for displaying? Discuss this with a partner.

WARM-UP ASSIGNMENT
Talk about Exam Question Challenges

Now it's your turn to research and present a short talk on exam question challenges.

A. Fill in the following table by rating how challenging exam questions for each level of learning are, according to the Likert scale (least to most challenging) as indicated. First, answer the question yourself; then, interview three other students.

Least Challenging   *Most Challenging*

| 0 | 1 | 2 | 3 | 4 | 5 | 6 | 7 | 8 | 9 | 10 |

LEVEL OF LEARNING	STUDENT 1 (YOU)	STUDENT 2	STUDENT 3	STUDENT 4
REMEMBERING				
UNDERSTANDING				
APPLYING				
ANALYZING				
EVALUATING				
CREATING				

B. Use the information from the table to complete the following radar chart.

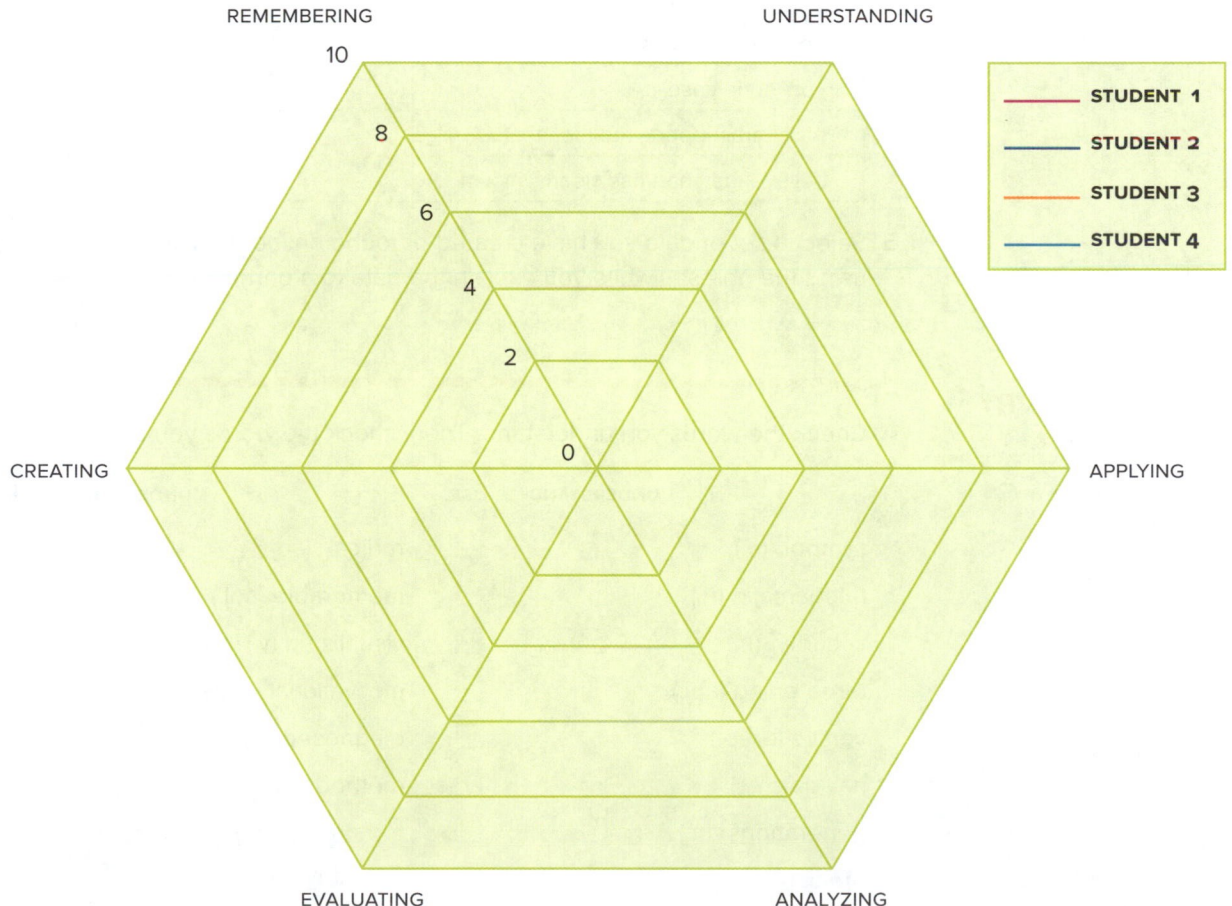

C. Use the information from your radar chart to prepare a compare and contrast presentation. Your presentation should last approximately five minutes. Write your notes on a separate sheet of paper. Use some of the following phrases to get started.

"Today, I'm going to discuss
how challenging exam questions ..."

"Most students think ..."

"Few students think ..."

"Only one student thinks ..."

"From this chart we can see ..."

D. Practise your presentation, using your notes to guide you.

FOCUS ON SPEAKING

Talking about Data

It's never enough to simply show a chart during a presentation: you have to explain the information, or data. When you talk about data, you need to explain findings that are significant or surprising. The data you discuss should support your points, but you should also consider and explain data that do not.

A. Consider the following phrases used to explain data. Write the purpose of each phrase.

PHRASE	PURPOSE
"Today, I'm going to discuss ..."	To introduce the data
"Most of the data shows ..."	
"The data shows few instances of ..."	
"In only one case, ..."	
"This chart supports the idea that ..."	
"I believe the chart has clearly shown ..."	

B. Select a set of data you have created or found online or elsewhere. Practise using the phrases while you explain the data to a partner.

VOCABULARY BUILD

A. Check the words you understand. Then, check the words you use.

	UNDERSTAND	USE		UNDERSTAND	USE
symbol* (n.)	☐	☐	radical* (adj.)	☐	☐
thingamajig (n.)	☐	☐	memorable (adj.)	☐	☐
security* (n.)	☐	☐	visualizing (v.)	☐	☐
threatening (adj.)	☐	☐	motivational* (adj.)	☐	☐
versus (prep.)	☐	☐	diagnosed (v.)	☐	☐
navigate (v.)	☐	☐	methods* (n.)	☐	☐
generations* (n.)	☐	☐	turnaround (n.)	☐	☐
precise* (adj.)	☐	☐	fairy dust (n.)	☐	☐

* Appears on the Academic Word List

B. Read the following sentences or phrases and then write a definition for each of the words in bold.

WORDS IN CONTEXT	DEFINITION
1 These memory masters are a **symbol** of us all ...	symbol: *something that stands for something else*
2 ... we can't remember the word for the **thingamajig** to wash the salad.	thingamajig:
3 ... from PIN numbers to alarm codes to personal **security** passwords ...	security:
4 ... we pay more attention to the act of forgetting as we get older because it's **threatening**.	threatening:
5 Memory is the greatest thing I have—**versus** money, ...	versus:
6 ... sailors learned to **navigate** by memorizing songs that gave directions.	navigate:
7 These songs were a kind of GPS for countless **generations**, ...	generations:
8 The points of the compass that are described in this song are very **precise**.	precise:
9 It's a **radical** sign.	radical:
10 Can we find other techniques that work as well as **memorable** songs?	memorable:
11 By **visualizing** something unique and different involving ...	visualizing:

WORDS IN CONTEXT	DEFINITION
⑫ ... where he is today's **motivational** speaker.	motivational:
⑬ ... he was **diagnosed** with two learning disabilities ...	diagnosed:
⑭ ... ancient Roman **methods** for mastering the mind.	methods:
⑮ And that's when I saw a huge **turnaround**.	turnaround:
⑯ It's not some sprinkling of **fairy dust** on some people that other people don't get ...	fairy dust:

C. Check your definitions with a partner. If you do not understand some words, look them up in a dictionary.

D. Words like *thingamajig* are used when you cannot remember or do not know the name of the thing you want to mention. What other words in English do we use in the same way?

_____gizmo_____ _____ _____ _____

_____ _____ _____ _____

E. Many words have related forms. When you learn one form, try to learn others, as well as phrases that use the word. Write a definition for each of the following.

❶ memory: _____

_____

❷ memorize: _____

_____

❸ memories: _____

_____

❹ walk down memory lane: _____

_____

❺ from memory: _____

_____

❻ in memory of: _____

_____

LISTENING ②   **Where Did I Put ... My Memory?**

Before You Listen

How good is your memory? Has your ability to remember things changed over the past few years? How do you remember best? If you think about the things you do remember, you might find that it is easy to remember subjects you are deeply interested in. But for most things, we need memory techniques to help us.

In this section, you will listen to a documentary about what some people do in order to remember. Before you listen, discuss what you know about memory with a partner. Then, read the following passage and compare your ideas about memory with those of the narrator.

> "It's a battle that's becoming tougher as we live to an older age and are overwhelmed by the information age. We meet people we know but can't recall their names. We forget where we put our purses, our wallets and our keys. Sometimes, we can't remember the word for the thingamajig to wash the salad. And by the way, where did I park my car?"

While You Listen

Take notes on each of the different methods for remembering things. Add details such as examples and your own opinions of how effective each method might be.

METHODS USED TO REMEMBER THINGS

After You Listen

Discuss the different methods with your partner. Which method is the most effective and which is the least effective? Why?

Academic
Survival Skill

Using Handouts

When you are using visual aids, like the radar chart in the Warm-Up Assignment, you have to make decisions about how you share the information. There is a couple of ways to do this, depending on what you want your audience to know and when you want them to know it. For example, you can project your chart as a slide from your computer or you can give it to your audience as a handout.

If you choose a handout, you will need to decide what other information it will contain and at what point in your presentation it should be handed out. If you hand it out at the beginning, your audience may read it before you start speaking or—even worse—while you are speaking. It's probably best to give the handout when you are ready for your audience to look at it.

A. In the Final Assignment, you will be asked to design a handout for your presentation. Decide what information you would want to have on it and what information you would not want to have on it. Give a reason for each choice.

		REASON FOR CHOICE
NAME	yes ☐ no ☐	
DATE	yes ☐ no ☐	
TELEPHONE NUMBER	yes ☐ no ☐	
E-MAIL ADDRESS	yes ☐ no ☐	

		REASON FOR CHOICE
COURSE TITLE	yes ☐ no ☐	
INTRODUCTION	yes ☐ no ☐	
CHART/LEGEND	yes ☐ no ☐	
CONCLUSION	yes ☐ no ☐	
SUMMARY	yes ☐ no ☐	
SOURCE/REFERENCE	yes ☐ no ☐	
OTHER	yes ☐ no ☐	

B. Now, consider how you will introduce your handout and what information will be presented at what points during your presentation.

	INFORMATION TO BE PRESENTED
INTRODUCTION	
BEFORE YOU SPEAK	
WHILE YOU SPEAK	
AFTER YOU SPEAK	

> When someone uses an unfamiliar term like "bucket list," listen to see if the context explains it, but if not, don't be afraid to ask: "Excuse me, what do you mean by ...?"

Before You Listen

Many people write a list of things they want to accomplish before they die or, as the saying goes, before they "kick the bucket." What have you always wanted to do? Perhaps travel, or write the great Canadian novel, learn a new skill, or maybe volunteer to work with less fortunate people or at a wildlife sanctuary?

Think of three things you want to do, before you listen to Oscar and Stella discuss their bucket lists and the kinds of things they would put on them.

① _____

② _____

③ _____

Here is the beginning of Oscar and Stella's conversation. Underline the words or ideas that are unfamiliar to you.

> OSCAR: So, what's on your bucket list, Stella?
>
> STELLA: Bucket list? What's that?
>
> OSCAR: Oh, it's kind of a crude term ... Do you know the expression, "Kick the bucket"? You know, when you don't want to say something unpleasant.
>
> STELLA: You mean a *euphemism*.
>
> OSCAR: Yes, a euphemism, for something you'd rather not say directly. So "kick the bucket" refers to dying.
>
> STELLA: And a bucket list?
>
> OSCAR: Oh, it's a list of things you want to do before you die.
>
> STELLA: Ah, well sure, I think everyone has a list of things they'd like to do. What sort of things are on your list?

Write the words or ideas that were unfamiliar to you. Then, discuss these with a partner and work together to write definitions or explanations.

WORD/IDEA: _____

DEFINITION/EXPLANATION: _____

_____

WORD/IDEA: _____

DEFINITION/EXPLANATION: _____

_____

WORD/IDEA: _____

DEFINITION/EXPLANATION: _____

_____

WORD/IDEA: _____

DEFINITION/EXPLANATION: _____

_____

WORD/IDEA: _____

DEFINITION/EXPLANATION: _____

_____

While You Listen

Oscar and Stella discuss a number of ideas of what to include on a bucket list. Take notes on the general categories.

_____

_____

_____

_____

_____

_____

_____

_____

_____

After You Listen

Work in a group. Compare lists from Before You Listen. Write the five most interesting or most unusual bucket list ideas.

1 _____

2 _____

3 _____

4 _____

5 _____

FINAL ASSIGNMENT
Give a Presentation

Now it's your turn. Use everything you have learned in this chapter to prepare for and give a longer presentation of up to ten minutes.

A. Choose a topic related to learning and what you would like to do in life. Write it below. You might want to take the ideas from your bucket list and think about what training or preparation it would take to achieve them, and then map your progress on a radar chart that you can add to your handout.

_____

_____

_____

B. Speak with your teacher. Ask for approval of your topic and advice on how to develop it.

C. Do your research. Find out interesting details about your topic from at least three sources.

SOURCE 1: _____

_____

SOURCE 2: _____

_____

SOURCE 3: _____

_____

D. Prepare your handout. Refer to the choices you made in Academic Survival Skill (page 36). Think about how you could use a radar chart. For example, your radar chart could have three legs, each one representing a different goal. Divide each leg into ten and use these numbers to indicate, in percentage points, your progress. If you haven't yet begun preparing for any of your goals, then make your chart for a year or five years from now and predict where you will be.

E. Plan your presentation. Use the following table to outline your script.

PRESENTATION STRUCTURE	NOTES
GREETING AND INTRODUCTION	
OBJECTIVE	

▶

PRESENTATION STRUCTURE	NOTES
ORGANIZATION	
POINT 1	
• EXPLANATION	
POINT 2	
• EXPLANATION	
POINT 3	
• EXPLANATION	
QUESTIONS	
THANKS	

F. Practise, practise, practise! Practise your presentation. Make sure your handout is complete and useful and find ways to refer to it during your presentation.

Some speakers may be nervous. If so, the handouts they are holding can flutter like leaves in the wind. If you are nervous, don't hold your handout; put it in front of you on a table or desk. But better yet, don't be nervous!

CHAPTER 3

Selling Dreams

It's hard for many of us to imagine life before the digital age. A lot of our personal communications, news and information gathering, shopping, self-expression, schooling and work are done online. We are influenced by what we see and do online, but we also help to shape the online world; when we write a blog, post a comment, make a purchase, recommend a website, we are working with millions of other people to define what is valuable and useful on the Internet.

Shaping ideas and opinions has always been important to companies and organizations, and now they are extending their influence online.

How much are you using the online world and how much is it using you?

- listen to an interview on stealth social marketing, a lecture on propaganda and a discussion on viral marketing;

- learn vocabulary related to propaganda techniques and viral marketing;

- organize your ideas using tables and timelines;

- learn the goals of persuasive speech and the steps to successful viral marketing;

- practise speaking skills individually, in pairs and in small groups;

- prepare and deliver one short and one longer presentation.

GEARING UP

A. Work with three other students and discuss reasons why you use the Internet and the kind of information it can provide.

B. List the five most popular reasons. For each reason, give an example.

REASONS FOR USING THE INTERNET	EXAMPLES OF INFORMATION FOUND
❶	
❷	
❸	
❹	
❺	

C. Was information you found useful? Did it help you make a decision about something? Explain your answer.

_____

_____

_____

A. Check the words you understand. Then, check the words you use.

	UNDERSTAND	USE		UNDERSTAND	USE
media (n.)	☐	☐	scope* (n.)	☐	☐
marketing (n.)	☐	☐	buzz (n.)	☐	☐
social networking (n.)	☐	☐	emulate (v.)	☐	☐
mirage (n.)	☐	☐	mundane (adj.)	☐	☐
stealth (adj.)	☐	☐	legitimacy (n.)	☐	☐
viral (adj.)	☐	☐	deception (n.)	☐	☐
subtle (adj.)	☐	☐	predators (n.)	☐	☐
identity* (n.)	☐	☐	ulterior motives (n.)	☐	☐
profiles (n.)	☐	☐	tension (n.)	☐	☐
pursuits (n.)	☐	☐	skeptical (adj.)	☐	☐

* Appears on the Academic Word List

B. Read the following sentences or phrases and then write a definition for each of the words in bold.

WORDS IN CONTEXT	DEFINITION
❶ But McLuhan's quips about ads ... were talking about *mass* **media** advertising.	media: *main means of mass communication (e.g., newspapers and broadcasting)*
❷ I wonder what he'd make of some of the dark corners of today's online **marketing**.	marketing:
❸ You're online, logged into a **social networking** site, and ...	social networking:
❹ ... he's a **mirage**, a fake account, a carefully crafted online persona ...	mirage:
❺ Sometimes it's called "**stealth** marketing," ... the account is just one of many in an army of fake profiles ...	stealth:

▶

WORDS IN CONTEXT	DEFINITION
6 I like to call it online **viral** marketing.	viral:
7 Emily agreed to ... give us a rare behind-the-scenes look at how this kind of **subtle** online persuasion happens.	subtle:
8 ... revealing her **identity** could affect her future employment.	identity:
9 ... Emily's job was to create a bunch of fake online **profiles** ...	profiles:
10 ... they would tell stories about their **pursuits** as a photographer ...	pursuits:
11 In the **scope** of between dozens and hundreds of different accounts ...	scope:
12 The goal was to create as much **buzz** as possible ...	buzz:
13 ... we would just try to **emulate** that.	emulate:
14 We would talk about **mundane** things ...	mundane:
15 ... because it adds a certain **legitimacy** to the product that is very difficult to replicate otherwise.	legitimacy:

▶

WORDS IN CONTEXT	DEFINITION
⑯ ... the work involves a level of **deception** that, of course, one would feel conflicted about doing.	deception:
⑰ ... it's not on the same scale as Internet **predators**.	predators:
⑱ ... trying to go out there and befriend strangers for **ulterior motives**.	ulterior motives:
⑲ ... highlights the strange **tension** that can happen when an online friendship is based on false premises.	tension:
⑳ ... I think maybe I'm over-**skeptical** ...	skeptical:

C. Check your definitions with a partner. If you do not understand some words, look them up in a dictionary.

D. Some words might be confusing when you hear them in different contexts. Fill in the blanks with vocabulary from the table.

① busy sound made by bees _____

② false vision, often of water in a desert _____

③ word used to describe a type of disease _____

④ animals that hunt other animals _____

⑤ state of something being stretched tight _____

> ❗ Learn to paraphrase: explain things in different ways. There are some words you understand but seldom use. Find synonyms to help you paraphrase.

E. There are often many ways to say similar things. Match each of the following phrases to its meaning.

① ulterior motives _____ motives that just aren't the same as yours

② self-serving motives _____ motives that are based on lies

③ different motives _____ motives that include and go beyond your own

④ additional motives _____ intentionally hidden motives

⑤ conflicting motives _____ motives that are opposite to your own

⑥ deceptive motives _____ motives that put your interests before others

Before You Listen

Social marketing, sometimes called *viral marketing*, makes use of networks of friends, relatives and associates to spread new ideas in much the same way as some diseases spread: quickly, from person to person. *Stealth* social marketing spreads new ideas in dishonest ways. Answer the following questions, and then discuss your answers with a partner. Think about your answers as you listen to a stealth marketer talk about her job.

❶   What is viral marketing?

_____

_____

❷   How are some messages spread virally?

_____

_____

❸   What sort of information is best suited to viral sharing?

_____

_____

❹   What is the difference between a rumour and a viral message?

_____

_____

❺   Why might companies adopt viral marketing techniques?

_____

_____

Here is the first segment of the interview you will listen to. Underline the words or ideas that are unfamiliar to you.

> **❶** Canadian educator and philosopher Marshall McLuhan (1911–1980) studied media, invented the term "global village" and predicted the World Wide Web, thirty years before it happened.

"First up, advertising. McLuhan studied advertising as a key to the culture. His 1951 book *The Mechanical Bride* focused on it. But McLuhan's quips about ads, like 'All advertising advertises advertising,' were talking about *mass* media advertising. I wonder what he'd make of some of the dark corners of today's online marketing. Like, tell me if this ever happens to you.

"You're online, logged into a social networking site, and seemingly out of nowhere, up pops a message or a friend request from a total stranger. 'Wait a minute, who's Rick G.?' you think to yourself. 'Is that the guy I met at Debbie's barbecue … maybe?' You squint at the profile picture. 'He looks kind of familiar.' So you click through to see the stranger's profile. 'Oh yeah, we live in the same city. And he has *Mad Men* listed as his favourite TV show. Oh, what the hey.' And you click to approve the friend request."

Write the words or ideas that were unfamiliar to you. Then, discuss them with your partner and work together to write definitions or explanations.

WORD/IDEA: _____

DEFINITION/EXPLANATION: _____

_____

WORD/IDEA: _____

DEFINITION/EXPLANATION: _____

_____

WORD/IDEA: _____

DEFINITION/EXPLANATION: _____

_____

WORD/IDEA: _____

DEFINITION/EXPLANATION: _____

_____

WORD/IDEA: _____

DEFINITION/EXPLANATION: _____

_____

While You Listen

First, read the following excerpts from the interview. The first time you listen, try to get the general idea. Listen a second time and number the excerpts in the correct order. Listen a third time to take notes and add details.

EXCERPTS	NOTES
_____ "Each of them would have, you know, dreams in life and things to talk about other than just the service or the product."	
_____ "For Facebook for sure, while it used to be really easy to befriend total strangers on Facebook—now there are all sorts of warning messages: 'Do you actually know this person?' "	
___1___ "You're online, logged into a social networking site, and seemingly out of nowhere, up pops a message or a friend request from a total stranger."	
_____ "It was a campaign that was running in the fall, we had a Facebook account—for somebody and—you know, they lived in a certain city and had—a certain history."	

▶

EXCERPTS	NOTES
_____ "Now sure, that total stranger could have been the *Mad Men*-loving guy you met ... but it's also possible that he doesn't exist at all."	
_____ "So—whenever I see a video that has ... clips of a band's music, I always wonder, you know, did—did someone really choose this song, or is this—is this just some advertising company?"	
_____ "To make a persona seem real, we would do things like deliberate typos. If we were in a certain region, we would look at what other people ... were saying and ... what sorts of slang they would use, and we would just try to emulate that."	
_____ "I think maybe I'm over-skeptical— just assume that things are online marketing, even when perhaps they aren't."	

After You Listen

Think about what you know about Emily's job. Write a short paragraph on a separate sheet of paper to describe what she does. Be sure to give examples.

FOCUS ON LISTENING

Working with Timelines

One of the most common ways to organize information, particularly information about changes over time, is to use a timeline. A timeline lets us see, chronologically, what has happened and when it happened in relation to other events. Timelines are often used to show historical events. It can be difficult to listen to, and remember, a series of dates, so drawing your own timeline in your notes can help you focus on the sequence of events as well as when events overlap.

A. Think of five events in your life from the past ten years. These events could be goals you've reached, places you've visited or people you've met. Record these events, and the dates on which they happened, on a timeline.

B. Use the Internet to research five world events during this same time period and record these on your timeline.

C. Explain your timeline to a partner. Use phrases such as, "In 2010, when Canada hosted the Winter Olympic Games, I was ..."

A. Check the words you understand. Then, check the words you use.

	UNDERSTAND	USE		UNDERSTAND	USE
phenomenon* (n.)	☐	☐	prejudice (n.)	☐	☐
concepts* (n.)	☐	☐	justify* (v.)	☐	☐
demonizing (n.)	☐	☐	protocols* (n.)	☐	☐
connotation (n.)	☐	☐	fraudulent (adj.)	☐	☐
cult (n.)	☐	☐	initiating* (v.)	☐	☐
fundamental* (adj.)	☐	☐	inclined* (adj.)	☐	☐
confine* (v.)	☐	☐	links* (v.)	☐	☐
persistence* (n.)	☐	☐	source* (n.)	☐	☐
instill (v.)	☐	☐	ideology* (n.)	☐	☐
advocated* (v.)	☐	☐	disseminated (v.)	☐	☐

* Appears on the Academic Word List

> Some topics, like propaganda, are full of jargon: specialized words or phrases that can be difficult to understand. When you study a new area of knowledge, try to find out what popular jargon is commonly used.

B. Read the following sentences or phrases and then write a definition for each of the words in bold.

WORDS IN CONTEXT	DEFINITION
❶ ... we will be examining an interesting **phenomenon** within the field of political science ...	phenomenon: *fact or condition that can be observed*
❷ To help you understand the **concepts** involved, I'm going to further define propaganda ...	concepts:
❸ Creating an impression of evil, or **demonizing** ...	demonizing:
❹ ... the word *propaganda* has not always had a negative **connotation**.	connotation:
❺ It is all part of a **cult** of leadership, a common propaganda technique.	cult:

WORDS IN CONTEXT	DEFINITION
6 The most brilliant propagandist technique will yield no success unless one **fundamental** principle is borne in mind ...	fundamental:
7 ... it must **confine** itself to a few points and repeat them over and over.	confine:
8 Cato's **persistence** in working for an end to Carthage was heavily laden with propaganda ...	persistence:
9 ... used ... to **instill** fear in the German public and to rally the German troops.	instill:
10 The book **advocated** the sterilization of German men to stop them from producing children ...	advocated:
11 ... another propaganda technique, an *appeal to **prejudice***, which is linked to both demonization and scapegoating.	prejudice:
12 ... in order to **justify** the horrors to which Jews were subjected.	justify:
13 A famous one was *The **Protocols** of the Elders of Zion*, a forgery ...	protocols:
14 Even though the document was clearly shown to be **fraudulent**, ...	fraudulent:
15 Hitler's primary justification for **initiating** the Holocaust ...	initiating:

WORDS IN CONTEXT	DEFINITION
⑯ ... might be more **inclined** to support the idea.	inclined:
⑰ If the political party **links** the message to other things that are positive, through photographs and other images ...	links:
⑱ These three colour codes refer not to the propaganda itself, but rather to each one's **source**.	source:
⑲ ... a so-called research organization whose only goal is to produce documents that secretly support their **ideology**.	ideology:
⑳ ... we can see that these can be **disseminated** in three ways ...	disseminated:

C. Check your definitions with a partner. If you do not understand some words, look them up in a dictionary.

D. Depending on the context, some words can be used to express positive or negative ideas. Look at the following words and write a sentence that is positive and another sentence that is negative for each word.

1 campaign

POSITIVE: We hope you'll join our campaign to clean up our beaches.

NEGATIVE: He is running a campaign to become mayor any way he can.

2 prestige

POSITIVE: _____

NEGATIVE: _____

3 instill

POSITIVE: _____

NEGATIVE: _____

4 ideology

POSITIVE: _____

NEGATIVE: _____

5 disseminated

POSITIVE: _____

NEGATIVE: _____

E. You can often understand a new word by an explanatory phrase that follows and helps to explain it. Match each of the following words to its explanation.

① ad nauseam _____ creating an impression of evil

② ameliorative _____ over and over, to an excessive degree

③ demonizing _____ expressing negative connotations

④ pejorative _____ making better or improving

⑤ propaganda _____ generalize from an individual or an individual incident to a larger group or pattern

⑥ transfer _____ information used deliberately and systematically to communicate a particular point of view

LISTENING ②

Understanding Propaganda

Before You Listen

Propaganda is all about shaping a message that will convince people to believe in certain things or to act in certain ways. There are many techniques, and being able to recognize when and how these are being used will allow you to make better decisions. Before you listen to a lecture on propaganda techniques, think about what the word *propaganda* means to you. Write two examples of occasions when you thought propaganda was used in an attempt to sway your thinking.

① _____

② _____

Here is the first segment of the lecture you will listen to. Read it carefully and underline the key words that indicate what you are likely to learn about.

> "Today, in this lecture, we will be examining an interesting phenomenon within the field of political science: propaganda. I would like to first give a general overview about what is meant by the term *propaganda*. Propaganda is the deliberate and systematic use of information to communicate a particular—often political—point of view. Propaganda is meant to shape public opinion, to influence and persuade, most often through emotional appeals and, frequently, by ignoring the truth, or at least the *whole* truth. A number of propaganda techniques have been identified. To help you understand the concepts involved, I'm going to further define propaganda by giving a few historical examples and by discussing how propaganda is used today. Please take notes and, if you have any questions, I will be happy to answer them at the end of the lecture."

Write three questions that you expect the lecture will answer. Discuss your questions with a partner.

1. _____

2. _____

3. _____

While You Listen

This lecture deals with several new ideas. While you listen, take notes on the different propaganda techniques and terms.

PROPAGANDA TECHNIQUES/TERMS	NOTES
DEMONIZATION	
CULT OF LEADERSHIP	
AD NAUSEAM STATEMENTS	
SCAPEGOATING	
APPEALS TO FEAR	
APPEALS TO PREJUDICE	
BANDWAGON	
SELECTIVE OMISSION	
GLITTERING GENERALITIES	
TRANSFER	
WHITE PROPAGANDA	

PROPAGANDA TECHNIQUES/TERMS	NOTES
BLACK PROPAGANDA	
GREY PROPAGANDA	

After You Listen

Read the slogans and identify which propaganda technique each is an example of.

❶ Polluters are monsters!

❷ Kill mosquitoes before they kill you!

❸ There's only one person to blame; that's Joe Kerr.

❹ You wouldn't want a homeless person in your basement, would you? Say "no" to homeless shelters.

❺ Joe Kerr for Mayor! He's the only one who can lead us!

❻ Everyone is having fun at Club Q!

_____ appeals to fear _____ bandwagon _____ demonization

_____ appeals to prejudice _____ cult of leadership _____ scapegoating

WARM-UP ASSIGNMENT

Use Propaganda Techniques to Persuade

Now it's time to research and present a short talk using propaganda techniques to persuade.

A. Choose and research one of the following topics.

- use less water
- drive carefully
- stop smoking
- volunteer
- donate money
- join a club
- play a sport

B. Take note of significant dates and organize them on a timeline that you can refer to in your presentation.

C. Prepare your presentation. Decide which propaganda technique(s) you will use to sway classmates to your point of view. Write your notes on a separate sheet of paper. Your presentation should last approximately five minutes. Don't read from your notes, but you may use cue cards to remind you of important points.

Academic
Survival Skill

Changing Minds Through Persuasive Speech

One of the most important things you do when you speak to a group of people is try to change their minds about something. Changing people's minds usually means addressing them through a persuasive speech. A persuasive speech has specific goals designed to capture the attention of an audience, to get them interested in the topic by seeing how it might affect them and to push them to some kind of action. Sometimes this action is physical; sometimes it is a change in beliefs or attitudes.

Choose a second topic from the Warm-Up Assignment or a topic of your own, and based on the goals of a persuasive speech, write an example that would illustrate each.

GOALS OF A PERSUASIVE SPEECH	EXAMPLE
Begin by getting the audience's attention. Ask a rhetorical question, make a surprising statement or open with a quotation or story.	
Motivate the audience by giving them a reason to keep listening. Assure the audience that the information you are going to give will be helpful.	
Let the audience know what you will talk about. Give the audience the main points, explaining any technical aspects.	

GOALS OF A PERSUASIVE SPEECH	EXAMPLE
Explain a need. Point out the change that needs to happen (or not happen) and support it with a fact.	
Present a solution. Explain the attitude, belief or action the audience needs to adopt in order to avoid negative consequences.	
Ask the audience to take action. Summarize the main points and remind the audience of what needs to be done. Be excited and positive about the outcome.	

LISTENING ③ A Mountain of Rice

Before You Listen

Did you know that in 1791, Richard Daly, an Irish theatre owner, bet he could make a nonsense word popular in his hometown? He had several people write the word *quiz* on walls around the city and within two days, it was being discussed by countless people and had taken on one of its modern meanings: *ask questions*. Now, this story may or may not be true, but it is a good example of how viral marketing works: something interesting is created that captures people's attention and they share it with others.

Before you listen to Stella and Oscar discuss viral marketing, write a text message about something you heard or saw or did online, such as listen to a song, watch a video or play a game, that might capture people's attention and be shared.

_____

_____

Working in a group, compare messages and discuss what might make one message more compelling than another.

While You Listen

Listen to the advice Oscar gives Stella on how to apply the six steps in viral marketing. Write notes to explain each of the steps.

STEPS IN VIRAL MARKETING	NOTES
OFFER SOMETHING FOR FREE.	

▶

STEPS IN VIRAL MARKETING	NOTES
MAKE SURE THE MESSAGE CAN TRAVEL EASILY.	
MAKE SURE THE MESSAGE, PRODUCT OR SERVICE CAN SCALE UP.	
CONSIDER HUMAN NATURE AND EMOTIONS.	
USE EXISTING COMMUNICATION NETWORKS.	
TAKE ADVANTAGE OF OTHER PEOPLE'S RESOURCES.	

After You Listen

Look at the six steps again. Think of your topic from Before You Listen. What could you do to ensure that your message would go viral?

STEPS IN VIRAL MARKETING	VIRAL MARKETING MY TOPIC
OFFER SOMETHING FOR FREE.	
MAKE SURE THE MESSAGE CAN TRAVEL EASILY.	
MAKE SURE THE MESSAGE, PRODUCT OR SERVICE CAN SCALE UP.	
CONSIDER HUMAN NATURE AND EMOTIONS.	
USE EXISTING COMMUNICATION NETWORKS.	
TAKE ADVANTAGE OF OTHER PEOPLE'S RESOURCES.	

FINAL ASSIGNMENT
Give a Persuasive Presentation

Now it's your turn. Use everything you have learned in this chapter to prepare and give a longer presentation of up to ten minutes.

A. Choose a topic related to an important issue that is of interest to you and that has a historical background. Write it below. Consider your point of view and think about how you could persuade others to adopt it.

_____

_____

_____

B. Speak with your teacher. Ask for approval of your topic and advice on how to develop it.

C. Do your research. Use at least three sources. Take note of significant dates and organize them on a timeline that you can refer to.

SOURCE 1: _____

_____

SOURCE 2: _____

_____

SOURCE 3: _____

_____

D. Plan your presentation. Use the following table to write your notes.

GOALS OF A PERSUASIVE SPEECH	NOTES
BEGIN BY GETTING THE AUDIENCE'S ATTENTION.	
MOTIVATE THE AUDIENCE BY GIVING THEM A REASON TO KEEP LISTENING.	
LET THE AUDIENCE KNOW WHAT YOU WILL TALK ABOUT.	
EXPLAIN A NEED.	
PRESENT A SOLUTION.	
ASK THE AUDIENCE TO TAKE ACTION.	

Good luck!

CHAPTER 4

Creating the "Me" Brand

How many brands do you know? The answer is probably a number in the hundreds or thousands. Businesses carefully create brands by shaping the messages associated with their products; if successful, these messages make you feel confident about the products' value.

In a competitive world, you need to think of yourself as a brand. Your qualities, skills and interests—that shape who you are—are differences that make you your own brand. The effort you put into improving yourself makes you a better brand.

- listen to a lecture on defining yourself, an interview on promoting yourself and a discussion on imagining your future;

- learn vocabulary related to image and career;

- organize your ideas using tables and flow charts;

- learn how to respond to different types of questions;

- practise speaking skills individually, in pairs and in small groups;

- prepare and deliver one short and one longer presentation.

GEARING UP

A. With a partner, discuss what skills and training you would need for each of the jobs pictured in the table below. Then, write two advantages and two disadvantages of each job.

	ADVANTAGES	DISADVANTAGES
1		
2		
3		
4		

B. Work in groups. Compare your answers with those of other students. Which job interests you most? Why?

_____

_____

_____

A. Check the words you understand. Then, check the words you use.

	UNDERSTAND	USE		UNDERSTAND	USE
series* (n.)	☐	☐	consultant* (n.)	☐	☐
principles* (n.)	☐	☐	individual* (n.)	☐	☐
branding (n.)	☐	☐	embraced (v.)	☐	☐
consumers* (n.)	☐	☐	ethnicity (n.)	☐	☐
logo (n.)	☐	☐	indication* (n.)	☐	☐
slogans (n.)	☐	☐	initial (adj.)	☐	☐
abandoned* (v.)	☐	☐	perceive* (v.)	☐	☐
minimized* (v.)	☐	☐	influence (v.)	☐	☐
recognition (n.)	☐	☐	fascination (n.)	☐	☐
projected* (v.)	☐	☐	sums up* (v.)	☐	☐

* Appears on the Academic Word List

> Although we talk about "ethnicity" in a general sense, it's seldom polite to ask someone directly about his or her ethnic background. If you're curious, ask, "Where did your family originally come from?"

B. Read the following sentences or phrases and then write a definition for each of the words in bold.

WORDS IN CONTEXT	DEFINITION
❶ Even as I say the words, you probably have a **series** of images appearing in your mind ...	series: *number of things happening one after the other*
❷ Essentially, I want to explore **principles** of business that have to do with **branding** and will ask you to consider yourselves in terms of a "me" brand.	principles:
	branding:
❸ ... a specific product or service that **consumers** connect with the company or organization ...	consumers:
❹ You might be thinking about a **logo**, or an image, that defines the company ...	logo:
❺ Both these companies are also identified by **slogans**, such as Nike's "Just Do It!"	slogans:

WORDS IN CONTEXT	DEFINITION
6 Other organizations have **abandoned** or **minimized** their slogans.	abandoned: minimized:
7 Brand **recognition** is tied up in many details beyond a logo, a slogan or a jingle.	recognition:
8 What kind of brand image is **projected**?	projected:
9 Tom Peters, a business **consultant**, wrote about the ways in which an **individual** could distinguish him- or herself in the workplace.	consultant: individual:
10 It's an interesting idea and one that a lot of people have **embraced** over the past few years, …	embraced:
11 These might include … **ethnicity** … and education.	ethnicity:
12 … if your clothing and overall appearance are an **indication**.	indication:
13 … people often make snap judgments based on **initial** perceptions.	initial:
14 Regardless of what you look like and how others **perceive** you, …	perceive:
15 The problems and successes you have over the years will **influence** who you are.	influence:

WORDS IN CONTEXT	DEFINITION
⑯ ... it was a **fascination** with computers and writing code for them.	fascination:
⑰ From this single concise sentence, write a slogan of a few words that **sums up** your brand.	sums up:

C. Check your definitions with a partner. If you do not understand some words, look them up in a dictionary.

D. Some verbs have a related noun form that describes the person performing the action. Write the jobs suggested by the following verbs and then write the definitions.

VERB	JOB	DEFINITION
analyze	analyst	someone who studies data and advises other people about it
conduct		
consult		
interview		
lecture		

E. Some words have a common *root* or base that gives clues to the meaning of other words. For example, the root of *project* is *ject*, which means "throw" and is also found in *eject*, *inject* and *interject*. Write three words with each of the following roots.

❶ *act* (do): _____

_____

❷ *ceive* (take): _____

_____

❸ *dict* (speak): _____

_____

❹ *port* (carry): _____

_____

> ❗ A good way to learn new words is to start a list, on paper or on your phone or computer. Add words, with their meanings, as you hear them, and review the list often.

Before You Listen

You may not realize it, but you are already branded: by the clothes you wear, your hairstyle, the food you eat, the items you own and use—even by the friends you make. But does this really represent you? In this section, you will listen to a lecture about how personal experiences shape us and play a part in creating what we can call our brands. Before you listen, answer the following questions.

❶ Name four brands you buy.

_____   _____

_____   _____

❷ In one or two words, how would you define each of the four brands?

_____   _____

_____   _____

❸ Who do you think these brands are most popular with, and why?

_____

_____

Famous people are their own brands. Their names and faces are their logos, promoting who they are and what they represent. When you consider the following categories, who are the people you think of?

• action hero _____   • musician _____

• athlete _____   • politician _____

• business person _____   • scientist _____

• inventor _____   • writer _____

Here is the first segment of the lecture you will listen to.

> "Today, in this lecture about business, we will be discussing marketing, but starting from an unusual point of view. That point of view is *you*. At some point in our life, each of us asks, 'Who am I?' Even as I say the words, you probably have a series of images appearing in your mind about who you are. We define ourselves in many ways: by nationality, by profession, by the things we like to do, be it riding motorcycles, playing hockey or studying dance. What I would like to do during this lecture is explore these and other qualities in terms of a *business* model. Essentially, I want to explore principles of business that have to do with *branding* and will ask you to consider yourselves in terms of a 'me' brand."

If you were a brand, what product or service would you represent? Think of adjectives that describe you, and then think of products or services those adjectives might also describe. Discuss your ideas with a partner.

While You Listen

While you listen to the lecture, take note of the different factors that shape us and write these in the first column. Listen a second time and take notes on the key ideas. Listen a third time to check your notes and add details.

FACTORS THAT SHAPE US	NOTES
PERSONAL APPEARANCE	
PERSONAL HISTORY	

After You Listen

Review your notes. Think about how each factor has shaped you. Add your thoughts in the second column of the table. Then, create a personal brand by completing the following steps.

1. Describe yourself in a couple of sentences.

2. Reduce those sentences to one sentence. Be as concise as possible.

3. From this single concise sentence, write a slogan of a few words that sums up your personal brand.

4. For a logo, draw a picture of yourself doing something, or some other image, that would represent who you are.

Working with Flow Charts

Whenever you create a presentation, you can use different types of charts to take notes. When you listen to a presentation, understanding different types of charts can help you follow the speaker's ideas and critically evaluate them. The choice of chart depends on the content of the presentation. If you are listening to a presentation on processes, a good chart type to use is a flow chart. Flow charts show how stages in a process are connected.

When the information is complex, such as in engineering, science and computer systems design and programming, standardized sets of symbols are used: boxes, rectangles, circles, diamonds and other shapes.

A. Look at the flow chart below. The top box is the starting point. It indicates the initial problem that needs a solution or a decision. The boxes that lead from the starting point represent possibilities, choices or steps, each of which lead in turn to different actions or results. Using a flow chart helps clarify what actually happens or what needs to happen. Flow charts allow you to quickly sort out your ideas, map the steps and see at a glance what your alternatives are.

B. Fill in the flow chart with some choices about what you might do next weekend. Include the actions or results each will lead to, and consider how each decision affects the others.

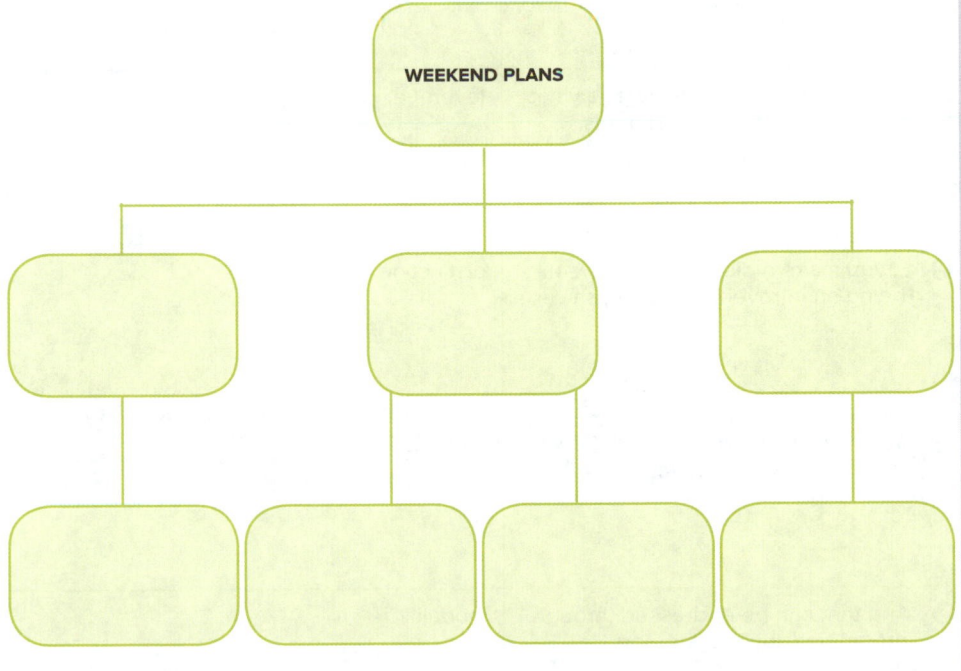

WEEKEND PLANS

A. Check the words you understand. Then, check the words you use.

	UNDERSTAND	USE		UNDERSTAND	USE
introverts (n.)	☐	☐	particular (adj.)	☐	☐
extroverted (adj.)	☐	☐	credit (n.)	☐	☐
leverage (v.)	☐	☐	mutual* (adj.)	☐	☐
distinction* (n.)	☐	☐	initiative (n.)	☐	☐
anxiety (n.)	☐	☐	connected (v.)	☐	☐
modalities (n.)	☐	☐	chairing (v.)	☐	☐
passions (n.)	☐	☐	committee (n.)	☐	☐
workplace (n.)	☐	☐	associated (v.)	☐	☐
visibility* (n.)	☐	☐	recommend (v.)	☐	☐
challenge* (n.)	☐	☐	entrepreneurial (adj.)	☐	☐

* Appears on the Academic Word List

> The words "introvert" and "extrovert" are opposites. When you learn a new word, try to learn its opposite as well.

B. Read the following sentences or phrases and then write a definition for each of the words in bold.

WORDS IN CONTEXT	DEFINITION
❶ **Introverts** tend to shy away from the limelight, and also, often, they get passed over for job offers and promotions while their more **extroverted** colleagues get all the attention.	introverts:
	extroverted:
❷ ... how introverts can **leverage** what she calls their "quiet strengths."	leverage:
❸ ... you make a **distinction** between being an introvert and being shy.	distinction:
❹ So being shy is something different; that's more social **anxiety**.	anxiety:
❺ And that can be addressed through **modalities** such as therapy.	modalities:

▶

WORDS IN CONTEXT	DEFINITION
6 If you're an introvert, you tend to dive deeply ... into whatever your **passions** are.	passions:
7 And how can you use those to your advantage in the **workplace**?	workplace:
8 So let's talk about that: gaining **visibility**.	visibility:
9 ... obviously a big **challenge** for introverts.	challenge:
10 You say, become known as an expert in a **particular** area.	particular:
11 ... getting known for what you've done, taking **credit** for your own work.	credit:
12 ... get to know and to build your network, and for **mutual** benefit.	mutual:
13 And another one is to chair **initiative**, so get your name **connected** with initiatives that are important at work.	initiative:
	connected:
14 So—whether that means **chairing** meetings or taking on a special **committee**, ...	chairing:
	committee:

WORDS IN CONTEXT	DEFINITION
⓰ ... it's just getting your name **associated** with things that are important ...	associated:
⓰ I don't **recommend** changing your personality.	recommend:
⓱ ... how to turn your **entrepreneurial** dreams into a successful small business.	entrepreneurial:

C. Check your definitions with a partner. If you do not understand some words, look them up in a dictionary.

D. Sometimes you learn new words and phrases in a particular context or situation. These words and phrases are often associated with other words that relate to the same situation. For example, both *chairing* and *committees* are commonly associated with holding meetings. Define each of the following words or phrases in the context of a meeting.

❶ secretary: <u>person who takes notes for the chair of the meeting</u>

❷ agenda: _____

❸ outstanding items: _____

❹ minutes: _____

❺ conference call: _____

❻ call to vote: _____

❼ any other business: _____

E. Often when we speak, we use metaphors to better explain the message we are trying to convey. The following sports metaphors are frequently used in a job-related context. Write the meaning of each expression.

❶ be a team player: _____

❷ score big: _____

❸ make a play: _____

❹ level playing field: _____

Self-Promotion for Introverts

Before You Listen

The way you perceive the world influences how you act in certain situations. In turn, your perception is determined partly by your personality. Different personality types exhibit different traits. Most people have a combination of traits, with one or two more prominent. Before you listen to an interview in which an author talks about introverts and how they can overcome shyness, complete the exercise below.

Some psychologists use the CANOE model to group personality traits. In the table on the right, write three examples of the opposite traits. Then, circle the words in each table that best describe you.

CANOE MODEL OF PERSONALITY TRAITS		EXAMPLES OF OPPOSITE TRAITS	
CONSCIENTIOUS	disciplined, organized, achievement-oriented	**CARELESS**	
AGREEABLE	helpful, cooperative, sympathetic	**DISAGREEABLE**	
NEUROTIC	emotional, impulsive, anxious	**RATIONAL**	
OPEN	intellectually curious, variety- and novelty-seeking	**CLOSED**	
EXTROVERTED	social, assertive, talkative	**INTROVERTED**	

Write three jobs and list the personality traits best suited to each one.

JOBS	PERSONALITY TRAITS

Here is the first segment of the interview. Cross out those phrases or sentences not essential to understanding the topic. Then, answer the questions that follow.

> "Welcome to the Useful Commute on B-net. I'm your host, Carmine Gallo. In today's show, how to get noticed and get ahead, especially if you're an introvert.
>
> "Introverts tend to shy away from the limelight, and also, often, they get passed over for job offers and promotions while their more extroverted colleagues get all the attention. But our guest today says it doesn't have to be that way. Nancy Ancowitz, author of *Self-Promotion for Introverts*, is here to tell us how introverts can leverage what she calls their 'quiet strengths.' Nancy, nice to have you on the program."

1. What is the interview about? _____

2. What do you expect to learn from this interview?
   _____
   _____

3. Do you think the interview will encourage introverts to become more extroverted? Explain your answer.
   _____
   _____
   _____

While You Listen

If you have the opportunity to listen to a recorded interview more than once, write down key questions, as in the table below, the first time you listen. The second time you listen, take notes on the answers. Listen a third time to check your notes and add details.

GALLO'S QUESTIONS	NOTES ON ANCOWITZ'S ANSWERS
"Nancy, you make a distinction between being an introvert and being shy. What's the difference between the two?"	
"OK, so for this topic, we're addressing that 50 percent of the population that see themselves as introverts."	
"What are these 'quiet strengths' that you say many introverts possess? How can we use those … to get ahead?"	
"What are some quick tips, then, that you can offer us for … helping us become more visible in the workplace?"	
"Those are some of the tips that you have for gaining visibility as an introvert."	
"It's not as though, Nancy, introverts have to change their personalities."	
"You talk about where to sit at business meetings. Tell us about that."	

After You Listen

In the interview, Ancowitz says, "You want to be really clear about what your accomplishments are and get ready to be able to talk about them ... just in a sentence or two." Write one or two sentences that summarize your accomplishments.

_____

_____

_____

_____

WARM-UP ASSIGNMENT
Talk about Time Travel!

Now it's your turn to research and present a short talk on why you should be part of a team that will be sent back in time to solve a problem. Teams need members with a wide range of skills. You need to convince team leaders that you belong on the mission.

A. Choose and research a period in history. Based on your research, write three problems people from that time period might have faced.

1 _____

_____

2 _____

_____

3 _____

_____

B. Choose one of the problems and think about ways in which you could use your skills and experience to find a solution. In the flow chart, write the problem, the steps you would need to take and the possible outcomes.

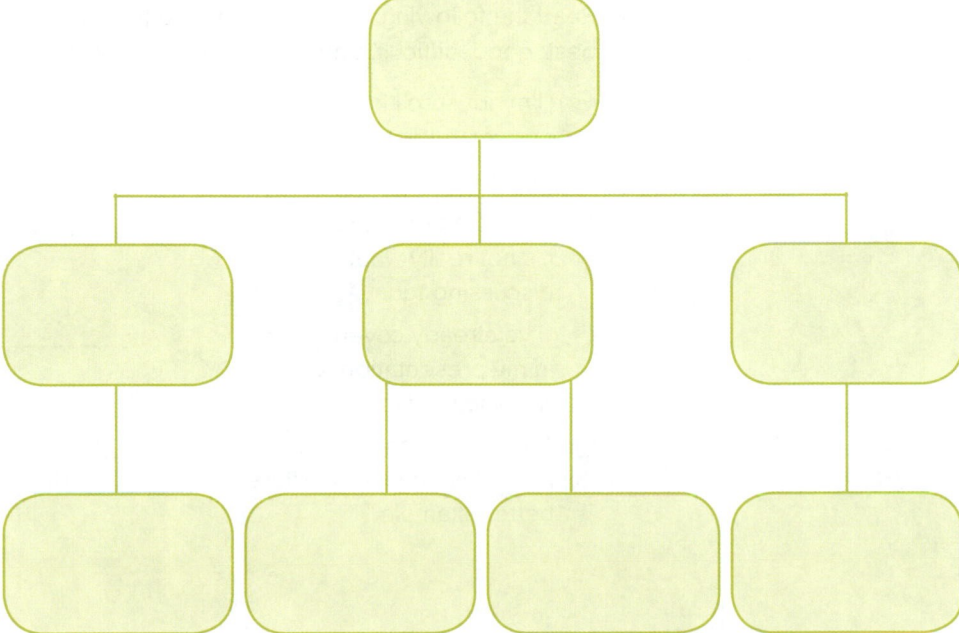

C. On a cue card, write three questions team leaders might ask you. Then, on a sheet of paper, prepare your answers. Your presentation should last approximately five minutes. Use information from your flow chart.

D. Using your questions and answers, practise with a partner. Then do your presentation for the class. Don't read from the page, but you may use cue cards with a few words to remind you of important points.

Dealing with Questions

No matter how much you prepare or practise, there is one part of your presentation that you cannot control: the question period. People have the right to question what you say, but sometimes the questions are not appropriate.

Questions asked after a presentation can be broken down into four kinds: good questions, difficult questions, unnecessary questions and irrelevant questions. Recognizing the difference will make dealing with each type easier.

Good questions give you an opportunity to explain your points more clearly. Difficult questions are also opportunities but might be harder to answer. Unnecessary questions are often asked by people who were not listening properly; they want you to repeat part of your presentation, but this can be boring for the rest of the audience. Irrelevant questions are about something other than what you spoke about, and for the most part, don't need to be answered at all.

A. Read the following responses and identify the kind of question each reply fits best: good, difficult, unnecessary or irrelevant.

① "I'm not sure I know the exact answer, but let me explain it this way." _____

② "That's a good question, but it's not really what we're discussing today." _____

③ "I've already covered that in my presentation. Could we discuss it later?" _____

④ "This gives me an opportunity to explain that point with a better example." _____

B. Write a response to each of the following questions.

1 You haven't mentioned anything about … I know it's not really part of what you're talking about, but could you say something about it?

_____

_____

2 Isn't everything you have said just your opinion?

_____

_____

3 Maybe this is hard to answer, but do you think … is also important?

_____

_____

4 I have a really funny story about something sort of similar. Shall I share it with everyone?

_____

_____

LISTENING ❸   Imagining Your Future

Before You Listen

Stella and Oscar are discussing an assignment for which they need to think about how their skills and interests might influence future work options. Here is the beginning of their conversation.

> OSCAR: Stella, do you ever think about what you're going to do in the future?
>
> STELLA: All the time, Oscar. What about you?
>
> OSCAR: Well, to be honest, I spend most of my time thinking about what I'm going to eat for my next meal, but you know that assignment we have, to put together a flow chart about our future options? Well, I haven't quite done it yet.
>
> STELLA: You haven't done it yet?
>
> OSCAR: Oh, don't tell me you've done it already?

▶

> STELLA: I just finished. What have you done so far?
>
> OSCAR: Done? Nothing. Nothing but questions, really. I know I have to start by reviewing my skill set.
>
> STELLA: That's right. That's what I did. You have to write about what you can do and, more importantly, what you are good at and, most importantly, what you enjoy.

Discuss with a partner what you can do, what you are good at and what you enjoy. Then, think of three possible careers that fit with your skills and interests. What further skills and training would be necessary for each one?

CAREERS	SKILLS	TRAINING

Work in a group. Discuss how different levels of education might allow for different types of careers. Based on the level of education, fill in the flow chart with some of the different careers you could have.

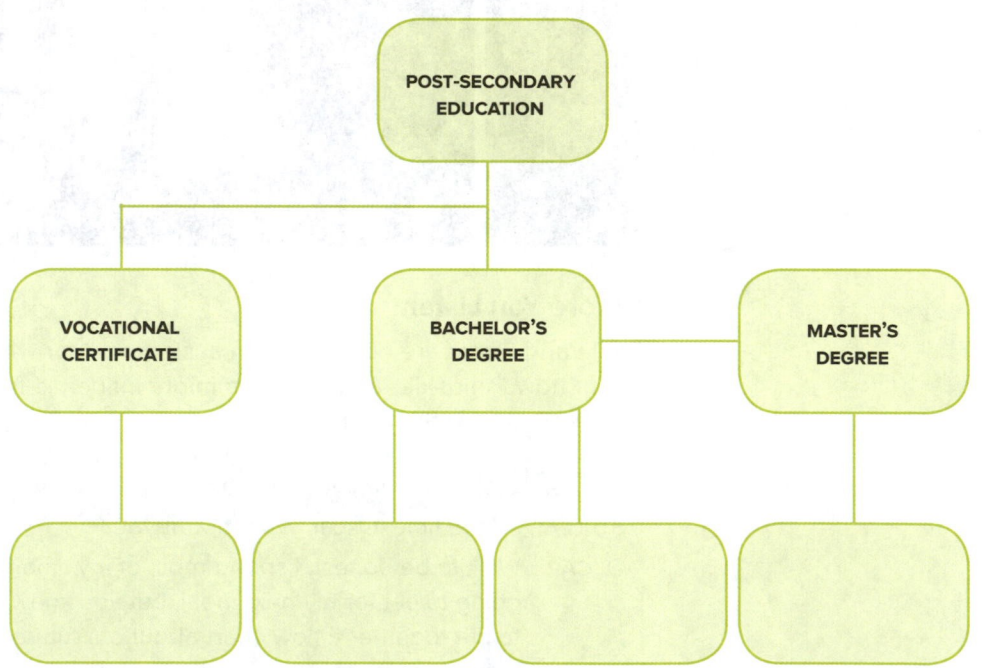

While You Listen

Listen to Stella and Oscar discussing skills, choices and careers. Write notes in the table that follows to explain the discussion points.

DISCUSSION POINTS	NOTES
reviewing your skill set	
what you can do	
what you are good at	
what you enjoy	
evidence for what you can do	
how skills and experiences open doors	
combining skills	
how some choices close doors	
making the most of your opportunities	

After You Listen

Review your notes. Think about what you've written. Has listening to the discussion between Oscar and Stella made any difference in the career choices you made in Before You Listen? Explain your answer.

_____

_____

_____

FINAL ASSIGNMENT
Give a Presentation

Now it's your turn. Use everything you have learned in this chapter to prepare for and give a longer presentation of up to ten minutes.

A. For your topic, choose a famous person. If possible, choose someone from your field of study. Write your choice below, along with a brief explanation of why you chose that person.

_____

_____

_____

B. Speak with your teacher. Ask for approval of your choice and advice on how to develop it.

C. Do your research. Use at least three sources.

SOURCE 1: _____

_____

SOURCE 2: _____

_____

SOURCE 3: _____

_____

D. Identify three critical points in the person's life or career when personal choices (or others' choices) were life-changing.

For example, Florence Nightingale (1820–1910) helped to establish the field of professional nursing and was an advocate for better sanitation in hospitals. Critical points in her life included her father's decision to have her learn advanced statistics, her medical training in Germany and her choice to do battlefront nursing during the Crimean War (1853–1856) when she statistically proved that proper sanitation saved lives.

CRITICAL POINT 1: _____

_____

CRITICAL POINT 2: _____

_____

CRITICAL POINT 3: _____

_____

E. Plan your presentation. Think about which questions your audience would want answered about the person you have chosen and the reasons for choices that were made. Use the following table to write your notes.

QUESTIONS	NOTES
WHO: Describe the person as fully as possible.	
WHEN/WHERE: When and where did the person live? Include cultural and social influences, if relevant.	
WHAT: Describe the person's failures (if any) and achievements.	
HOW: Note decisions taken, or events that happened, that led to the person's achievements.	
WHY: Describe why those decisions or events were important.	

F. On the following chart, name the person you chose, show the three critical points, or events that happened, and the resulting achievements. Refer to it during your presentation.

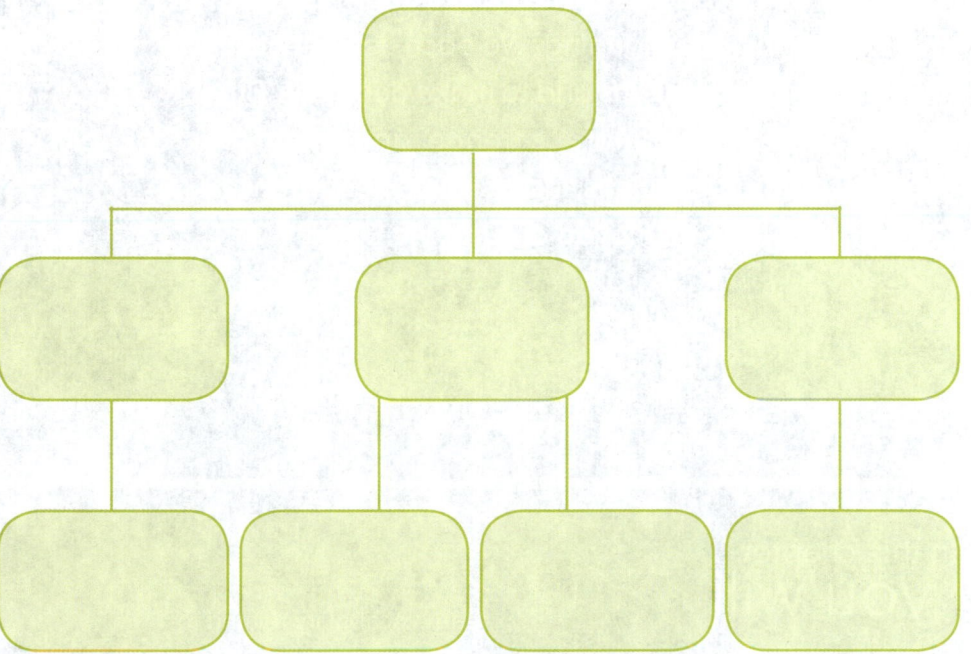

G. Prepare cue cards, and practise your presentation. Good luck!

CHAPTER 5

Putting the Scientific Method to Work

What kind of thinker are you? How do you make decisions about what you do and what you believe?

The scientific method evolved as a way of better understanding the world through careful observation, measurement and experimentation. These processes help us develop theories. The scientific method is also vital to inventing new devices and processes and improving old inventions.

Scientific thinking begins with curiosity and, if all goes well, ends with understanding. We each use scientific thinking to solve problems and to make decisions. But people sometimes ignore science and cling to ignorance and superstitions, just as some people once believed that the Sun moved around the Earth.

In this chapter,
you will

- listen to a lecture on the scientific method, an interview about innovation and a conversation about urban legends;

- learn vocabulary related to science, innovation and myths;

- organize your ideas using tables and Venn diagrams;

- learn how to use persuasive language;

- practise speaking skills individually, in pairs and in small groups;

- prepare and deliver one short and one longer presentation, with a partner.

GEARING UP

A. Sometimes experts make mistakes. Read these statements and consider why each was made and why each was proven wrong.

B. Discuss your answers with a partner. Pick the best ones and write them in the table below.

	WHY THEY THOUGHT THIS	WHY THEY WERE WRONG
"It is unlikely that anyone could find unknown lands of any value." —Committee reporting on a proposal by Christopher Columbus (1486)		
"Heavier-than-air flying machines are impossible." —Lord Kelvin, British mathematician and physicist (1895)		
"Television won't last." —Mary Somerville, radio broadcaster (1948)		
"Nuclear-powered vacuum cleaners will probably be a reality in ten years." —Alexander M. Lewyt, vacuum cleaner company president (1955)		

C. Work in groups. Compare your answers with other students. What prediction would you make about a technology that is familiar to you?

_____

_____

_____

_____

_____

When you learn new nouns, note whether they are count or noncount nouns. "Feedback" and "consensus" are non-count nouns, so they have no plural form.

A. Check the words you understand. Then, check the words you use.

	UNDERSTAND	USE		UNDERSTAND	USE
lecture* (n.)	☐	☐	inquiry (n.)	☐	☐
solved (v.)	☐	☐	incorporating* (v.)	☐	☐
observation (n.)	☐	☐	literature review (n.)	☐	☐
hypothesis* (n.)	☐	☐	consensus* (n.)	☐	☐
conducted* (v.)	☐	☐	revolutionary* (adj.)	☐	☐
published* (v.)	☐	☐	obvious* (adj.)	☐	☐
feedback (n.)	☐	☐	scrutiny (n.)	☐	☐
intermittently (adv.)	☐	☐	offend (v.)	☐	☐

* Appears on the Academic Word List

B. Read the following sentences or phrases and then write a definition for each of the words in bold.

WORDS IN CONTEXT	DEFINITION
❶ Welcome to this first **lecture** on the history of science.	lecture: *educational talk*
❷ Okay! It works. You've **solved** the problem.	solved:
❸ The first step is to identify a problem, a question or an **observation** that somehow excites your curiosity.	observation:
❹ Based on your research, in the third step, you constructed a **hypothesis** …	hypothesis:
❺ The fourth step was when you **conducted** an *experiment*.	conducted:
❻ Finally, as a sixth step, you **published** your findings.	published:
❼ It's important because you can get **feedback** from people who examine your problem …	feedback:

▶

WORDS IN CONTEXT	DEFINITION
8 Perhaps the problem was with the light switch: it contains a loose wire and works only **intermittently**.	intermittently:
9 Now, Plato had another view of scientific **inquiry**.	inquiry:
10 Aristotle challenged this notion by **incorporating** measurement into his method.	incorporating:
11 First, he studied existing writings about a subject—we now call this a *literature review*.	literature review:
12 Second, he looked for general **consensus** ...	consensus:
13 ... an Arab scientist, Ibn al Haytham ... wrote a **revolutionary** book on optics ...	revolutionary:
14 On the surface, it made **obvious** sense, but Galileo's experiments showed that the objects fell at the same rate.	obvious:
15 ... Galileo's greatest contribution ... was to challenge widely held beliefs and hold them to scientific **scrutiny**.	scrutiny:
16 The priest would ... ask whether the man had done anything to **offend** the gods.	offend:

C. Check your definitions with a partner. If you do not understand some words, look them up in a dictionary.

D. *Feedback* is an example of a compound word. Compound words can be confusing because their meanings are not necessarily obvious from their component parts.

Some of the following compound words have obvious meanings, and some do not. Match the words to their definitions.

1. backstroke   _____ minor or remote place

2. pushback   _____ place where development is not taking place

3. backup   _____ courage

4. backbone   _____ backward current of water or air

5. backlight   _____ negative response

6. backtrack   _____ opposite effect to the one intended

7. backstreet   _____ retrace one's steps

8. backfire   _____ swimming style

9. backwater   _____ person or thing that can be called upon

10. backwash   _____ illumination from behind

E. When hearing about or reading experimental research, it is helpful to understand key concepts. Read this paragraph about an experiment and use the context to explain the words in bold.

> **In our experiment, we had a control group to compare to an experimental group. We wanted to know if students who drank camomile tea at bedtime slept more than seven hours.**
>
> So drinking camomile tea was our **independent variable**, and our **dependent variable** was the number of hours of sleep. All the other variables, such as the subjects' age and gender and the amount of tea, were identical.
>
> We used a **double-blind test**, so no one knew who belonged to the control group or the experimental group. This helped to reduce **experimental bias** and make our results more reliable.

1. control group: _____

2. experimental group: _____

3. independent variable: _____

4. dependent variable: _____

5. double-blind test: _____

6. experimental bias: _____

LISTENING ① Introduction to the Scientific Method

Before You Listen

What do you know about the scientific method? From its roots with the Greek scientist Aristotle (384–322 BCE), the scientific method emerged over the course of centuries as people explored new ways to measure and understand the natural world. Before listening to a lecture on the scientific method, discuss this question with a partner.

• Think of three common problems. What different approaches might you take to solving each one?

Here is a segment from the beginning of the lecture, describing a common problem. The words and phrases in bold indicate the different steps to solving it. In the table below, write explanations for why you might follow each step.

> "You enter your home—let's say your front hallway—and it's *dark*. You try to turn on a light switch but no light comes on. Not having any light in the hallway is a problem, so you **consider** a few things that might be **causing** it. You **do a little research** and see if other lights in your home work. They do. You then **decide that the problem might be** that the hallway light bulb has burned out. You find a new light bulb and change it. Okay! It works. You've **solved** the problem. Later, you run into a friend and casually **mention** that the light wasn't working but that you identified and solved the problem."

KEY WORDS OR PHRASES	EXPLANATION
consider	Before you can find the cause of a problem, or a solution to it, you have to think about it.
causing	
do a little research	
decide that the problem might be	
solved	
mention	

While You Listen

Because this lecture describes a method, you can expect to learn about some steps Involved. While you listen, list the steps in the table and then write notes to define each.

STEPS IN THE SCIENTIFIC METHOD	NOTES
STEP 1: _____ _____ _____	
STEP 2: _____ _____ _____	
STEP 3: _____ _____ _____	
STEP 4: _____ _____ _____	
STEP 5: _____ _____ _____	
STEP 6: _____ _____ _____	

After You Listen

Review your notes. Think about what you've written. Add other details or thoughts to your notes, such as examples that help you understand.

Working with Venn Diagrams

A Venn diagram is a set of circles used to show the relationships between two or more things that have characteristics in common. Where the circles overlap, indicate characteristics that are similar. Where the circles do not overlap, indicate characteristics that differ. Venn diagrams are often used in presentations to compare information.

A. Here is an example of a Venn diagram and a list of some of the characteristics of three different species. Where the circles overlap, write the characteristics that they have in common.

FROG
cold-blooded
lays eggs
four legs

CHICKEN
warm-blooded
lays eggs
two legs

PLATYPUS
warm-blooded
lays eggs
four legs

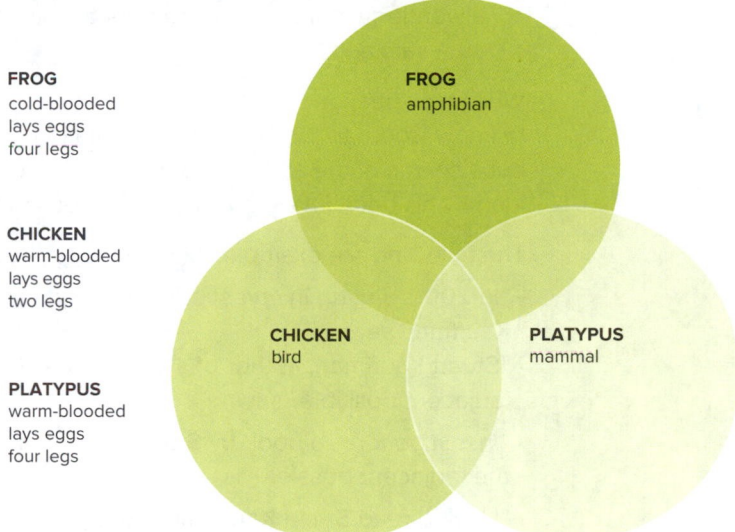

FROG
amphibian

CHICKEN
bird

PLATYPUS
mammal

B. In the following Venn diagram, under each heading list four characteristics. Then, where the circles overlap, write the characteristics they have in common.

ROWBOAT
_____
_____
_____

BICYCLE
_____
_____
_____

BUS
_____
_____
_____

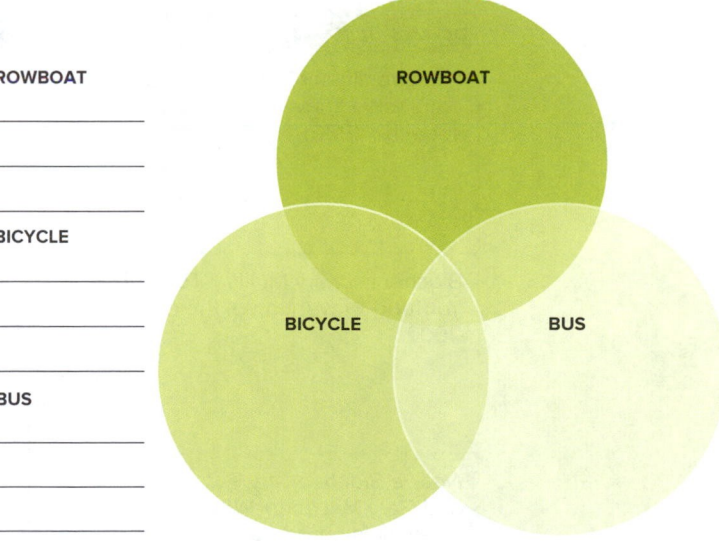

ROWBOAT

BICYCLE

BUS

C. Write three other examples of topics where Venn diagrams could be used.

1 _____

2 _____

3 _____

Referencing Speeches

Speeches or lectures often feature evidence in the form of a reference to content from a book, video, article or other media. When you refer to such content, both when talking and writing, it's important to give credit to the author or authors and to give your audience or readers an opportunity to follow up on the reference if they're interested in getting more information.

Consider the following excerpt from Listening 2, which you will hear later in this chapter:

> "... one of the opening chapters is called 'The Adjacent Possible,' and this is a wonderful phrase from the scientist Stuart Kauffman that I first read about ten years ago."

While the speaker correctly credits the author for the borrowed phrase, it's hard to know where to look for more information. The phrase "ten years ago" is vague, but a search of the author's name and the words "adjacent possible" helps identify his book *Investigations*, published in 2000.

The following are examples of more complete references to this source:

• "In 2000, writing in *Investigations* about the 'adjacent possible,' Stuart Kauffman says ..."
• "Stuart Kauffman, author of a 2000 book, *Investigations*, writes about the 'adjacent possible,' saying ..."
• "*Investigations*, a book by Stuart Kauffman published in 2000, suggests that the 'adjacent possible' is ..."
• "Having read Stuart Kauffman's 2000 book, *Investigations*, I know that his idea of the 'adjacent possible' ..."

A. Read the following details about three sources and write an informative sentence for each, incorporating the relevant details.

DETAILS	REFERENCE SENTENCE
"Human dignity is better served by embracing knowledge." + John Polanyi + speech + 1986	_____ _____ _____
Biochemist Kary Mullis + TED Talk + YouTube + invention of the experiment + 2002	_____ _____ _____
Nature Biochemistry + Mark Noseda and Gary McLean + Where did the scientific method go? + 2008	_____ _____ _____

B. Work with a partner and compare how you referred to each source.

WARM-UP ASSIGNMENT
Talk about Science

Now it's your turn to research and present a short talk on a scientific topic.

A. With a partner, choose one of the following topics.

- genetically modified foods and organic foods
- traditional medicine and modern medicine
- igneous and metamorphic rock
- cross-pollinating and self-pollinating flowers
- planets and asteroids

B. Decide which subject each partner will take. Do the research independently. Write notes on your subject in one of the circles of a Venn diagram.

C. Compare notes and, in the overlapping part of the diagram, write those characteristics or features that the subjects have in common.

D. Prepare your presentation. Some of the following phrases may be useful.
- "Today, we would like to compare two ..."
- "I will begin by telling you what is unique about ... then my partner will explain what is unique about .... After, I will explain what both ... and ... have in common."
- "As you can see in the Venn diagram, ..."

E. Structure your presentation by taking turns with your partner to explain your side of the issue. One partner should give the introduction and the other the conclusion.

VOCABULARY BUILD

❗ The word "edge" is often combined with other words to describe limits, as in "cutting-edge." For example, "leading edge" and "trailing edge" are both used to describe parts of an airplane's wing. The term "bleeding edge" describes new but imperfect technology.

A. Check the words you understand. Then, check the words you use.

	UNDERSTAND	USE		UNDERSTAND	USE
culture* (n.)	☐	☐	crucial* (adj.)	☐	☐
innovative* (adj.)	☐	☐	collaborated (v.)	☐	☐
predictable (adj.)	☐	☐	adjacent* (adj.)	☐	☐
mainstream (n.)	☐	☐	cutting-edge (adj.)	☐	☐
case studies (n.)	☐	☐	mechanism* (n.)	☐	☐
core* (adj.)	☐	☐	solitary (adj.)	☐	☐
medium* (n.)	☐	☐	spontaneous (adj.)	☐	☐
enabled* (v.)	☐	☐	evolutionary (adj.)	☐	☐
quantum leap (n.)	☐	☐	theory* (n.)	☐	☐
capacity* (n.)	☐	☐	hunch (n.)	☐	☐

* Appears on the Academic Word List

B. Read the following sentences or phrases and then write a definition for each of the words in bold.

WORDS IN CONTEXT	DEFINITION
1 Steven's the author of a number of books about science and **culture** …	culture: *beliefs, way of life and customs shared and accepted by people in a society*
2 … a book about spaces in history and in biology that have been unusually **innovative** …	innovative:
3 … for much of the twentieth century, innovation … happened at a very measured, very **predictable** speed.	predictable:
4 Technologies … took about two decades to go from the laboratory to the **mainstream**.	mainstream:
5 … that's one of the kind of **case studies** … that the book begins with …	case studies:
6 … all these kind of **core** elements of the **medium** have changed and been created in fifteen years.	core:
	medium:
7 … and so part of the question of the book is what is it about the Web that's **enabled** this …	enabled:
8 … what is it about the Web that's enabled this kind of **quantum leap** in the **capacity** for innovation?	quantum leap:
	capacity:

▶

WORDS IN CONTEXT	DEFINITION
9 ... it was **crucial** that he didn't have to invent the Internet first.	crucial:
10 I mean he **collaborated** with some people ...	collaborated:
11 ... an idea isn't a single thing, that it's more like a network or a swarm of ... **adjacent** ideas.	adjacent:
12 So Gutenberg ... had done amazing **cutting-edge** work with metallurgy and developing his movable type ...	cutting-edge:
13 ... he really didn't have a kind of, an actual printing **mechanism** or press ...	mechanism:
14 But yet as a culture ... we are just in love with this idea of the **solitary** inventor ...	solitary:
15 Why do you think we love ... the sort of **spontaneous** good idea ...	spontaneous:
16 It was a much more **evolutionary** process, the idea of coming up with the **theory** of evolution.	evolutionary:
	theory:
17 I want to talk about one in particular, which is the **hunch**.	hunch:

C. Check your definitions with a partner. If you do not understand some words, look them up in a dictionary.

D. The suffix *-ary* turns some nouns into adjectives, for example, *planet* to *planetary*. Less often, the suffix *-ary* turns adjectives into nouns, for example, *adverse* to *adversary*. And sometimes it creates words of more than one category, such as *documentary*, which can be an adjective or a noun. Match each newly formed adjective (or noun) to its definition.

1 discipline → disciplinary   _____ basic

2 document → documentary   _____ (person) having progressive ideas about the future

3 element → elementary   _____ describing a process of change

4 evolution → evolutionary   _____ related to punishment

5 revolution → revolutionary   _____ alone

6 solitude → solitary   _____ (person) involved in creating political or other major change

7 vision → visionary   _____ (presenter) communicating information or a type of evidence

LISTENING ❷ — Fostering Innovation

❗ Knowing a word's history can help you remember it. "Bricolage" in this listening comes from the French "bricoler" and means "to do crafts, odd jobs or repairs." A "bricolage" is a mix of ideas or things.

Before You Listen

How often has someone's great idea inspired you? Many innovations happen because people believe that they can improve on existing inventions or processes. A hundred years ago, if you wanted to launch a new product that everyone would want, you probably needed a factory. Today, people use the Internet to learn about, create and share new ideas.

Before you listen to an interview about how innovations occur, discuss these questions with a partner.

What did each of the following innovations replace? In your opinion, have these made life better or worse? How?

- Velcro, invented in 1948
- mobile telephone, invented in 1973
- plastic water bottles, invented in 1975

Here is the beginning of the interview you will listen to. Read the passage and try to guess what Steven Johnson's first two books are about.

> YOUNG: Well, Steven Johnson's been thinking a lot about that [innovation] lately. Steven's the author of a number of books about science and culture, such as *The Ghost Map* and *Everything Bad Is Good for You*. His latest is *Where Good Ideas Come From: The Natural History of Innovation*.
>
> JOHNSON: *Where Good Ideas Come From* is a book about spaces in history and in biology that have been unusually innovative and the patterns that we see in all those spaces.

The Ghost Map

_____

Everything Bad Is Good for You

_____

Check your answers by looking the books up online. Based on the information you find, would you want to read these books? Why or why not? Discuss your reasons with your partner.

While You Listen

During the interview, ten individuals are mentioned. Match each individual to the phrase that describes his contribution to the field of science.

While you listen, take notes, particularly of questions you might want to ask. Use a few words to remind you of your question rather than writing long notes.

1. Steven Johnson   _____ discovered the law of gravity
2. Tim Berners-Lee   _____ discovered how cholera was spread
3. Gutenberg   _____ discovered the idea of displacement
4. Isaac Newton   _____ came up with the theory of evolution
5. Archimedes   _____ collaborated with John Snow
6. Charles Darwin   _____ invented the printing press
7. John Snow   _____ came up with the idea of the programmable computer
8. Henry Whitehead   _____ came up with the idea of with the World Wide Web
9. Charles Babbage   _____ wrote books on science and culture
10. Malcolm Gladwell   _____ wrote about a kind of hunch or "blink" idea

Steven Johnson talks about different ideas, theories and inventions worked on over the course of more than 500 years. Number the following in the order in which they were developed. Check your answers with your partner. If your answers disagree, do some research to find the correct answer.

_____ AM radio   _____ colour TV   _____ printing press

_____ theory of evolution   _____ VCR   _____ World Wide Web

After You Listen

Based on what you have heard Steven Johnson explain, what do you think would be a good way to foster innovation? Discuss this in a group.

Using Persuasive Language

In Chapter 3, you learned about the goals of persuasive speech. In this chapter, you will learn how to use persuasive language to convince others to give you the things you want or to do the things you want them to do. Persuasive language is all about changing people's minds and making them do or believe something different. When making a persuasive speech, there are techniques you can use. Understanding these techniques also helps when you listen to persuasive speeches: you will see how they try to convince you with certain kinds of arguments, manipulate your emotions and encourage you to take action.

A. Look at the following photographs and think about how using persuasive language could convince someone to do something he or she might not want to do. Write a short persuasive sentence for each.

_____   _____   _____

_____   _____   _____

_____   _____   _____

B. Persuasive speech, in which the speaker tries to convince people to take action or think in a certain way, is different from informative speech, in which the speaker wants only to explain ideas or options. Read the following statements and decide which are persuasive and which are informative.

STATEMENT	PERSUASIVE	INFORMATIVE
1 You can choose between two theories.	☐	☐
2 Don't you think that it's a good theory?	☐	☐
3 The obvious solution to the problem is …!	☐	☐
4 When you review the experimental results, you'll agree with me.	☐	☐
5 Let me explain the hypothesis of each theory.	☐	☐
6 I'll explain each step and then you can reach a conclusion.	☐	☐
7 Only a fool would think that this theory is true.	☐	☐
8 If you agree, I'll be your friend forever.	☐	☐

Discuss your answers with a partner. If you disagree, explain your reasons—and try to sway your partner to your way of thinking!

C. There are many ways to express the same idea. We often include weak—or tentative—expressions when we are not sure of our idea, are being polite or are concerned the listener might not like the suggestion. In persuasive speech, we avoid tentative expressions and use commands that make our suggestions stronger and more direct. Rewrite the following sentences using persuasive language to change them from weak to strong.

1 I believe it would be better if we recycled more plastic.

_____

_____

2 I'm wondering if you've considered trying three wheels instead of four.

_____

_____

3 You might want to think about changing the mixture of chemicals.

_____

_____

4 Wouldn't it be better if you checked the electricity first?

_____

_____

5 I'm not sure but maybe it's time to work on another project.

_____

_____

D. Imagine you have encountered a group of people who refuse to believe in scientific facts and will not save their lives by taking action. Choose a situation with the potential to kill a lot of people such as a volcano about to erupt, a radiation leak or poisoned water supplies.

Keeping in mind the goals of persuasive speech, use the persuasive techniques in the table to convince the group to take action. Write your notes in short sentences and use persuasive language.

PERSUASIVE TECHNIQUES	PERSUASIVE SENTENCES
Start with the problem: explain the facts clearly and concisely.	
Motivate with emotional appeals: address things people care about.	

PERSUASIVE TECHNIQUES	PERSUASIVE SENTENCES
Talk about similar experiences: explain decisions taken or not taken and the results.	
Critique the alternatives: explain options and show how each is unsatisfactory.	
Point to the future: explain how life will improve.	
Ask for a commitment: elicit a promise to take action.	

LISTENING ③   Urban Legends

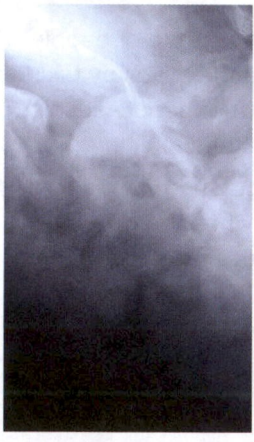

Before You Listen

Urban legends are a modern form of tall tales, parts of which sound as though they could be true. You've probably heard lots of such stories about unbelievable events and surprising cures. How do you decide what to believe?

Before you listen to Stella and Oscar discuss urban legends, read the following statements and indicate whether you think each one is true or false.

		TRUE	FALSE
❶	Chocolate causes acne.	☐	☐
❷	Spacecraft returning to Earth heat up because of air friction.	☐	☐
❸	Chameleons change colour for camouflage.	☐	☐
❹	People evolved from monkeys.	☐	☐
❺	Henry Ford invented the automobile assembly line.	☐	☐
❻	A duck's quack doesn't echo.	☐	☐

Working in a group, compare answers. Discuss which statements you could prove or disprove by research and which you could prove or disprove by experimentation.

		RESEARCH	EXPERIMENTATION
❶	Chocolate causes acne.	☐	☐
❷	Spacecraft returning to Earth heat up because of air friction.	☐	☐
❸	Chameleons change colour for camouflage.	☐	☐
❹	People evolved from monkeys.	☐	☐
❺	Henry Ford invented the automobile assembly line.	☐	☐
❻	A duck's quack doesn't echo.	☐	☐

While You Listen

Listen to the advice Stella gives Oscar about the dangers of believing in urban legends. Using the key phrases below, take notes while you listen. Add Stella's examples.

KEY PHRASES	NOTES
... makes you feel smart because it makes someone else look stupid.	
... the story usually has to do with a so-called friend of a friend.	
... something humorous that doesn't hurt anyone ...	
... the more details you throw in, the more likely it seems.	
... makes you think badly of other people for cultural or even racist reasons.	

KEY PHRASES	NOTES
The third type ... make people feel good about doing nothing, or worse than nothing.	
... the most terrible ones are those that give bad advice ...	
... don't believe it until you check the facts for yourself.	

After You Listen

Work in a group and discuss Stella's examples of urban legends. Which are the more believable; which the least? Why? If you know any other urban legends, share them with the group.

FINAL ASSIGNMENT

Give a Persuasive Presentation

Now it's your turn. Use everything you have learned in this chapter to prepare for and give a longer presentation of up to ten minutes.

A. Work with a partner to imagine a situation in which people must make a decision on a scientific topic or issue with at least two choices or points of view. Each partner will argue in favour of one point of view, but the two sides to the topic should share some characteristics. For example, clean energy is a topic with many options that share a core of common characteristics. For this example, you might create a scenario in which local residents must choose between a wind farm and a tidal energy project for power generation.

B. Speak with your teacher. Ask for approval of your topic and advice on how to develop it.

C. Research your point of view independently. Use at least three sources.

SOURCE 1: _____

_____

SOURCE 2: _____

_____

SOURCE 3: _____

_____

D. With your partner, draw a Venn diagram and each write notes on your point of view in one of the circles. Compare notes and, in the overlapping part of the diagram, write those characteristics or features that are in common.

E. Working with your partner, plan your presentation. Use points from the following table. You may wish to rearrange the order to better suit your topic.

GOALS OF A PERSUASIVE SPEECH	NOTES
Begin by getting the audience's attention. Ask a rhetorical question, make a surprising statement or open with a quotation or story.	
Motivate the audience by giving them a reason to keep listening. Assure the audience that the information you are going to give will be helpful.	
Let the audience know what you will talk about. Give the audience the main points, explaining any technical aspects.	
Explain a need. Point out the change that needs to happen (or not happen) and support it with a fact.	
Present a solution. Explain the attitude, belief or action the audience needs to adopt in order to avoid negative consequences.	
Ask the audience to take action. Summarize the main points and remind the audience of what needs to be done. Be excited and positive about the outcome.	

F. Introduce your topic and use your Venn diagram to highlight the similarities between the two points of view. Taking turns with your partner, explain your side of the issue. One partner should give the introduction and the other the conclusion. Use persuasive language to convince your audience of the relevance of your arguments.

Good luck!

CHAPTER 6

Saving the World, One Child at a Time

Imagine if a deadly new disease was rapidly spreading across the world and no one quite understood how. What do you think would be the best way to uncover its secrets?

Cholera is a terrible—and often fatal—disease. In 1854, British doctor John Snow (1813–1858) disagreed with so-called experts who thought cholera was spread through "bad" air; he thought it was spread through polluted drinking water. To prove his theory, he mapped cases of cholera during a London outbreak and found that 500 of them occurred within 225 metres of a single common water pump. The pump was closed—after much opposition—and the number of cholera cases dropped dramatically. Mapping became an important new tool for fighting old and new diseases.

- listen to a podcast about smallpox, a report on malaria and a conversation about debating skills;

- practise debating skills;
- learn vocabulary related to different diseases and their treatment;
- organize your ideas using tables and maps;

- practise speaking skills individually, in pairs and in small groups;
- prepare and participate in one short presentation and one longer team debate.

GEARING UP

A. Pictured here are different ways in which diseases can spread. Name three diseases that are spread in each of these ways.

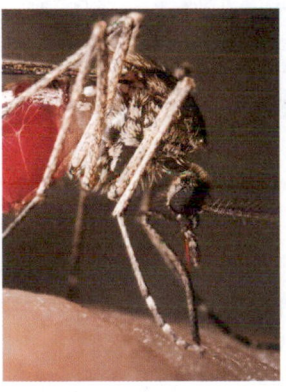  

_____ _____ _____

_____ _____ _____

_____ _____ _____

B. In what other ways are diseases spread? Discuss your answers with a partner.

_____

_____

C. Work in groups. Compare your answers with those of other students. Based on your discussion, what are possible ways of battling the spread of different diseases?

_____

_____

_____

> Learn word histories. The word "decimate" comes from the Roman army's practice of killing one in ten people to punish the group.

A. Check the words you understand. Then, check the words you use.

	UNDERSTAND	USE		UNDERSTAND	USE
unprecedented (adj.)	☐	☐	epidemiology (n.)	☐	☐
eradication (n.)	☐	☐	daunting (adj.)	☐	☐
contagious (adj.)	☐	☐	afflicted (v.)	☐	☐
devastating (adj.)	☐	☐	testimony (n.)	☐	☐
epidemics (n.)	☐	☐	deemed (v.)	☐	☐
decimated (v.)	☐	☐	vaccine (n.)	☐	☐
marginalized* (adj.)	☐	☐	transmission* (n.)	☐	☐
nomadic (adj.)	☐	☐	immunization (n.)	☐	☐
attributed* (v.)	☐	☐	ensure* (v.)	☐	☐
component* (n.)	☐	☐	emerged* (v.)	☐	☐

* Appears on the Academic Word List

B. Read the following sentences or phrases and then write a definition for each of the words in bold.

WORDS IN CONTEXT	DEFINITION
❶ In this episode, we look at an **unprecedented** achievement in the history of the World Health Organization, the **eradication** of smallpox.	unprecedented: *never having happened before*
	eradication:
❷ Smallpox is an acute **contagious** disease caused by the variola virus.	contagious:
❸ ... smallpox is one of the most **devastating** diseases known to mankind.	devastating:
❹ For centuries, repeated **epidemics** swept across continents and **decimated** populations.	epidemics:
	decimated:

▶

WORDS IN CONTEXT	DEFINITION
❺ The disease ... left survivors blind, disfigured and **marginalized**.	marginalized:
❻ ... from **nomadic** tribes in remote mountain areas to permanent dwellers in ... Asia's slums.	nomadic:
❼ Success has been **attributed** to a strong research **component**, an emphasis on **epidemiology** and surveillance, and the flexibility to adapt to new findings and change course when needed.	attributed:
	component:
	epidemiology:
❽ He spoke of the **daunting** challenges faced by health workers at that time.	daunting:
❾ ... conflict in so many areas and with large populations **afflicted** by natural disasters ...	afflicted:
❿ I think it is a **testimony** to the skill and creativity of the international advisers ...	testimony:
⓫ ... staff who managed to overcome all of these and achieve what had been **deemed** impossible.	deemed:
⓬ Dr. Peter Carassco is a WHO Policy Adviser for **vaccine** security.	vaccine:
⓭ We were able to track down what we call the chains of **transmission**, shut them down with vaccination ...	transmission:

▶

WORDS IN CONTEXT	DEFINITION
⑭ ... the Assembly agreed to set in motion an expanded programme on **immunization** whose goal was to **ensure** that the world's children would also be protected ...	immunization:
	ensure:
⑮ ... a new era has **emerged** for public health achievement through vaccination.	emerged:

C. Check your definitions with a partner. If you do not understand some words, look them up in a dictionary.

D. Knowing one word can often help you understand other words derived from it. Give the definition for each of the following words. Then, indicate if the words are nouns, verbs or adjectives.

❶ margin: _____

_____

❷ marginal: _____

_____

❸ marginalize: _____

_____

❹ marginalization: _____

_____

> ❗ Two words that don't follow the negative suffix rule are "flammable" and "inflammable"; they both mean the same thing: "likely to catch fire."

E. The prefix *un-* is added to the word *precedent* (meaning "an earlier example that is used as a guide") to form the negative adjective *unprecedented*. In some—but not all—cases, the prefixes *in-, ir-, im-, il-* and *un-* are used to indicate a negative or opposite meaning. Write the negative form of each of the following words and then give the definition.

	NEGATIVE FORM	DEFINITION
legal		
material		
relevant		
satisfactory		
sufficient		

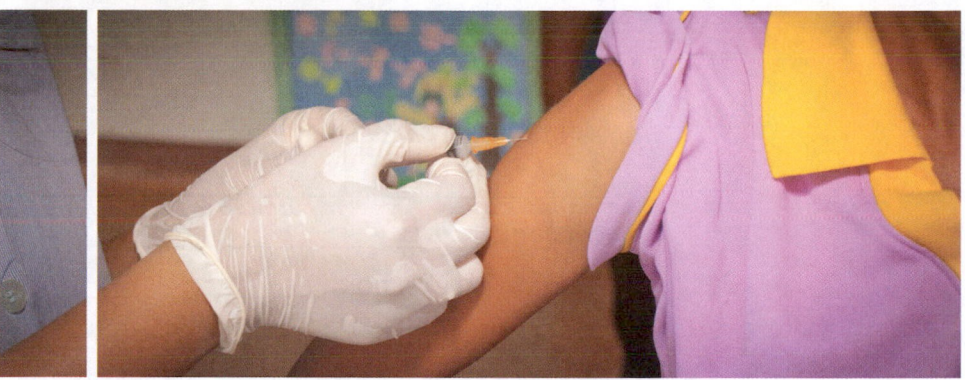

Before You Listen

Do you believe that science and medicine can protect us from diseases and epidemics? Let's hope so. A lot of work goes into identifying, battling and eradicating diseases. The World Health Organization (WHO) is among several groups working to track and treat different diseases. In this podcast, you will hear about some of the challenges faced in eradicating one of the world's deadliest diseases: smallpox.

Before you listen to the podcast, discuss these questions with a partner.

• What do you know about smallpox?

• How do epidemics spread?

• How are diseases and epidemics eradicated?

Here is the opening segment of the podcast you will listen to. Underline the words or ideas that are unfamiliar to you.

> "Smallpox is an acute contagious disease caused by the variola virus. Having originated over 3,000 years ago in India or Egypt, smallpox is one of the most devastating diseases known to mankind. For centuries, repeated epidemics swept across continents and decimated populations. The disease, for which there was no effective treatment, killed as many as 30 percent of those infected and left survivors blind, disfigured and marginalized.
>
> "In 1967, when the disease threatened 60 percent of the world's population, WHO launched an intensified plan to eradicate smallpox. Through the success of the global eradication campaign, smallpox was finally pushed back to the Horn of Africa, with the last recorded case in Somalia in 1977. The World Health Assembly in 1980 declared smallpox eradicated from the face of the Earth."

Write the words or ideas that were unfamiliar to you. Then, discuss these with your partner and work together to write definitions or explanations.

WORD/IDEA: _____

DEFINITION/EXPLANATION: _____

_____

WORD/IDEA: _____

DEFINITION/EXPLANATION: _____

_____

▶

WORD/IDEA: _____

DEFINITION/EXPLANATION: _____

_____

WORD/IDEA: _____

DEFINITION/EXPLANATION: _____

_____

WORD/IDEA: _____

DEFINITION/EXPLANATION: _____

_____

While You Listen

While you listen, try to understand the process involved in eradicating a disease by noting the challenges mentioned in the interview and the solutions applied to address those challenges. Listen a first time to get the general idea. The second time you listen, take notes on the solutions. Listen a third time to check your notes and add details.

CHALLENGES	SOLUTIONS
Disease threatening 60 percent of the world's population	WHO launched an intensified plan to eradicate smallpox.
Making eradication possible	
Facing floods, famines, civil war, refugees and a lack of technology	
Tracking down and containing the last outbreak	
Protecting against measles, polio, diphtheria, pertussis (whooping cough) and tetanus	

After You Listen

Review your notes. Think about what you've written. Add other details or thoughts to your notes.

FOCUS ON LISTENING

Working with Maps

Maps are a powerful way to enhance a presentation. When you listen to a presentation that includes maps, you need to be critical about what kind of map is being used and whether the information is properly represented. Sometimes, maps can mislead an audience, either accidentally or by design. It's important to properly interpret what is being expressed.

A. Look at the following map. It shows outbreaks of H1N1, commonly known as *swine flu*, in cities around the world. With a partner, discuss which factors might explain the spread of this disease.

B. This map differs from some other maps that show outbreaks of disease because it identifies the cities in which the outbreaks occurred rather than the whole countries. What makes the city approach useful and what makes it problematic, in terms of mapping diseases?

_____

_____

_____

C. You can use different types of maps, depending on the kind of information you want to provide. What kind of information might each of the following types of maps give? How can the information on them be ambiguous or difficult to interpret?

TYPE OF MAP	INFORMATION	AMBIGUITIES
HISTORICAL		
POLITICAL		
ROAD		

TYPE OF MAP	INFORMATION	AMBIGUITIES
THEMATIC		
TOPOGRAPHIC		

D. Review the following data about the incidence of Acquired Immunodeficiency Syndrome (AIDS) in the four most populated provinces of Canada.

AIDS CASES BY PROVINCE/TERRITORY

PROVINCE	NEW CASES IN 2009	CUMULATIVE TOTAL UNTIL END 2009 (OVER 1,000)
British Columbia	56	4,377
Alberta	36	1,462
Ontario	114	8,546
Quebec	—	6,098*
Total (for Canada)	224	21,681

* Quebec AIDS data have not been available since June 2003.

Adapted from Public Health Agency of Canada. (2010). HIV and AIDS in Canada: Surveillance report to December 31, 2009. Retrieved from: http://www.phac-aspc.gc.ca/aids-sida/publication/survreport/2009/dec/7-eng.php#table18a

E. Present the data on the following map outline. Then, complete the legend for your map and give it a title.

TITLE: _____

_____

LEGEND	

❗ A legend explains the meaning of symbols and colours used on a map.

F. Discuss with a partner what is clear and what is controversial about the map. How might it misrepresent the data?

WARM-UP ASSIGNMENT
Talk about Maps

A. Poverty and death are closely related. Look at these two maps of the world: one shows countries suffering from poverty; the other shows countries where common vaccines could prevent many deaths, particularly in children. Think about the distribution on each map. What do they have in common? What is different?

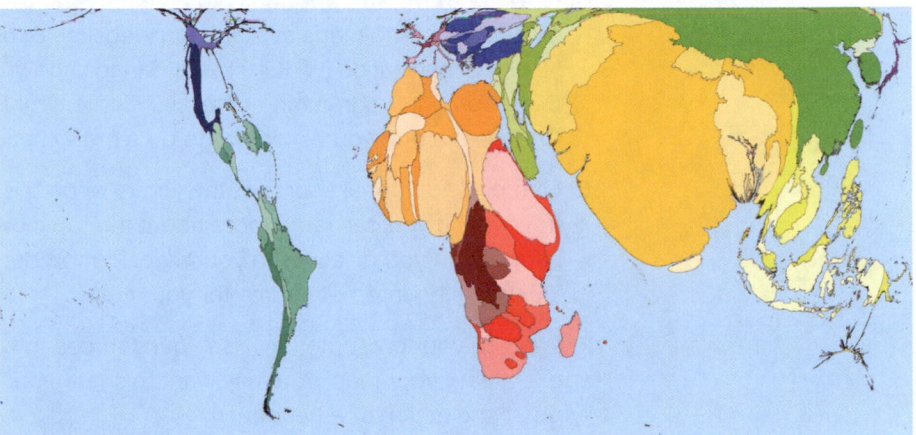

Territory size shows the proportion of the world population living in poverty there.

Worldmapper. (n.d.) Human poverty: Map no. 174. Retrieved from: http://www.worldmapper.org/display.php?selected=174

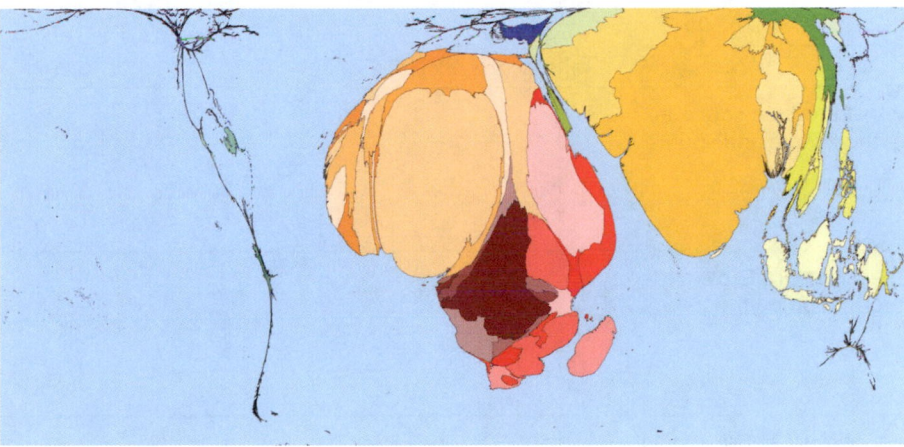

Territories are sized in proportion to the absolute number of people who died from childhood cluster disease in one year.

Worldmapper. (n.d.) Vaccine preventable deaths: Map no. 380. Retrieved from: http://www.worldmapper.org/display_extra.php?selected=380

B. Discuss your ideas with a partner. Then, answer the following questions.

1 What do the areas have in common?

_____

_____

2 How do the areas differ?

_____

_____

3 What reason(s) might explain the distributions?

_____

_____

_____

C. Work in groups. Compare your answers with those of other students.

D. Now you have an opportunity to research and give a short presentation on a map. Look at the maps available on websites of organizations such as the World Health Organization (WHO), Health Canada, the World Bank, the United Nations Development Programme or the U.S. Centers for Disease Control and Prevention. Choose the one you would like to do a presentation on.

E. Find one additional source in the library or on the Internet (other than _Wikipedia_) from which you can learn more about the topic of your map. Add any new information you discover to your map. Remember to cite your sources correctly including the Internet source for your map.

F. Prepare your presentation. Use your sources to write notes for a short speech explaining your map. You may want to share your map with the class as a computer projection or a handout.

	NOTES
PURPOSE: What is your presentation about?	
MAP: Introduce your map, giving its title and source.	
EXPLANATION: Explain the key information on the map.	
SIGNIFICANCE: Talk about the importance of the data represented: what impact does the phenomenon have on the world?	
SUPPORT: Mention the information you found in your additional source.	
CONCLUSION: Show why the audience should be concerned about this data.	

VOCABULARY BUILD

A. Check the words you understand. Then, check the words you use.

> We all understand more words than we use. A word like "efficacy" is a synonym for the more common "effectiveness." As long as you understand both, you can use the one you prefer.

> WHO and MSF (Médecins Sans Frontières) are initialisms. In English, Médecins Sans Frontières translates to Doctors Without Borders.

	UNDERSTAND	USE		UNDERSTAND	USE
humanitarian (adj.)	☐	☐	parasite (n.)	☐	☐
severe (adj.)	☐	☐	alternative* (adj.)	☐	☐
clinical trials (n.)	☐	☐	efficacy (n.)	☐	☐
administer* (v.)	☐	☐	potent* (adj.)	☐	☐
endemic (adj.)	☐	☐	neutral* (adj.)	☐	☐
transformative* (adj.)	☐	☐	subsidy* (n.)	☐	☐
convulsions (n.)	☐	☐	reluctance* (n.)	☐	☐
infusion (n.)	☐	☐	implement* (v.)	☐	☐
monitor* (v.)	☐	☐	intervention* (n.)	☐	☐
vertigo (n.)	☐	☐	mortality (n.)	☐	☐

* Appears on the Academic Word List

B. Read the following sentences or phrases and then write a definition for each of the words in bold.

WORDS IN CONTEXT	DEFINITION
❶ MSF is an independent medical **humanitarian** aid organization.	humanitarian: *concerned with promoting human welfare*
❷ ... the disease progresses to a **severe** form of malaria ...	severe:
❸ ... there's a drug that has been proven in **clinical trials** to be a major improvement ...	clinical trials:
❹ ... the new medication is also far simpler and safer to **administer** than quinine ...	administer:
❺ ... the countries where the disease is **endemic** also need to make the move ...	endemic:
❻ Making the switch would be **transformative** for many communities ...	transformative:

WORDS IN CONTEXT	DEFINITION
7 ... rushed her to the local health centre because she was having **convulsions** ...	convulsions:
8 It's a drug that's administered through an **infusion** ...	infusion:
9 That's a very demanding twenty-four-hour process for health staff to **monitor** ...	monitor:
10 The side effects caused by an overdose of quinine include **vertigo**, nausea and vomiting ...	vertigo:
11 Under dosing, however, means that the malarial **parasite** isn't knocked out by the medicine ...	parasite:
12 ... newer treatments, **alternative** treatments, are much more effective than quinine.	alternative:
13 ... a Chinese plant whose **efficacy** against malaria was rediscovered in the 1980s has proved itself in clinical trials.	efficacy:
14 ... it's more effective and **potent** than quinine ...	potent:
15 ... the difference in cost between quinine and artesunate is **neutral** ...	neutral:
16 The way forward ... is an initial **subsidy** on the higher costs ... from the international community ...	subsidy:
17 There will be an initial **reluctance** ... but that initial reluctance has to be overcome ...	reluctance:

WORDS IN CONTEXT	DEFINITION
⑱ ... offer countries technical support and training in how to **implement** the new drug.	implement:
⑲ To my mind this is a very, very precise **intervention** with a massive reduction in **mortality** ...	intervention:
	mortality:

C. Check your definitions with a partner. If you do not understand some words, look them up in a dictionary.

D. Euphemisms are expressions we use to avoid directly naming a stark or unpleasant reality. There are many euphemisms that avoid direct mention of bodily functions and many formal, religious and humorous ones for referring to mortality or death. Which type is each of the following expressions?

EXPRESSION	FORMAL, RELIGIOUS OR HUMOROUS?
lives with the angels	
passed away	
gone to meet his maker	
kicked the bucket	
no longer with us	
pushing up daisies	
resting in peace	

> ❗ Some euphemisms are quite specific; "Davy Jones's locker" is an expression used to refer to the bottom of the sea or the resting place of drowned sailors.

E. Use these words to fill in the blanks in the following paragraph.

administer	clinical trials	humanitarian	mortality
alternative	efficacy	monitor	reluctance

Despite high rates of _____, many people show a _____ to accept _____ medicines to those they have used for years. Of course, _____ organizations like the Red Cross are active in conducting _____, in which they _____ new medicines to groups of people and _____ the effects, but even if there was proof of a new drug's _____, people tend to prefer the drugs they already know.

Before You Listen

What do you know about malaria? It's hard for most of us to understand the fear associated with diseases such as malaria. In different parts of the world without access to proper medicine, falling victim to malaria, or any number of other diseases, can be a death sentence. In 2009, malaria was responsible for an estimated 781,000 deaths, mostly among poor African children. In this section, you will listen to a report on the availability of a new drug for treating malaria.

Here is an excerpt from the report you will listen to. Read the passage and discuss it with a partner by comparing your ideas about the treatment of malaria. Why do you think it has taken centuries to develop a new treatment for the disease?

> ❗ When you take notes, if there is a repeated phrase or an unusual word, you can use a symbol to write it more quickly, e.g., "artesunate" = @. After, convert the symbols you've used to the appropriate phrase or word.

"The drug quinine, also pronounced *qui-neen*, has been used to treat malaria for centuries. It's been the main weapon in the battle against the disease, which is carried by mosquitoes and kills close to one million people every year.

"The vast majority of the victims are children in Africa, and they die after the disease progresses to a severe form of malaria where their internal organs come under attack. At the moment, the treatment these children receive is quinine.

"But now, there's a drug that has been proven in clinical trials to be a major improvement on quinine. It's called *artesunate*. And not only is it more effective, but the new medication is also far simpler and safer to administer than quinine, especially in the often remote places where malaria causes the greatest toll. Most importantly, artesunate could save 200,000 lives per year."

While You Listen

The first time you listen, try to get the general idea. In the following table, a variety of situations are listed in the order they are discussed in the report. When you listen the second time, identify either the solution to, or the consequence of, each situation and take notes to explain. Listen a third time to check your explanations or add details.

SITUATION	SOLUTION OR CONSEQUENCE
Countries where malaria is endemic need to move from quinine to artesunate.	SOLUTION: *The support of the international community*
Child seriously ill with severe malaria	SOLUTION:

▶

SITUATION	SOLUTION OR CONSEQUENCE
Not a comfortable procedure, especially for young children	CONSEQUENCE:
Delivering the correct dose of quinine	SOLUTION: Four-hour infusions three times a day until the child is well enough to swallow tablets
Child has to stay in bed quiet, not moving.	CONSEQUENCE:
An overdose of quinine causes side effects.	CONSEQUENCE: Vertigo, nausea and vomiting, and some patients experience problems with their sight and hearing
An under dose means the malaria parasite is not destroyed.	CONSEQUENCE:
Girl looked after in an MSF-supported health centre	CONSEQUENCE:
Villagers can't go to the hospital.	CONSEQUENCE:
Alternative treatments are much more effective than quinine.	SOLUTION:
Artesunate can be delivered by injection.	CONSEQUENCE:
Shorter time to give the medicine	CONSEQUENCE:
Initial reluctance because of cost	SOLUTION: Subsidies from the international community: $30,000,000

▶

SITUATION	SOLUTION OR CONSEQUENCE
Nurses, doctors and patients reluctant	SOLUTION:
Several African countries interested in artesunate	CONSEQUENCE: *WHO is making artesunate the preferred choice and providing training and technical support.*

After You Listen

With your partner, discuss solutions to treating malaria. Which problems do you think are the greatest barriers to treating the disease? What do you think are some of the economic, social and emotional impacts of a malaria epidemic?

FOCUS ON SPEAKING

Working with Analogies

One way to strengthen your arguments is through the use of analogies. Analogies are comparisons that make your points more obvious. Often, analogies are in the form of similes, using *like* to compare things.

A. Create similes by matching the following words with the people or events they can be compared to.

1 A war is like
_____ a mechanic who evaluates the problem and tries to fix it.

2 An epidemic is like
_____ an uninvited and unwelcome guest in your home.

3 A doctor is like
_____ a flood that starts slowly but spreads quickly.

4 A vaccine is like
_____ a game in which the losers die.

5 A parasite is like
_____ an umbrella, stopping diseases from touching you.

B. When you critique an analogy, look for something weak or false about it that does not make for a convincing comparison. Work with a partner and discuss what is imperfect about each of the above analogies and how they could be improved.

Academic
Survival Skill

How to Debate

Debating is an extension of persuasive speech. You use facts to support your point of view, but you also use techniques like offering analogies that compare the specifics of your arguments to something that is easier to understand.

A. There are many different structures for debates, but an informal one features a proposition that one side supports and the other tries to refute, or argue against. An example of a proposition is:

Many poor countries have no reason to develop their own medical infrastructure because foreign organizations and volunteers contribute so much.

Consider this proposition and the structure for debating it below. Complete the notes.

DEBATE STRUCTURE	NOTES
State the proposition and explain your point of view (for or against the proposition).	We reject the proposition that many poor countries have no reason to develop their own medical infrastructure because foreign organizations and volunteers contribute so much.
Offer an argument in three points. Strengthen your arguments with analogies. Produce and explain any visual aids that can support your point of view.	POINT 1: There are examples of poorer countries that have developed their own medical systems, including some based on traditional medicine such as _____ _____ POINT 2: Costa Rica and Cuba are both poor countries, but both have some of the highest percentages (give the percentage) of doctors per capita in the world. POINT 3: _____ _____ _____ _____
Anticipate the other side's arguments against your points and think of counter-arguments.	POINT 1: _____ _____ _____ POINT 2: You may argue that Cuba and Costa Rica are only isolated examples, but _____ _____ POINT 3: _____ _____ _____
Offer a conclusion.	Our arguments make it clear that the proposition is false and _____ _____ _____
Anticipate the other side's arguments in support of their points and consider objections.	POINT 1: Few countries in Africa have strong medical systems. POINT 2: Mortality rates for infants and women have not been improving _____ _____ _____ POINT 3: _____ _____ _____

B. Rebuttals are your arguments or evidence refuting or disproving the other side's points. It's tempting to go through the arguments point by point, but it's better to summarize them and take a thematic approach. Look at the following arguments, identify the general theme and write a rebuttal.

ARGUMENT	THEME	REBUTTAL
The lack of medical infrastructure is due to the politicians, the army and poverty.	Other forces are to blame.	Although our opponent tries to blame outside forces, …
Without organizations like the WHO, subsidies from international donors and volunteers …	Lumping together many factors makes the arguments seem stronger.	
Education, not medical care, will save people.		

LISTENING ③   Barriers to Solutions

Before You Listen

When you know you are going to have a discussion in which you will need to persuade another person, how do you prepare? Do you make a list of points and think about any objections the other person might have?

Before you listen to Stella and Oscar as they prepare for their class debate, think about the use of evidence in a debate. Write three issues you and your friends or family might debate because you hold opposing points of view. Then, think of evidence you could use to support your point of view.

❶ _____

❷ _____

❸ _____

Here is the beginning of Stella and Oscar's conversation about their debate topic. Think about whether or not you agree with the quotation by the philosopher Bertrand Russell (1872–1970).

STELLA: We start with Bertrand Russell's quotation, "Every advance in civilization has been denounced as unnatural while it was recent." Basically, he's saying that new ideas and innovations have always been criticized. People criticized everything from cars to rock 'n' roll music.

OSCAR: That's right, and some people still do. In any case, we're on the supporting side, which means we need to make points that agree with the quotation.

STELLA: And do you?

OSCAR: Do I what?

STELLA: Do you agree with the quotation? Do you really think that every advance in civilization has been criticized?

OSCAR: Stella, in a debate, it doesn't matter what you think; you just have to support your side of the argument as best you can.

Write an example and an explanation for opposite points of view on the quotation.

	AGREE WITH THE QUOTATION	DISAGREE WITH THE QUOTATION
EXAMPLE		
EXPLANATION		

While You Listen

Oscar and Stella discuss a number of principles and examples. The first time you listen, fill in the missing examples. The second time you listen, write an explanation for each example. Listen a third time to add details.

PRINCIPLE	EXAMPLE	EXPLANATION
self-interest or greed	slavery in the United States before the Civil War	
ignorance		
wilful ignorance		
greed, ignorance and wilful ignorance	Andrew Wakefield on vaccines	

After You Listen

Imagine you had an opportunity to debate the value of vaccines with Andrew Wakefield. What information might you want to find out before you met?

_____

_____

_____

FINAL ASSIGNMENT
Prepare for a Debate

Now it's your turn. Use everything you have learned in this chapter to prepare for and participate in a debate.

A. Working in a group of six or eight people, choose one of the following topics:

- the Bubonic Plague of 1338–1351, which killed 100,000,000 in Europe and Asia
- the Great Plague of London in 1665–1666, which killed 100,000 in England
- European diseases such as smallpox, measles and typhoid, which were spread by colonists in North and South America between 1500 and 1900 and which killed 1,500,000
- the third cholera pandemic, which killed 1,000,000 in Russia between 1852 and 1860
- the 1918 flu pandemic, which killed 50–80,000,000 people worldwide
- AIDS, which has affected or killed 25,000,000 since 1981

B. Match your topic to a proposition and write it below:

- The _____ led to social changes that improved life for most people.

- The _____ would not have happened today because of (changes in science, better sanitation, new medicines, government policies ...).

- The _____ might one day be developed into a weapon to attack other countries.

- _____ would be cured if it occurred in wealthy industrialized nations instead of in poor countries.

PROPOSITION: _____

_____

_____

_____

C. As a group, speak with your teacher. Ask for approval of the proposition and advice on how to prepare for the debate. Divide your group into two teams and flip a coin to decide which team will argue *for*, and which team will argue *against*, the proposition.

D. Working with your team, do the research. Use at least three sources and try to include a map. Remember to cite your sources correctly.

SOURCE 1: _____

_____

SOURCE 2: _____

_____

SOURCE 3: _____

_____

E. Plan your presentation. Use the following table to organize your arguments.

DEBATE STRUCTURE	NOTES
State the proposition and explain your point of view (for or against the proposition).	
Offer an argument in three points. Produce and explain any visual aids that can support your point of view.	
Anticipate the other side's arguments against your points and think of counter-arguments.	
Offer a conclusion.	
Anticipate the other side's arguments in support of their points and consider objections.	

In a debate, it's easy to forget to listen because you're thinking of what you will say next. Listen to the other side! They might say something important that you need to argue against.

F. Practise your debate within your team. Take turns acting as the opposite side to critique and improve your points. Divide responsibility for the presentation of your arguments and the rebuttal of the challenges among team members. Work with your teacher and the other groups to agree on a set number of minutes for each stage of the debate.

G. Review notes from previous chapters on persuasive language to help you prepare for and participate in a convincing debate presentation.

Good luck!

CHAPTER 7
Embracing Risk

How comfortable are you with taking risks? How much are you willing to gamble to get what you want?

If you're young, you probably have a high threshold for taking risks. The older you get, the less likely you are to take risks because you have more responsibilities and, in many cases, you have more to lose, such as a comfortable home, a secure job and long-term relationships. When you're young, however, you may feel almost invincible and able to do anything you want. You can gamble with career choices, experiences and even your physical limits because you may not understand—or care about—the risks involved.

People who are willing to take risks are sometimes foolhardy, yet at other times pioneering, taking advantage of opportunities to achieve greatness.

In this chapter,
you will

- listen to a lecture about a rebel artist, a podcast on risk-taking and a conversation about learning from failure;

- learn vocabulary related to innovation, risk-taking and overcoming failure;

- organize your ideas using tables and line charts;

- practise speaking skills individually, in pairs and in small groups;

- prepare and deliver one short and one longer presentation.

GEARING UP

A. Each of us has different tolerance levels for risks related to physical activities, money and jobs. Answer the following questions. Give an example of the riskiest thing you would be willing to do in each situation and explain why. Then, discuss your answers with a partner.

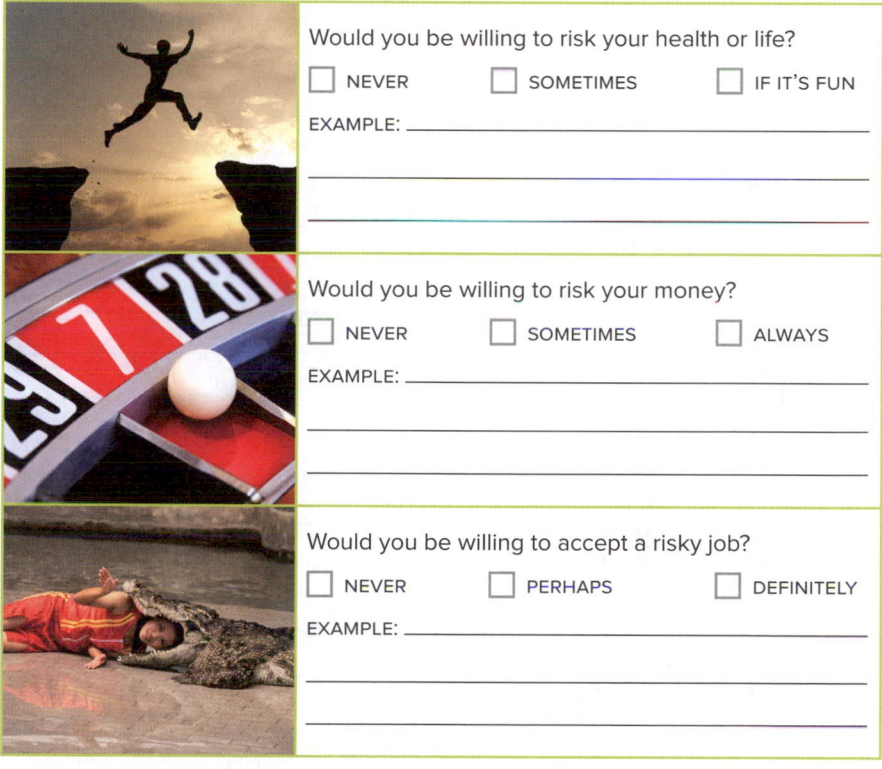

Would you be willing to risk your health or life?

☐ NEVER   ☐ SOMETIMES   ☐ IF IT'S FUN

EXAMPLE: _____

_____

_____

Would you be willing to risk your money?

☐ NEVER   ☐ SOMETIMES   ☐ ALWAYS

EXAMPLE: _____

_____

_____

Would you be willing to accept a risky job?

☐ NEVER   ☐ PERHAPS   ☐ DEFINITELY

EXAMPLE: _____

_____

_____

B. Who is more willing to take risks, you or your partner? What type of risks are you each willing to take and why?

_____

_____

_____

A. Check the words you understand. Then, check the words you use.

In 1492, Christopher Columbus thought he had reached India. So he called the people he met "Indians." The Aboriginal peoples of North America usually prefer other names.

	UNDERSTAND	USE		UNDERSTAND	USE
rebels (n.)	☐	☐	grandeur (n.)	☐	☐
remote (adj.)	☐	☐	inadequate (adj.)	☐	☐
First Nations (adj.)	☐	☐	gestures (n.)	☐	☐
accounts (n.)	☐	☐	appreciated* (v.)	☐	☐
immigrated* (v.)	☐	☐	collapsed* (v.)	☐	☐
plaster casts (n.)	☐	☐	schemes* (n.)	☐	☐
anatomy (n.)	☐	☐	documented* (v.)	☐	☐
conservative (adj.)	☐	☐	idealized (adj.)	☐	☐
income* (n.)	☐	☐	resent (v.)	☐	☐
embarked (v.)	☐	☐	vision* (n.)	☐	☐

* Appears on the Academic Word List

B. Read the following sentences or phrases and then write a definition for each of the words in bold.

WORDS IN CONTEXT	DEFINITION
❶ We often call such people *rebels*.	rebels: *people who resist authority, control or convention*
❷ ... there was a great deal of such exploration ... in **remote** parts of Asia, Africa and the Middle East.	remote:
❸ ... she travelled to remote areas ... her love of painting and her interest in **First Nations** culture.	First Nations:
❹ Her paintings and written **accounts** of her travels have delighted and inspired others for generations.	accounts:
❺ Emily Carr was born ... to English parents who had **immigrated** to Canada.	immigrated:
❻ Carr saved and bought **plaster casts** of sculptures from the local tombstone maker.	plaster casts:

WORDS IN CONTEXT	DEFINITION
7 Carr used these plaster casts to draw from and to learn about **anatomy**.	anatomy:
8 ... to study art at the somewhat **conservative** California School of Design.	conservative:
9 ... she realized that she needed to put her skills to use in earning an **income** ...	income:
10 ... she **embarked** on a study trip to England to learn more about European painting styles.	embarked:
11 Carr was amazed at the **grandeur** of the totem poles and other structures ...	grandeur:
12 "More than ever was I convinced that the old way of seeing was **inadequate** ..."	inadequate:
13 ... she got by with **gestures** and her good nature.	gestures:
14 ... they were little **appreciated** and didn't sell.	appreciated:
15 ... the rental market **collapsed**: people were unwilling to pay high rents ...	collapsed:
16 ... she invented several **schemes** to make money ...	schemes:
17 ... she turned her hand to writing and **documented** her time among the First Nations peoples.	documented:

▶

WORDS IN CONTEXT	DEFINITION
⑱ ... European-trained painters were sketching **idealized** versions of Canada ...	idealized:
⑲ "The men **resent** a woman getting any honour in what they consider is essentially their field."	resent:
⑳ Carr's **vision** of the First Nations peoples and the Canadian landscape helped to raise awareness ...	vision:

C. Check your definitions with a partner. If you do not understand some words, look them up in a dictionary.

D. Write one or more noun forms for each of the following words.

❶ appreciated: _____

❷ collapsed: _____

❸ documented: _____

❹ idealized: _____

❺ immigrated: _____

E. Both facial expressions and gestures are important parts of body language and help convey meaning. Which gestures might you use to express the following? (Note: Some gestures might have different meanings to different cultures.)

❶ agreement: _____

❷ disagreement: _____

❸ enthusiastic support: _____

❹ not understanding: _____

❺ can't hear: _____

LISTENING ❶

Emily Carr: A Life Less Ordinary

Before You Listen

Hearing about the lives of famous or inspiring people is fascinating. Perhaps you sometimes compare yourself to them and wonder what you might have done in their place. You may be struck by the physical, emotional and social challenges they faced and the risks they took to overcome those challenges.

Answer the following questions, and then discuss your answers with a partner. Think about your answers as you listen to a lecture on the Canadian artist Emily Carr (1871–1945).

1 Name a famous or inspiring person who you admire.

_____

2 What major challenge did this person face?

_____

3 What risks did the person take to overcome that challenge?

_____

_____

4 What did the person achieve by taking a risk?

_____

_____

Here is the first segment of the lecture you will listen to. Read it carefully and underline the key words that indicate what you are likely to hear and learn about.

> The expression "at one's doorstep" refers generally to something nearby, not necessarily outside one's house.

"Many of us long to live what we call _a life less ordinary_. The phrase _a life less ordinary_ refers to someone who has made interesting choices about what to do in life. Usually, such people have avoided the safe and traditional path that most of us follow and set out to do something extraordinary, something far different from the expectations of those around them and, even, something shocking. We often call such people _rebels_."

Predict what the lecture on Emily Carr will reveal. Discuss your prediction with your partner.

While You Listen

Read the following segments of the lecture. Then, listen a first time to get the general idea. While you listen a second time, number the segments in their correct order. Listen a third time to take notes and add details.

SEGMENT	NOTES
___1___ Some rebels set out to be consciously and deliberately different, for example, by travelling to a far country and perhaps living with and learning from the local people.	
_____ After five more years in Victoria, Carr was beginning to become aware of the new European art movements.	
_____ Carr's life might well have been quite ordinary.	

▶

SEGMENT	NOTES
_____ Emily Carr was born in Victoria, British Columbia, in 1871, to English parents who had immigrated to Canada.	
_____ In 1912, she set off on a six-week summer trip by steamer and canoe, exploring villages on the west coast of Vancouver Island, sketching and painting everywhere she went.	
_____ In other cases, a rebel does not set out to be so different but, in slow stages and through countless choices, achieves fame for doing great and different things.	
_____ In the 1870s, Victoria, on British Columbia's Vancouver Island, was a rather wild place.	
_____ One of her first choices as a student was to turn down a traditional class in drawing from plaster models— she'd done too much of that already— and instead take life-drawing classes.	
_____ The paintings she created were exceptional and, today, may sell for more than a million dollars.	
_____ As I mentioned earlier, while growing up in Victoria, Carr would have had contact with First Nations peoples.	
_____ Today, with so many popular women artists, it's difficult for us to understand that, as a rebel, Emily Carr did something quite different.	
_____ When both her parents died while she was still a teenager, she was placed in the care of guardians.	
__13__ Carr died on March 2, 1945, at the age of seventy-three, having lived *a life less ordinary*, true to a rebel vision she embraced as a young woman.	

After You Listen

Working in a group, discuss what you now know about Emily Carr. What did she do that was considered risky for her time? Would her decisions and actions be considered risky today? Why or why not?

Working with Line Charts

When you are listening to a presentation, or giving one yourself, the right chart can be an effective tool that helps to inform or convince the audience. One of the most common chart types is a *line chart*, also called a *line graph*. Line charts or graphs typically show the relationship of one set of data to another.

A. Look at the following line chart. It illustrates dangerous driving-related offences for different age groups. The x-axis shows the independent variable—age—and the y-axis shows the dependent variable—rates of different driving offences.

Dangerous Driving-Related Offences in Australia, 2006–2007

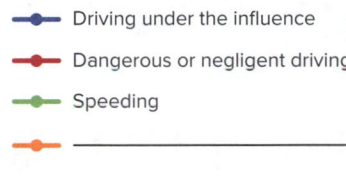

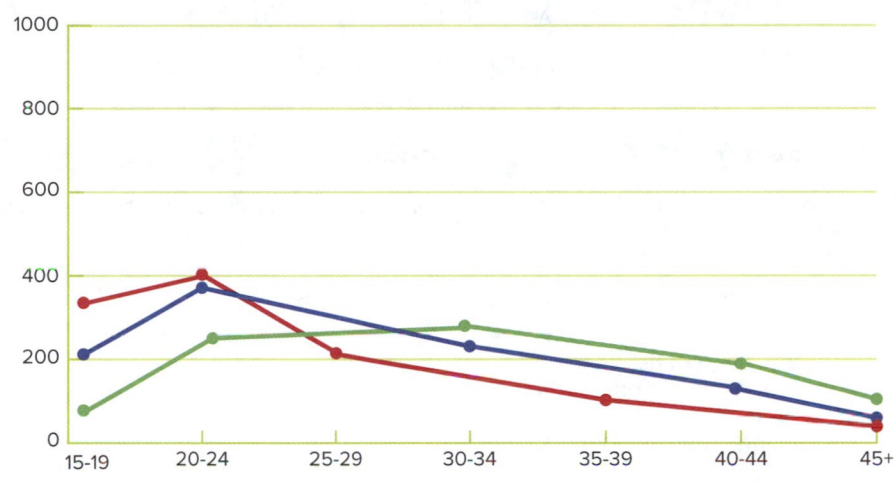

Australian Bureau of Statistics. (2009, December). Risk taking by young people. Retrieved from: http://www.abs.gov.au

B. Add the following data for exceeding the alcohol limit to the line chart above. Indicate the rate of offences for each age group and connect the points with lines. Add a line to the legend to identify the data.

EXCEEDING THE LEGAL ALCOHOL LIMIT

AGE GROUP (YEARS)	15–19	20–24	25–29	30–34	35–39	40–44	45+
RATE	400	900	700	600	500	400	200

C. With a partner, discuss the information on the line chart by answering the following questions.

- Which age group is responsible for the highest rate of dangerous driving offences?
- Which age group is responsible for the lowest rate?
- Why is it important to express the numbers of offences as rates and not simply as totals?

> "*Comfort zone*" *is an example of an expression that is open to individual interpretation; most people are aware of a zone or range of activities in which they feel comfortable.*

A. Check the words you understand. Then, check the words you use.

	UNDERSTAND	USE		UNDERSTAND	USE
killer idea (n.)	☐	☐	comfort zone (n.)	☐	☐
investing* (v.)	☐	☐	unnerving (adj.)	☐	☐
convincing* (v.)	☐	☐	neutralize (v.)	☐	☐
hesitate (v.)	☐	☐	pitching (v.)	☐	☐
reaction* (n.)	☐	☐	spouse (n.)	☐	☐
surveyed* (v.)	☐	☐	decision-maker (n.)	☐	☐
outcomes* (n.)	☐	☐	adrenaline rush (n.)	☐	☐
dramatically* (adv.)	☐	☐	paralyzing (adj.)	☐	☐
previously* (adv.)	☐	☐	warranted (adj.)	☐	☐
doomed (adj.)	☐	☐	perspective* (n.)	☐	☐

* Appears on the Academic Word List

B. Read the following sentences or phrases and then write a definition for each of the words in bold.

WORDS IN CONTEXT	DEFINITION
1 At some point, in the life of a **killer idea**, you're going to have to take a risk …	killer idea: *slang term for an important idea that will bring about significant change*
2 Now, the range of risks can go from **investing** your entire retirement fund to quitting your job, to **convincing** others to take risk with you …	investing: convincing:
3 But then you **hesitate**: the risk seems huge …	hesitate:
4 And immediately, your **reaction** is to retreat back to the comfort of the safe option.	reaction:
5 Back in 2005, a German researcher **surveyed** 20,000 people about their risk behaviour.	surveyed:

WORDS IN CONTEXT	DEFINITION
⑥ Now, there's some interesting **outcomes** from this that may not seem logical.	outcomes:
⑦ And a willingness to take risks decreases **dramatically** with age.	dramatically:
⑧ ... they'd had success **previously** in their lives—were more willing to take more risk.	previously:
⑨ ... are you **doomed** to realize your killer idea ...?	doomed:
⑩ The risk profiles—what I would refer to is that **comfort zone** ...	comfort zone:
⑪ Ask yourself why the potential for risk is so **unnerving** for you.	unnerving:
⑫ Then come up with ideas that **neutralize** each concern.	neutralize:
⑬ ... going through and evaluating the risk of an idea that you're **pitching**?	pitching:
⑭ How do you convince your **spouse** to take a little bit of that money ...?	spouse:
⑮ ... look at the risk profile for the key **decision-maker**—your boss, your spouse ...	decision-maker:

WORDS IN CONTEXT	DEFINITION
⑯ Some people climbing rocks, that fear is an **adrenaline rush**, it gives them energy ...	adrenaline rush:
⑰ For others, that fear of heights is **paralyzing** ...	paralyzing:
⑱ ... what is causing that deep-seated fear and see if it's **warranted**.	warranted:
⑲ Get a realistic **perspective** of what it is you are truly risking ...	perspective:

C. Check your definitions with a partner. If you do not understand some words, look them up in a dictionary.

D. A Tom Swift joke is a play on words that consists of an invented quotation followed by a punning adverb. Use these adverbs to fill in the blanks.

convincingly	dramatically	haltingly	hesitatingly	unnervingly

❶ "I'm thinking of becoming an actor," said Tom _____.

❷ "This injection will take away any feeling of pain," said Tom _____.

❸ "Vince is a liar," said Tom _____.

❹ "Maybe I should wait," said Tom _____.

❺ "I'm at the stop sign," said Tom _____.

LISTENING ❷ Getting Comfortable Taking Innovation Risks

Before You Listen

If you had a really great, but risky, idea that you think could change your life, what would you do? Would you take the risk? Or would you do nothing, perhaps simply talk about the idea to a friend without taking it further? What would stop you from taking a risk? You might have many reasons, and your list of reasons is likely to grow as you get older and become more reluctant to try new experiences. Before you listen to a podcast on taking innovation risks, discuss these questions with a partner.

• What big idea have you had in the past that you never got around to trying? What stopped you? Are you sorry or glad you did not pursue the idea?

Here is a segment from the beginning of the podcast you will listen to. Underline the words or ideas that are unfamiliar to you.

> "So, you've come up with that killer idea. To move it forward, you need to take a risk. Now, the range of risks can go from investing your entire retirement fund to quitting your job, to convincing others to take risk with you, where you're asking them to risk *their* retirement fund, *their* job security. But then you hesitate: the risk seems huge, and you start to second-guess the original idea. You ask yourself: 'Is the potential value of what this killer idea is worth the risk?' And immediately, your reaction is to retreat back to the comfort of the safe option. Stay where you're at and do nothing. Before you give up, let's understand how our mind processes risk."

Write the words or ideas that were unfamiliar to you. Then, discuss these with your partner and work together to write definitions or explanations.

! The expressions "losing face" and "saving face," used in this listening, both relate to embarrassment.

! The expression "twenty-five-year gold watch" is a metaphor for a conventional reward after years of loyalty to the same company.

WORD/IDEA: _____

DEFINITION/EXPLANATION: _____

_____

WORD/IDEA: _____

DEFINITION/EXPLANATION: _____

_____

WORD/IDEA: _____

DEFINITION/EXPLANATION: _____

_____

WORD/IDEA: _____

DEFINITION/EXPLANATION: _____

_____

WORD/IDEA: _____

DEFINITION/EXPLANATION: _____

_____

While You Listen

Read the questions in the following table. Then, listen a first time to get the general idea. While you listen a second time, answer the questions. Listen a third time to check your answers and notes and add details, such as examples that help you understand.

QUESTIONS	ANSWERS AND NOTES		
1 According to Phil McKinney, which characteristics make people more likely risk-takers?	female ☐ male ☐	older ☐ younger ☐	short ☐ tall ☐

▶

QUESTIONS	ANSWERS AND NOTES
❷ Why do older people avoid risk?	
❸ Which of these does McKinney say are concerns that may prevent people from taking risks?	home ☐ money ☐ saving face ☐ family ☐ nationality ☐ sports ☐
❹ What does he say people should do about each concern?	
❺ What does he say people need to do about their boss' or spouse's unwillingness to take a risk?	
❻ Why does McKinney talk about rock climbing?	
❼ What does McKinney mean by "take the plunge"?	

After You Listen

Review your notes. Think about what you've written. Write a short paragraph on a separate sheet of paper that defines your risk profile.

FOCUS ON SPEAKING

Paraphrasing

When we explain an idea and it's difficult for listeners to understand, we often *paraphrase*. The purpose of paraphrasing is to restate your ideas in ways that are easier for your audience to understand. You can still use the original phrase, but it's sometimes useful to say it another way, to add clarity.

A. Complete the following sentences with paraphrases for the vocabulary in bold.

❶ This is a **killer idea**; by that I mean it's _____.

❷ Skydiving is out of his **comfort zone**; it's _____ _____.

❸ We have to **neutralize**, or _____, this threat.

❹ She gets an **adrenaline rush** from skiing; in other words, _____ _____.

❺ That plan is **doomed**; that is to say, _____.

B. Paraphrasing is also a way to avoid plagiarism. Put the ideas behind the following quotations in your own words by paraphrasing.

1 "Only those who will risk going too far can possibly find out how far one can go." —T.S. Eliot (1888–1965)

_____

_____

2 "What you risk reveals what you value." —Jeanette Winterson (1959–)

_____

_____

3 "We took risks. We knew we took them. We have no cause for complaint." —Robert Frost (1874–1963)

_____

_____

WARM-UP ASSIGNMENT
Talk about Risk-Taking

Now it's your turn to research and present a short talk on risk-taking.

A. Choose a topic related to taking risks from the following:
- investments
- physical activities
- travel destinations
- types of jobs
- types of transportation

B. For your chosen topic, think of a range of examples that show different degrees of risk for different age groups. For instance, for the topic "physical activities," one example could be horseback riding, for which the risk might be higher for younger children and the elderly but lower for age groups in-between. If your topic was table tennis, on the other hand, the risk would be low across all ages.

1 _____

2 _____

3 _____

4 _____

5 _____

C. Draw a line chart to show your examples. On the x-axis, show a range of ages similar to the age groups in the Focus on Listening line chart (page 129). On the y-axis, show degrees of risk: no risk, little risk, medium risk, serious risk, extreme risk. For each activity, plot a series of points on the chart according to your perception of the associated risk for each age group. Use a different coloured line to connect each series of points and create a legend to identify the data.

D. Prepare your presentation by writing notes for the following speaking points.

SPEAKING POINTS	NOTES
Introduce your topic.	
Explain that examples within your topic represent varying degrees of risk to different age groups.	
Explain each example in terms of its degree of risk and identify potential positive or negative consequences, depending on which age group undertakes it.	
Explain why some people might ignore the risks involved with the more dangerous choices.	
For the more dangerous choices, explain how you or others might neutralize concerns about one or more of the risk factors.	

Help yourself remember! Use your line chart and cue cards to remind you of the most important points.

Academic
Survival Skill

Mind maps are a good way to capture and organize brainstorming ideas.

Beyond Basic Brainstorming

Brainstorming is a group activity used for generating new ideas. Once a task has been identified, a group assembled and a recorder appointed (to write down each idea), group members are encouraged to contribute new ideas and to build on the ideas of others.

A. Basic brainstorming is largely a spoken activity, but there are many different brainstorming techniques, some of which involve writing. Read about the following techniques and then write an advantage for each.

TECHNIQUE	KEY POINTS	ADVANTAGE
BRAIN-NETTING	Instead of writing notes on a white board, a shared computer interface is used.	

TECHNIQUE	KEY POINTS	ADVANTAGE
BRAIN-WRITING	Instead of speaking, group members write their ideas on individual notes that are then passed around.	
CRAWFORD'S SLIP	Group members write their ideas on notes that are then put up on a wall.	
ROUND-ROBIN	Each group member speaks in turn before ideas are debated by the group.	

B. Imagine the concerns you might have about going on a hiking trip in an interesting but dangerous region. Pick a region, and working in a group, identify the three most important concerns. Then, use basic brainstorming to generate ideas on how you might neutralize each concern.

C. Try again, but this time select a different region and use one of the above techniques. When you have finished, as a group, compare your experience using the second technique with that of basic brainstorming. Which do you prefer? Why?

_____

_____

_____

LISTENING ③   First Comes Failure

Before You Listen

History is full of individuals who have first suffered failure then gone on to enjoy success. Some failures lead directly to success, but in unexpected ways. Harry Brearley (1871–1948) worked for the British military, trying to create stronger steel for weapons. He reportedly threw out one failed experiment only to notice, several days later, that the metal had kept its silver sheen and did not rust. Almost every kitchen in the world now includes objects made of Brearley's discovery: stainless steel.

Before you listen to Stella and Oscar talk about overcoming failure, think of other ways in which failure might lead to success. Discuss these with a partner.

While You Listen

Stella and Oscar talk about many individuals and either explain what those individuals said about failure and success or show how their lives provided examples of facing risk and overcoming failure to go on to success. Write notes to explain each individual's role in the discussion.

SUCCESSFUL INDIVIDUALS	NOTES
Winston Churchill	
Terry Fox	
Roberta Bondar	
Abraham Lincoln	
Charles Darwin	
Masaru Ibuka and Akio Morita	
Mary Pickford	

After You Listen

Which person mentioned in this listening do you most admire? Discuss why with your partner.

FINAL ASSIGNMENT

Give a Presentation

Now it's your turn. Use everything you have learned in this unit to give a longer presentation of up to ten minutes.

A. Work in a group and brainstorm the names of famous people who took risks and experienced both success and failure. For example, Steve Jobs (1955–2011) co-founded Apple computers in 1976 but was forced out of the company in 1985. He went on to build Pixar, which became the world's largest computer-animated movie company, then returned to Apple in 1997 and helped turn it into one of the largest technology companies in the world.

Select one famous person and briefly explain your choice.

_____

_____

_____

B. Speak with your teacher. Ask for approval of your topic and advice on how to develop it.

C. Do your research. From at least three sources, note significant risks, failures and successes the person you chose experienced and the dates on which these occurred.

SOURCE 1: _____

_____

SOURCE 2: _____

_____

SOURCE 3: _____

_____

D. Organize the information you've collected on a line chart with events in the person's life by year or decade on the x-axis and the degree of risk, failure and success (low, medium and high) on the y-axis. Remember to add a title and a legend to identify your data.

E. Plan your presentation. Paraphrase to avoid plagiarism.

GOALS OF YOUR SPEECH	NOTES
Give a biographical introduction. Explain that the person's life included risk, failure and success.	
Draw the audience's attention to your line chart. Explain that you will discuss five (or more) incidents in the person's life.	
Explain each incident, pointing out the relationship between risk, failure and success.	
Draw one or more conclusions about why the person succeeded despite having first failed.	

F. Instead of taking questions at the end of your presentation, select a brainstorming technique from the Academic Survival Skill in this chapter and conduct a brief brainstorming session on a related question, such as: What other choices might this person have made, and how might those choices have changed the course of events?

Good luck!

CHAPTER 8

Slow Food, Please!

Everyone needs to eat, but not everyone needs to eat the same foods prepared in the same way. If you eat rice, you might enjoy it steamed, boiled, in paella, pilaf, risotto, sushi, pudding or any number of other dishes. We make a lot of choices about which foods to eat, how to prepare them, how to serve them and how to eat them.

Although you may have choices, many people do not. They eat seasonal foods, grown locally and prepared and served in traditional ways. **Some people now believe that this is the best way to eat, both for the quality of the food and for the social and environmental benefits that result from choosing foods "closer to home."**

In this chapter, **you will**

- listen to a lecture on the Slow Food movement, an interview with local-food activists and a conversation about food security;

- learn vocabulary related to food issues;

- organize your ideas using tables and pie charts;

- learn how to develop arguments in a debate;

- practise speaking skills individually, in pairs and in small groups;

- prepare and deliver one short presentation;

- prepare for and participate in a formal debate.

GEARING UP

A. With a partner, discuss different dishes you eat that contain each of the ingredients pictured in the table below. Then, write the names of the dishes in the appropriate column, depending on whether they reflect traditional or non-traditional preparations.

	TRADITIONAL	NON-TRADITIONAL

B. Working in groups, compare your answers with those of other students. Which are the most popular ways of preparing the above foods?

_____

_____

_____

A. Check the words you understand. Then, check the words you use.

	UNDERSTAND	USE		UNDERSTAND	USE
nutrition (n.)	☐	☐	slavery (n.)	☐	☐
manifesto (n.)	☐	☐	discarded (adj.)	☐	☐
consumption* (n.)	☐	☐	petrified (adj.)	☐	☐
welfare* (n.)	☐	☐	bonding* (n.)	☐	☐
accessible* (adj.)	☐	☐	savour (v.)	☐	☐
economies of scale* (n.)	☐	☐	calories (n.)	☐	☐
corporations* (n.)	☐	☐	authoring* (v.)	☐	☐
livestock (n.)	☐	☐	launched (v.)	☐	☐
organic (adj.)	☐	☐	positioning (v.)	☐	☐
pollution (n.)	☐	☐	regional* (adj.)	☐	☐

* Appears on the Academic Word List

B. Read the following sentences or phrases and then write a definition for each of the words in bold.

WORDS IN CONTEXT	DEFINITION
❶ ... the concept of a quick bite prepared with more concern for speed and budget than for **nutrition** has been around for much longer.	nutrition: *process of finding food necessary for health and growth*
❷ ... became a movement in 1989, when he and others created a **manifesto** that laid out general principles ...	manifesto:
❸ *Clean* refers to food production and **consumption** that do not harm the environment, animal **welfare** or our own health.	consumption:
	welfare:
❹ *Fair* refers to **accessible** prices for consumers and fair conditions and pay for small-scale producers.	accessible:
❺ Often, the **economies of scale** ... means that many traditional farmers cannot compete.	economies of scale:

▶

> The word "manifesto" has a negative connotation or meaning for some because it's associated with radicalism. Political parties often prefer the word "platform."

WORDS IN CONTEXT	DEFINITION
6 ... the ability of large **corporations** to use their vast sales ...	corporations:
7 Many small farmers are trying to bring back ... a wide variety of other fruits, vegetables and **livestock**.	livestock:
8 However, although **organic** is a preference, many Slow Food advocates favour locally produced foods ...	organic:
9 ... foods that are imported over great distances, with the additional costs and **pollution** of shipping.	pollution:
10 The conditions for workers are often appalling: closer to **slavery**.	slavery:
11 Deep piles of **discarded** wrappers and boxes grew.	discarded:
12 ... Michelle's two dogs, who took advantage of car trips to forage for what she characterized as **petrified** fries ...	petrified:
13 Michelle enjoyed dinnertime **bonding** as a family, which she explains is a "slow-food-ish" thing to do.	bonding:
14 ... most North Americans are unable to **savour** the moment, really tasting food ...	savour:
15 Too many people are so obsessed with **calories** ... they've forgotten how to enjoy themselves ...	calories:
16 ... she also wrote food reviews, which led to her **authoring** a guidebook for dining ...	authoring:

WORDS IN CONTEXT	DEFINITION
⑰ He had just **launched** a community support agriculture co-op.	launched:
⑱ But rather than **positioning** slow food as a chore, …	positioning:
⑲ … to host do-it-yourself feasts using as many local or **regional** ingredients as possible.	regional:

❗ *French has influenced the names of foods in English. We say "beef" rather than "cow" because of the Old French word "boef." We say "pork" and "poultry" instead of "pig" and "fowl" for the same reason.*

C. Check your definitions with a partner. If you do not understand some words, look them up in a dictionary.

D. Unusual words are sometimes chosen to add interest when speaking and writing, but if you are taking notes, it is better to summarize the information in clear language.

Make the following sentences clearer by choosing words from the box to replace the underlined words or phrases in each sentence.

appreciate	concerned	developed	problem	traditional

❶ The french fries were <u>petrified</u>. _____hardened over time_____

❷ She explains bonding as a "<u>slow-food-ish</u>" thing to do. _____

❸ Too many people are <u>obsessed</u> with calories. _____

❹ Growing chili peppers <u>blossomed</u> into other activities. _____

❺ Most North Americans are unable to <u>savour</u> the moment. _____

❻ She'd like to work on this particular <u>piece of the puzzle</u> next. _____

E. Adjectives like *regional* describe a particular region. Write three adjectives used to describe each of the following.

❶ city _____urban_____ _____ _____

❷ state _____ _____ _____

❸ province _____ _____ _____

❹ country _____ _____ _____

❺ world _____ _____ _____

Before You Listen

You eat each day, but the food you choose—or that is chosen for you—is likely different from what other people eat. You may base your decisions on memories of childhood dinners, on your budget, on the foods that are locally and seasonally available or on how interested you are in trying the foods of other cultures. Before you listen to a lecture about the Slow Food movement, consider your own food choices.

Describe one meal you ate yesterday.

_____

Was this meal prepared for you or did you make it yourself?

_____

If you bought the ingredients and/or prepared the meal, what influenced the choices you made?

_____

_____

Locals in Southern China joke that they eat anything with four legs except a table and anything that flies except an airplane. What are the most unusual foods that you have heard about or seen people eat? Why might that food be eaten?

FOOD ITEM	REASON WHY IT MIGHT BE EATEN

Here is the first segment of the lecture you will listen to.

"I imagine that most of you have had a fast-food meal this month, this week or maybe even today. The term *fast food* has been in popular use for more than sixty years although the concept of a quick bite prepared with more concern for speed and budget than for nutrition has been around much longer. Today, I'd like to persuade you that you should seriously consider following the opposite trend, the Slow Food movement. After, I'd like to make sense of it with an example of one individual's journey from fast food to slow food."

What are the most nutritious foods you eat? What are the least nutritious? What is the fastest meal you eat? What is the slowest? Discuss your answers with a partner.

While You Listen

While you listen to the lecture the first time, try to understand the relationship between the two main subjects: the Slow Food movement and Michelle Pentz Glave's community food initiatives. When you listen a second time, write notes on the key words and ideas. Listen a third time to check your notes and add details.

KEY WORDS AND IDEAS	NOTES
the term *fast food*	
Carlo Petrini	
good	
clean	
fair	
Michelle's food history	
shift to fresh foods	
bonding	

KEY WORDS AND IDEAS	NOTES
savouring the moment	
authoring a guidebook	
Farmer Monte	
Bowfeast	
connecting with students	
harvest box program	
working with farmers	
be part of a miracle	

After You Listen

Review your notes. Think about how one person can make a difference. Add examples to help you understand and remember.

FOCUS ON LISTENING

Working with Pie Charts

A pie chart is used to show statistical proportions as percentages. Added together, segments of the pie chart equal a total of 100 percent. Individual pie charts never show changes over time; instead, several pie charts might show changes when set side by side. The attraction of a pie chart is that it is often easier to understand at a glance than some other types of charts.

When people talk about pie charts, listen carefully to make sure they are not distorting the percentages by excluding some information or combining unlike categories into one percentage or slice of the pie. The opposite can also be confusing, where there are so many slices of the pie that it becomes difficult to understand their relationships to each other.

Consider the following daily serving recommendations from Health Canada.

Recommended Number of Food Guide Servings per Day

	ADULTS (19–50 YEARS)	
	FEMALE	**MALE**
VEGETABLES AND FRUIT	7–8	8–10
GRAIN PRODUCTS	6–7	8
MILK AND ALTERNATIVES	2	2
MEAT AND ALTERNATIVES	2	3

Health Canada. (2007, May). Food and nutrition: Canada's food guide. Retrieved from: http://www.hc-sc.gc.ca

The table is useful in some ways, but does not give a sense of the proportions the way a pie chart does.

The following pie chart shows the rounded averages of daily servings for males, ages 19–50. To make the pie chart even more effective, segments might be filled with photographs of the appropriate foods, such as vegetables and fruit in the appropriate segment.

Rounded Average Servings for Males, Ages 19–50

1. Vegetables and fruit
2. Grain products
3. Milk and alternatives
4. Meat and alternatives

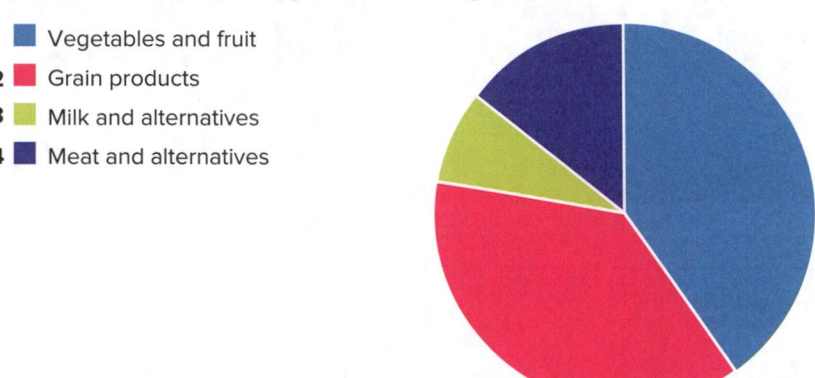

There are two ways to create pie charts. You can convert a set of statistics into percentages and turn those percentages into degrees of a circle. For example, in the chart above, the rounded averages for males are nine servings of vegetables and fruit, eight servings of grain products, two servings of milk and alternatives and three servings of meat and alternatives for a total of twenty-two servings. To create the pie chart by hand, you divide the twenty-two servings by 360 degrees and will find that you need to measure out 16.36 degrees for each serving.

The second, and much simpler, method is to enter the data into a spreadsheet program. In a few clicks, it will create the pie chart for you, with options for tailoring the colours.

Consider your meals from one day during the past week. On the pie chart on the next page, show the average number of servings you had of vegetables and fruit, grain products, milk and alternatives and meat and alternatives.

Add a title and complete the legend to explain what the pie segments represent. If you are comfortable using a spreadsheet program, use the information to create a pie chart on a computer.

TITLE: _____

1 ☐ Vegetables and fruit
2 ☐ Grain products
3 ☐ Milk and alternatives
4 ☐ Meat and alternatives

VOCABULARY BUILD

❗ "Souls" can be a synonym for "individuals" but is usually only used in certain contexts, such as when talking about character or strengths.

A. Check the words you understand. Then, check the words you use.

	UNDERSTAND	USE		UNDERSTAND	USE
souls (n.)	☐	☐	apparently* (adv.)	☐	☐
midst (n.)	☐	☐	protein (n.)	☐	☐
preserved (v.)	☐	☐	inspired (v.)	☐	☐
bounty (n.)	☐	☐	fertile (adj.)	☐	☐
naively (adv.)	☐	☐	artisans (n.)	☐	☐
burst (v.)	☐	☐	respectable (adj.)	☐	☐
lingered (v.)	☐	☐	re-energized* (adj.)	☐	☐
lean (adj.)	☐	☐	generated* (v.)	☐	☐
definitely* (adv.)	☐	☐	peak (v.)	☐	☐
borscht (n.)	☐	☐	impressive (adj.)	☐	☐

* Appears on the Academic Word List

B. Read the following sentences or phrases and then write a definition for each of the words in bold.

WORDS IN CONTEXT	DEFINITION
❶ About a year and a half ago, I met two brave **souls** …	souls: *individuals*
❷ They were right in the **midst** of attempting to spend a whole year …	midst:
❸ This is what's left of what we **preserved** in the summer and fall.	preserved:

▶

WORDS IN CONTEXT	DEFINITION
4 The contents of the cupboards sounded pretty good, but that was after living through the **bounty** of summer and fall.	bounty:
5 We **naively** thought that the first day of spring was when the first green shoots would **burst** from the earth, and within two weeks we'd be having spring green salads.	naively:
	burst:
6 ... the winter just **lingered**, and the rain, and the cold, and that was a long, **lean** period for us.	lingered:
	lean:
7 ... that was when I **definitely** got sick of beets because beets were one of the few things we could buy in the store ...	definitely:
8 ... all kinds of **borscht** was had around here, and I normally like it a lot, but ...	borscht:
9 ... potatoes I can have in endless quantities, but **apparently** beets is not one of those things.	apparently:
10 ... there were no fish being caught in the spring, so we were really— for **protein**, we were running on— on eggs, pretty much.	protein:
11 There I met Jenn Lamm, who was **inspired** by the couple to create a website encouraging a 100-mile diet ...	inspired:
12 ... we live in such a **fertile** area, and we've forgotten how fertile it really is and what it can really produce ...	fertile:
13 ... I want there to be, you know, apple orchards, and cheese **artisans**, and you know, locally grown vegetables ...	artisans:

▶

WORDS IN CONTEXT	DEFINITION
⑭ ... Jenn Lamm was able to put together a pretty **respectable** resource list of foods for people to taste ...	respectable:
⑮ ... who have become **re-energized** by being able to discover the bounty that's right next door to their homes ...	re-energized:
⑯ The excitement level **generated** by this diet has not started to **peak** by any means.	generated:
	peak:
⑰ ... an **impressive** ranking considering how many books are released in Canada each week.	impressive:

C. Check your definitions with a partner. If you do not understand some words, look them up in a dictionary.

D. Use these words to fill in the blanks in the paragraph that follows.

borscht	fertile	inspired	peak	protein
bounty	impressive	lean	preserved	

In Victoria, British Columbia, a young vegetarian was _____ to live on the _____ of his own small but _____ yard. He grew an _____ amount of beans (for _____), tomatoes and other vegetables, picked them at their _____ of freshness and _____ them. He dried some produce like the beans and canned or froze other vegetables. One of his popular dishes was _____, which he made with beets, onions, tomatoes, cabbage, potatoes and carrots. He even ground wheat and made bread. Summers were great, but winters were _____ times, times when he may have been tempted to give up and go grocery shopping.

E. Some words, such as *peak*, can be nouns, verbs or adjectives. Underline the word or phrase in each sentence that could be replaced with *peak*.

❶ Healthy eating has helped keep him at his highest level of fitness.

❷ Sadly, fast food has not yet reached its greatest degree in popularity.

❸ These herbs were gathered just below the top of the mountain.

❹ At the busiest hours, the lines at the farmer's market are quite long.

❺ Her business began to become its most successful three months ago.

Before You Listen

Are you a *vegetarian*, a *vegan*, an *omnivore* or a *locavore*? There are many ways to describe the type of diet you might follow; even within these categories, definitions vary. *Vegetarians* generally don't eat meat but might or might not eat fish and/or dairy products. *Vegans* eat nothing but vegetables and fruit while *omnivores* eat everything. *Locavores* is a new term to describe people who eat only food that has been produced near to their homes. Other terms to describe people's diets include *fruitarian*, someone who eats mostly—or only—fruit. Before you listen to an interview with local-food activists, discuss with a partner what you know about these different types of eating choices.

Here is the first segment of the interview you will listen to. Underline the foods that are mentioned. Then, with your partner discuss the answers to the questions that follow.

> GENOVA: About a year and a half ago, I met two brave souls named James MacKinnon and Alisa Smith. They were right in the midst of attempting to spend a whole year eating meals made with ingredients that were produced no more than 100 miles away from their home in downtown Vancouver.
>
> SMITH: Um, well, here's the cupboards. This is what's left of what we preserved in the summer and fall. And we've got pickles here, uh, ketchup, although my first time making ketchup, it's very watery, I didn't boil it long enough. Tomatoes and these are plums from our tree up in northern British Columbia, our cabin in Doreen. And this is crabapple jelly, also from our trees up in Doreen. And strawberry preserves, we did a u-pick, probably in Delta.

Would you want to make your own ketchup, crabapple jelly and strawberry preserves? Why or why not? Why do you think some people might want to make their food from scratch?

While You Listen

The first time you listen, try to get a general idea of the kind of food Smith and MacKinnon eat and why they talk about each one. Listen a second time and write notes about what is significant about each food mentioned. Listen a third time to check your notes and add details.

FOODS	NOTES
spring green salads	
beets	
borscht	
potatoes	
eggs	
fritters	
milk	
apples	
cheese	
locally grown vegetables	
cranberries	
cranberry sauce (ingredients)	
kiwi fruit	

100 miles =
160 kilometres

After You Listen

Discuss the foods listed above with your partner. Which of these foods do you commonly eat? Which do you rarely eat? What would be easy about following a 100-mile diet? What would be difficult?

WARM-UP ASSIGNMENT
Your 100-Mile Diet

Now it's your turn to research and present a short talk on what following a 100-mile diet would mean for you.

A. Think about the kind of foods you usually eat. Then, research the sources of these foods and, on a map, indicate which are available within 100 miles (160 kilometres) of your home. Consider seasonal foods such as grains, fruits and vegetables, as well as foods that can be preserved and foods from indoor hydroponic farms, fish farms, poultry farms and traditional livestock farms. Also, consider any foods you can obtain from the wild. If you are unsure of which fresh foods you can preserve, research methods of preservation such as salting, freezing, canning and drying. Preserving fresh food when in season allows for a variety of food throughout the year.

Use the following table to categorize the food that would be available to you within your 100-mile limit.

SEASONAL FOODS	PRESERVED FOODS	FARM FOODS	WILD FOODS

B. Based on your research, and using the Health Canada food categories of vegetables and fruit, grain products, milk and alternatives and meat and alternatives, draw a pie chart to show the average number of servings in your 100-mile diet for one day. In your presentation, compare this new chart to the one you created in Focus on Listening.

C. Prepare your presentation. Explain where you live and what food sources are available to you within the 100-mile limit. Organize your content logically, such as by food categories, by distance from your home or by season. Use your pie charts and annotated map to remind you of important points.

Academic
Survival Skill

Learning About Formal Debates

You have already practised debating skills in informal debates in Chapter 6. In this chapter, you have the opportunity to participate in a formal debate. In a formal debate, there is a judge, sometimes called an adjudicator, who awards points for *matter*, *manner*, *method* and *conduct*.

Matter is the arguments presented by each speaker on each team. Good arguments include well-researched content, such as statistics, and clearly presented examples. Content should be presented logically so both the audience and the other team find it difficult to disagree.

In a debate, pay attention to the *manner* of the presentation. Good manner means appropriate gestures and body language, particularly since in a debate members face and speak to the audience, not the other team. Speaking clearly and confidently without rushing is important, as is varying rhythm, tone and volume so arguments sound more like a conversation and less like reading aloud. Humour sometimes helps engage the audience.

Method refers to the way debate arguments are structured and how well members work together as a team. Arguments should be consistent, easy to understand and clearly related, particularly if several people on the team are presenting different points.

A final concern is *conduct*. Conduct refers to individual behaviour during a debate. It's common to become excited, but in a debate, members should not mix passion with anger and lose control of their temper. Nor should members lose track of time and speak longer than allowed.

A. For the following proposition, fill in the blank and then prepare and practise a one-minute argument in support of your statement.

_____ is a perfect food and should be a part of everyone's diet.

B. Work in a group and take turns presenting your argument. When others are presenting, mark them using notes and the table to guide you. Compare your marks with the members of your group to reach a consensus.

JUDGE ON ...	NOTES	POINTS
MATTER		____/25
MANNER		____/25
METHOD		____/25
CONDUCT		____/25
TOTAL		____/100

Before You Listen

Not all debates are easy to prepare for; in one format, you receive the position you will argue only minutes before the debate begins. Generally, however, you have more time, and preparing for a debate can be an enjoyable team research task in which you consider the meaning of the proposition, formulate arguments to support or refute it, and find evidence that will encourage the judge and audience to agree with your position.

In this opening segment, Stella and Oscar are discussing a debate topic.

OSCAR: Stella, what do you know about *food security?*

STELLA: Ugh, I hate that term. It sounds like the war on terror. It sounds like something to get people scared.

OSCAR: Maybe, but it's the topic of the debate we're going to have next week.

STELLA: A debate? I missed that. When did the teacher talk about a debate?

OSCAR: It must have been the day you were at the dentist.

STELLA: Mm ... Okay, tell me all the details about the debate. Let's start with the proposition.

OSCAR: Sure. The proposition in a debate is the statement put forth that one team argues *for* and one team argues *against*.

STELLA: And are we for or against?

OSCAR: We won't know until we get there, unfortunately. We might be on the affirmative—agreeing with the proposition—or on the negative—disagreeing with the proposition—but the teacher wants us to prepare for both sides of the debate. In other words, we have to be prepared to argue either for or against the proposition.

Working in a group, think of a proposition related to food. Discuss some arguments that could be presented in support of your proposition and some that would refute it.

While You Listen

Read the following questions, then, listen to Stella and Oscar as they discuss the proposition that food security is essential to world peace. Listen a first time to get the general idea. While you listen a second time, answer the questions. Listen a third time and, on a separate sheet of paper, take note of examples of matter, manner, method and conduct.

1 Why does Stella think that the proposition is interesting?

_____

_____

2 Food security is based on three needs. Explain each one.

• food availability: _____

_____

• food access: _____

_____

• food use: _____

_____

3 What is odd about prisoners in the 1800s complaining about their food?

_____

_____

4 What three issues does Oscar have?

• There is enough food in the world but _____

_____

• Whether or not future food needs _____

_____

• Globalization/international _____

_____

5 Fill in the missing words: "Food security challenges affect everyone and, in the absence of food security, _____

_____."

6 Three things are important to making an argument. When discussing tea, what arguments are given for each of the following?

• being logical: _____

_____

_____

• being factual: _____

_____

_____

• being emotional: _____

_____

_____

After You Listen

Working in your group, compare your notes and discuss examples of when Stella or Oscar illustrated good manner, matter, method and conduct.

Using Your Senses

An important part of speaking is creating a clear and memorable image in your audience's minds. However, some speakers and writers focus only on simple descriptions. A good speaking technique, when preparing your speech, is to go beyond the ordinary and think imaginatively. Consider hunger. You can say, "I felt hungry," or you can say, "Hunger growled like a wolf in my stomach." Which is more memorable for the audience? You can also go beyond *seeing* by speaking about what you *hear*, *feel*, *taste* and *smell*.

A. One way to make your speech more interesting is to use synonyms for common words. Write two or more synonyms for each of the following.

1. eat _____ _____ _____
2. taste _____ _____ _____
3. say _____ _____ _____
4. feel _____ _____ _____
5. smell _____ _____ _____

B. Rewrite the following sentences to make them more imaginative or sensual.

1. I ate some cut mango.

   _____

   _____

2. I visited a cornfield on a sunny day.

   _____

   _____

3. I carried a big pumpkin into the house.

   _____

   _____

C. Share your descriptions with your classmates. Which are the most imaginative or sensual?

FINAL ASSIGNMENT

Participate in a Formal Debate

Now it's your turn. Use everything you have learned in this chapter to prepare for and participate in a team debate.

A. For your debate, work with other students to choose an issue related to food and formulate a proposition. The proposition is a statement that the affirmative team argues to support and the negative team argues to refute.

> Example: Fast food should be banned in all publicly funded institutions to reduce obesity and other related health risks.

_____

_____

_____

B. Speak with your teacher. Ask for approval of your proposition, the make-up of your teams and advice on how to develop your debate arguments.

C. Do your research, giving different roles or areas of research to each team member. Examine your topic in detail and collect statistical information that supports or refutes the proposition.

D. Use a pie chart or other visual aid to support your arguments during the debate.

E. Plan your side of the debate. Use constructive arguments to build your case. Contentions are arguments supporting your team's point of view, and attacks are arguments against contentions, given in the cross-examinations and rebuttals.

F. In a team debate, each member takes a turn speaking. On a separate sheet of paper, use the format in the table to prepare your side of the debate, giving each team member a role. Review the Academic Survival Skill and be sure to consider how each of your team members can make an impression with matter, manner, method and conduct. If your team is not participating in the debate, use the notes and table to rate the performance of one of the teams.

DEBATE TEAM	DEBATE STRATEGIES
Affirmative constructive 6 minutes	• Introduce the proposition and your role (*for* the proposition). • Explain your contentions with examples; then, conclude.
Negative team cross-examines 3 minutes	• Ask questions to show problems with the affirmative's reasoning.
Negative constructive 6 minutes	• Introduce your role (*against* the proposition). • Explain your contentions with examples. • Question and attack the affirmative's contentions and examples; then, conclude.
Affirmative team cross-examines 3 minutes	• Ask questions to show problems with the negative's reasoning.
Second affirmative constructive 6 minutes	• Outline the issues again and re-explain your contentions with new examples and offer new contentions and examples. • Respond to negative's arguments/attacks. • Question and attack the negative's contentions and examples; then, conclude.
Negative team cross-examines 3 minutes	• Ask questions to show problems with the affirmative's reasoning.
Second negative constructive 6 minutes	• Outline the issues again and re-explain your contentions with new examples and new contentions and examples. • Respond to affirmative's arguments/attacks; then, conclude.
Affirmative team cross-examines 3 minutes	• Ask questions to show problems with the negative's reasoning.
First negative rebuttal 4 minutes	• Rebuild the negative case. • Summarize how the negative has made its case and the affirmative has not; then, conclude.
First affirmative rebuttal 4 minutes	• Respond to the negative's arguments. • Rebuild the affirmative case. • Extend arguments and give additional examples and explanations; then, conclude.
Second negative rebuttal 4 minutes	• Respond to the affirmative's arguments. • Explain that the negative has proved its case and the affirmative has not. • Summarize the debate. • Ask the audience to agree.
Second affirmative rebuttal 4 minutes	• Respond to final negative's arguments. • Summarize the debate and explain how the affirmative position has made its case. • Ask the audience to agree; then, conclude.

"Be ready when opportunity comes ... luck is the time when preparation and opportunity meet." —Canadian Prime Minister Pierre Elliot Trudeau (1919–2001)

AUDIO SCRIPTS

CHAPTER 1
Playing to Win

LISTENING 1: Tai Chi: A Healthy Exercise for All Ages

Hello, everyone, and welcome to Being Healthy for Busy People. I hope you all had a great week full of healthy food choices and fun physical activity.

Today's show was inspired by a trip that I took to Beijing about three years ago. I was reminded of the trip a few days ago when I was looking through some photos and came across some of the many photos we took during that trip.

It was a wonderful ten-day trip and we had a fantastic time visiting places, such as the Great Wall, the Forbidden City, the Summer Palace, the Beijing Zoo, etc. Being who I am, the one thing from the trip that really stuck in my mind, besides the amazing historical sites, was our walk through what I believe was the Temple of Heaven Park. As we walked through that impressive park, I noticed that there was a bunch of people in the middle of the park performing slow dance-like flowing movements. When I asked our tour guide what they were doing, he told us that the group of people were practising tai chi. The graceful images of those people gliding through different poses made an impression on me. So, when I came home I started **researching** tai chi. I was interested to find out what the practice of tai chi was all about and how it could be beneficial to one's health.

So today, I want to share with you my findings. I will go over what tai chi is, the health **benefits** and how to get started. So, let's begin.

So, what is tai chi? Tai chi is actually a martial arts form. I know some people might be surprised by that if they've seen tai chi because most people picture martial arts as being aggressive, full of quick kicks, punches, blocks and throws; not slow, rhythmic meditative body movements that **promote** relaxation and peace, the way tai chi does.

Despite what some people might think tai chi is not a new form of exercise mixed with meditation. It actually originated many centuries ago in China. At that time it was used both as a form of self-defence and to promote inner peace.

However, today tai chi is largely practised as a form of non-competitive, gentle, low-**impact** physical exercise and stretching that creates a deeper connection between your mind and body. Practising tai chi takes a person through a series of postures or movements in a slow, graceful manner, which is **coordinated** with their breathing. Each posture is supposed to flow into the next one without pausing. There isn't one **unified** style of tai chi, though. There are many different **styles** of tai chi. And some of the forms of tai chi are more **intense** than others. Most of the traditional forms of tai chi have about a hundred possible movements to explore. So, it is hard to get bored. Of course, most people tend to find a few movements that they prefer and stick to those in their exercise routines. So, you don't have to worry about memorizing and mastering every single movement in order to enjoy tai chi.

And luckily, you don't have to be an elite athlete to perform tai chi. Almost anyone can practise it, even older adults, because it is considered a safe, gentle exercise that puts **minimal** stress on your joints and muscles. That is because tai chi **focuses** on technique and movement, not on **utilizing** sheer strength.

With that being said, even though tai chi is considered safe and has a low risk of injury, please talk to your doctor before starting a program to see if it is an appropriate exercise for you, especially if you suffer from any medical issues.

So what are the benefits of tai chi? Even though tai chi has been practised for centuries, its health benefits have only recently been studied, scientifically. So, studies are still limited. But there is some evidence that tai chi is a great way to reduce stress because it creates a state of relaxation and calm. It seems that the mind and body connection required to perform tai chi may be just what is needed to distract from the stress of a hectic life. Research is also showing that tai chi may also have other benefits beyond **stress** reduction, such as reducing anxiety and **depression**, improving balance, coordination, sleep quality, muscular strength, cardiovascular fitness, endurance, flexibility and reducing the frequency of falls, slowing bone loss in women after menopause, lowering blood pressure and helping to relieve chronic pain.

So, how do you get started? The great thing about tai chi is that you don't need any special clothing or **equipment**. You do, however, want to wear comfortable clothing that won't restrict your movements. Sweatpants, tights, shorts and T-shirts are all good choices. But don't overdress. Even though the movements are slower, it is possible to work up a sweat.

It's not enough to have the right clothes though. To really understand how to do the movements correctly, I would recommend joining a tai chi class in your community so that you can be guided by a qualified tai chi **instructor**. Luckily, tai chi is pretty popular, so it is usually fairly easy to find an instructor teaching classes in your area. If you don't know of a local place giving classes, you can always call your local health club, community education centre or look in the phone book to find a tai chi class.

Once you've joined a class, the fun can begin! The instructor will teach you how to do the movements safely and teach you to regulate your breathing. If you have injuries, chronic conditions or balance or coordination issues, the instructor will help you do the movements properly, so that you don't injure yourself. Even though tai chi is slow and gentle with no negative health impacts, if you have balance issues, you could still fall and hurt yourself while practising it. And while it is unlikely, you could injure yourself if the movements are done improperly.

Another great thing about having an instructor is that they will correct any errors in your posture or movements before they become ingrained in your routine. That is important because tai chi is all about doing the forms correctly. After you have mastered the forms, you may feel confident enough to do it on your own. At that point, you will be able to practise tai chi anywhere or anytime safely.

That is another advantage to tai chi. Unlike other forms of exercise, tai chi requires very little space to practise. So, even if you live in a small apartment, you really can't use not having enough space as an excuse not to practise. Since space is not really an issue, the most important thing to look for when choosing a place to practise tai chi, is to find somewhere quiet so that you can practise without disturbances or **distractions**.

And don't forget, in order to reap the greatest benefits of tai chi you have to practise it on a regular basis. If you do, it will help you to improve your cardiovascular fitness, muscular strength, flexibility and balance as well as decrease your stress and improve your **overall** well-being. So, give tai chi a try. It is a great exercise to add into your routine since it doesn't take a large investment in equipment and it is a gentle enough exercise for almost everyone, at almost any age. Plus, you won't get bored, because the many different movements that you can use in your routines should keep you interested for a long time. So, at the very least, maybe borrow a tai chi DVD from the library. That way you can give it a try to see how you like it from the comfort of your own home without even spending a penny. You have nothing to lose and everything to gain.

LISTENING 2: Talking about Library Resources

Hello, and welcome to Central Library. My name is Joseph Cornell and I am a reference librarian. Today, I will talk about how to get information from a variety of **resources** and, most importantly, identify which ones are good **academic** sources, suitable for college or university research. If you have any questions, please take notes and save them until the end.

I understand that for your class you have to do a **presentation** on some kind of extreme sport. As an example today, I'm going to talk about extreme sports and show you how you can narrow down the topic and find the information you need. This approach will be useful for anything you need to research at the library or even for researching information online.

The first thing you need to do is to look for key words that will help you in your search. The term *extreme sport* is a general description, but you need to be more specific. A few years ago, I would have suggested you look at the subject index or even a dictionary, but now I know most of you will turn first to the Internet and, on the Internet, you'll look first at *Wikipedia*.

Now, *Wikipedia* is a great **source**, but it's not a particularly academic one. It's not academic because a lot of the information on the website is neither written nor edited by experts. It is general information, and it is also quite **unstable**. It's unstable because anyone can edit a *Wikipedia* entry and add his or her own ideas. When this happens, the content changes. Anyone who looks up the reference after an edit might find different or even **contradictory** information. This is one reason for noting the date you retrieve information whenever you look up a website. In any case, you're certainly not going to get high marks for including *Wikipedia* as a source for an essay or for quoting it in a speech.

Still, *Wikipedia* can be a useful starting point for looking elsewhere. By the way, this is true for dictionaries and encyclopedias as well. When your instructors see a sentence beginning "According to the Oxford Dictionary" they are already lowering your mark. Don't do it.

But back to *Wikipedia*. Our **objective** is to find some basic terms we can follow up with in more academic sources. When you use an Internet search engine to look for information on extreme sports, one of the first website hits is usually a *Wikipedia* page. This page features a brief overview, including a list of forty or so extreme sports. And, in terms of your presentations on extreme sports, they're even grouped in a useful way, into *air sports*, *land sports* and *water sports*.

Air sports include hang-gliding, bungee jumping and BASE jumping. For those of you who are unfamiliar with the sport, the BASE in BASE jumping is an acronym for a special kind of skydiving. BASE stands for the different starting points for a parachute jump: *buildings*, *antennae*, *spans* (which refers to bridges) and *earth* (which usually refers to cliffs).

For the land sports, the list includes caving. Caving is also known by the more technical name *spelunking*. Two other land sports are skateboarding and ice yachting. Ice yachting involves small sailboats with skates or sleds fitted to them so they can race across a frozen lake or river, using wind power. There's a similar version in which the boat has wheels and goes across flat beaches, roads or plains; this extreme sport is called *land yachting*.

For the water sports, the list includes cliff diving—that's diving off high cliffs into the ocean or a lake—whitewater kayaking on fast-flowing rivers and free diving. You'll have heard about many of these sports and can guess the meaning of others, but this last extreme sport, *free diving*, can be a bit confusing if you're not familiar with it. So this is an example of a term you might need to research more, even if you think you can guess the meaning. Free diving refers to diving down from the surface of the water to great depths on a single breath of air. How deep? The record is 264 metres. That's deep.

Okay, so far we have a range of extreme sports. Now, I will talk about some different ways to present the information you find.

If you simply want to explain a particular sport, you might write a definition essay or notes for a definition presentation. These notes might typically include the history of the sport, perhaps illustrated, but when you prepare a definition presentation, a good way to start is to try to answer those *W-H* questions: *who*, *what*, *when*, *where*, *why* and *how*.

In a compare and contrast essay or presentation, you might talk about two or more sports and say what they have in common and how they differ. For example, from the list of extreme sports we've mentioned so far, I think we can agree that some are more *competitive* than others.

An expository essay is another type. In an expository essay, you could talk about the **process**, that is, how to do the particular sport.

For your presentation, you need to talk about only one extreme sport, and you need some kind of point you want to make. We call this point a **thesis** statement. A thesis statement is often a kind of argument or point of view and is central to an argumentative essay or presentation. An argumentative presentation takes one side of an argument—although it might include the other side if for no other reason than to criticize it. To create or find a thesis, you can start by asking yourself what you know about an extreme sport and what would be interesting about it for other people.

Let's take BASE jumping as an example. Like many extreme sports, it's dangerous. So, for your thesis statement, you might say, "BASE jumping is an extreme sport that attracts people who enjoy danger."

Now that's an *okay*, but not great, thesis statement because it still sounds very much like a simple definition. What else can you add? First, you can say that it's a *new* sport; that signals to the readers or listeners that you will talk about the history. Second, once you start reading about it, you'll probably discover that BASE jumping is *illegal* in many places. Now you have more to talk about! To your thesis statement, you can also add your personal opinion or your side of an argument. For example, your new thesis statement might be "BASE jumping is a *new* extreme sport that attracts people who enjoy danger but that *should* be *illegal*." Or you could argue that it should *not* be illegal. It's your opinion after all. You just have to back it up. And to back it up, you need to add examples and explanations.

In this case, you might want to write a cause and effect essay. In a cause and effect essay, you are saying that one thing causes another; you're showing the impact of one action on another. For example, you might say that BASE jumpers encourage people to try foolish stunts for which they don't have the skills. But you need evidence. And when you need evidence, that's where the library comes in.

Now, we have a good idea of what you are going to research, so let's go back to the library. What resources are available to you? If you go to the electronic catalogue, you now have some search terms that you can use to find books and other sources. These terms include *BASE jumping, extreme sports, illegal sports* and *new sports*. There may or may not be a book or other publication on BASE jumping, but you might find general books on extreme sports with chapters on BASE jumping. There are other sources as well. The library has a wide collection of videos, computer programs and **journals**. Journals are monthly or semi-annual publications written by academics. You might, for example, find an article on injuries from BASE jumping in a journal of sports medicine. Newspaper stories stored electronically and on microfilm might also be useful for finding people who have been arrested for BASE jumping off public buildings and bridges. Which reminds me, don't forget biographies. There might be a biography of a famous extreme athlete that would help you. And remember, in every book you read, look at the references in the back. They may lead you to something else that is interesting and useful.

So, that's almost enough of an introduction to the library; there's just one more extremely important source to consider: the librarian. I expect most of you won't remember all the information I've given you here, so drop by any time you need some help. Now, let's hear some of your questions and then we can ...

LISTENING 3: Signposts to a Great Speech

STELLA: Hey Oscar, how's it goin'?

OSCAR: Ah, you know ... busy as usual. I've got so much work to do.

STELLA: Really? I don't know why. We take most of the same courses.

OSCAR: Don't tell me you've already finished your presentation!

STELLA: Of course. Haven't you?

OSCAR: I've barely started.

STELLA: You're joking.

OSCAR: I wish. Anyway, can you help me?

STELLA: No problem. How far along are you?

OSCAR: I chose the topic. You remember we're supposed to talk about a sport with both competitive and non-competitive versions. I guess every sport can be either competitive or non-competitive.

STELLA: Uh, I'm not sure about that. I'm thinking of bobsledding. You know, where you jump on a sled and hurtle down a track. I'd say that it was purely competitive. I'm not sure people just do it for fun in their backyards.

OSCAR: Maybe not, but for comparison, there's tobogganing, you know, sliding down a snowy hill on a sled. That's pretty close and it's non-competitive.

STELLA: I guess so. Anyway, what sport did you choose?

OSCAR: I picked swimming because, well, you know, I'm a swimming **instructor**. So I know something about it. It should be easy for me. I'm not sure I even need to prepare notes.

STELLA: Really? You think so? Let's see. Why don't you practise on me?

OSCAR: Practise? What? You mean, right now?

STELLA: Sure. Go ahead.

OSCAR: Ah, okay. Swimming is a competitive and a—

STELLA: Stop!

OSCAR: What?

STELLA: You can't start like that.

OSCAR: What do you mean? How am I supposed to start?

STELLA: You're supposed to say "hello." You should always greet the audience.

OSCAR: Uh, oh yeah. Okay. Yeah. Hello. Swimming is a compet—

STELLA: No!

OSCAR: What? I said "hello"!

STELLA: Yes, but you can't just *jump into* the topic. You should introduce yourself, and then you have to tell us what you're going to say. Something like "Hello. My name is Oscar, and today I'm going to talk about swimming."

OSCAR: Oh, okay. And I remember something about *signposting*. Isn't that about letting listeners know where they are and where they're going?

STELLA: That's right. For example, when you read something, there are usually lots of clues to let you know where you are and what's coming next. There are chapter titles, subheadings and paragraphs. You know where an idea starts and ends and if you don't understand something, you can read more slowly or go back and check some details.

OSCAR: But speeches are different.

STELLA: Yes, very different. So the best thing to do is to signpost your talk in other ways.

OSCAR: Oh, I remember now. Yeah, this is the thing about "first tell them what you will tell them, then tell them, and then tell them what you told them."

STELLA: Exactly. It means you explain what you will be talking about then, you give your talk, and at the end, you summarize the points in a conclusion. But this is just one part of what you should do. When you explain what you're going to say, try to give your listeners a certain number of points so they can keep track.

OSCAR: So, you mean something like "I am going to talk about three aspects of competitive swimming and three aspects of non-competitive swimming."

STELLA: Yes, although I'd probably **stress** the points about non-competitive swimming first.

OSCAR: Well, what's the difference? Why mention non-competitive swimming first?

STELLA: It's just a question of logic. People swim for pleasure—non-competitively—before they swim competitively.

OSCAR: Oh yeah, okay, I get it. But I'm starting to think I should probably write this all out first.

STELLA: Sure, you can do that, but don't read your speech. Nothing is worse.

OSCAR: But lots of people read their speeches.

STELLA: And it's almost always boring when they do. You want a speech to sound like a casual but convincing explanation. The best speeches sound so natural that you begin to believe the person is thinking of great new ideas just as he or she is telling them to you.

OSCAR: So you're saying I should be natural?

STELLA: Yep, even if you have to fake it. But the point is, if you write it all out and read from your notes, you will sound like you're reading from a book. Famous actors can do it and sound natural, but you probably can't.

OSCAR: Okay, so I need three points for non-competitive swimming and three points for competitive swimming.

STELLA: And an introduction.

OSCAR: An introduction, too?

STELLA: Preparing an effective introduction is an important part of the speech-writing **process**. You get people's attention and give them a general sense of the topic. What do you know generally about swimming? What are some interesting facts?

OSCAR: Well, this is something I do know. People have been swimming for a long time—thousands of years.

STELLA: You'll have to be more specific and give some evidence from reliable **sources**.

OSCAR: Got it. How's this? Cave paintings of swimmers were discovered in the Sahara Desert in 1933. The paintings are more than 10,000 years old.

STELLA: Very impressive! That's great for your introduction or part of it. Any other interesting facts to **promote** swimming?

OSCAR: Um, drowning is the third leading cause of death in Canada. If more people learned how to swim, fewer people would die.

STELLA: This is good. Now, if you tie this to fitness, you can also talk about competitive swimming.

OSCAR: Ah, this is shaping up. Should I give it a try?

STELLA: Sure. Go ahead.

OSCAR: Hello. My name is Oscar. In 1933, a cave was discovered in the Sahara Desert, and inside there were pictures of people swimming. These pictures were painted on the cave walls more than 10,000 years ago. Swimming has changed a lot over the years, but it is more popular than ever. However, even more people need to learn how to swim because drowning is the third leading cause of death in Canada. Today, I'd like to talk about swimming and share three points about non-competitive swimming and three points about competitive swimming.

STELLA: Oscar, that's fantastic! I'm hooked and can't wait to hear more.

OSCAR: Well, you'll have to wait. I'm not sure what points I'm going to say. I'll have to make some notes.

STELLA: Great, but remember, if you're going to use cards or a sheet of paper to remind yourself of the main ideas, just keep it simple, without **distractions**, and put a word or two to help you remember what you want to say.

OSCAR: Will do. Hey, is this the way you organized your presentation?

STELLA: No, not exactly. I like your story about the cave and the fact about drownings in Canada being an important reason for learning how to swim, but I started my presentation with a rhetorical question.

OSCAR: A what?

STELLA: A rhetorical question. A rhetorical question is a kind of question that listeners aren't really expected to answer either because the answer is obvious or because the speaker assumes they couldn't guess it.

OSCAR: I still don't get it. Can you give me an example?

STELLA: Uh, sure. An obvious rhetorical question is something like "Would you like to earn a million dollars?" No one is really going to say "no" even though they know there's some kind of catch that makes it unlikely they will get the money. For the other kind of rhetorical question, if I were doing your swimming presentation, I might say, "I see several people here today with stripes on their clothes. Do you know why?"

OSCAR: No, why?

STELLA: You see. It's a rhetorical question that I don't expect you to answer, but I've got you interested and you will wait for me to tell you the reason.

OSCAR: Stella!

STELLA: Okay, okay. Until recently, say in the last hundred years, sailors were **intensely** divided about the **benefits** of learning how to swim. Some said that if you fell overboard, you could stay afloat until someone saved you. Others said that it was better to accept your fate and drown as quickly as possible so you did not suffer too long. In any case, sailors started to wear clothes with stripes because it made them easier to spot if they fell overboard. This was before bright orange lifejackets.

OSCAR: Okay, but why do we wear stripes now?

STELLA: In the 1800s, when it became fashionable to go to seaside resorts—you know, grand hotels on the coast—people started seeing lots of sailors in their striped clothes, and the **style** caught on for kids' clothing and bathing suits. Today, people don't realize they wear stripes for this reason.

OSCAR: That's great! I think I'll steal that idea.

STELLA: Just as long as you don't get a mark that is even **minimally** better than mine! Now, I know you can handle the middle points; just make sure you give clear points and examples and then you explain them. At the end, you need to draw a conclusion.

OSCAR: More than a summary?

STELLA: Yes, in a short speech you don't have to repeat what you've said. Instead, make sure you say something new ... something that builds on your main points. A conclusion that features a suggestion for action is always a good idea.

OSCAR: Oh, something like "Swimming has many benefits. Swim today, swim every day!"

STELLA: Uh, I'm not sure. It sounds a bit like an advertisement. Maybe mention something about how learning to swim is a good idea.

OSCAR: I get it ... "Learn to swim to get fit, to be social and to gain a skill that might save your life!"

STELLA: Perfect. I think you're ready!

CHAPTER 2
Lifelong Learning

LISTENING 1: The Best Way to Learn

Hello, everyone, and welcome to our first class in Educational Psychology. Today, we're going to talk about the work of Benjamin Bloom, and those who followed him, in creating the *taxonomy of cognitive objectives*. Before we begin, let's make sure we all understand the terms. A *taxonomy* is a way of classifying and organizing characteristics of and ideas about something. In biology, for instance, taxonomies group and categorize plants and animals based on similarities and differences and on relationships. In **psychology**, and most especially in educational psychology, Bloom's interest was with the *cognitive*—and *cognition*—both of which refer to how we learn: the **mental** processes we use in perceiving the world and in understanding and remembering it.

In the 1950s, Bloom was working at the University of Chicago and was involved in **evaluating** examinations. He looked at the exams being developed by university professors at the time and tried to see general patterns in the kinds of questions that students were being asked. He thought that if he could organize the questions in a **logical** way, then professors could write better exams with clearer objectives of what was expected from students. What he ended up with was a set of six levels of questioning, along with sub-questions, from which he developed his taxonomy of cognitive—or learning—objectives that has since been used internationally to create teaching and learning materials. Now, what's interesting for you, as a student, is Bloom's **conjecture** that learning is hierarchical in nature—that learning progresses from the simple to the **complex**. This idea is a useful way for you to see how you understand and **interact** with knowledge, and if applied, a practical way to learn, and to learn better.

Bloom's taxonomy has been refined; we now use a model **adapted** by one of his partners, David Krathwohl, and one of his students, Lorin Anderson. The six levels are *remembering,*

*understanding, applying, **analyzing,** evaluating* and *creating*. We're going to spend a little time looking at each of these in turn, and I want you to understand that the hierarchy, in these terms, means that you have to get to the first level before you can go on to the second level and so on. That is, you have to *remember* before you can *understand*, and you have to *understand* before you can *apply*. So, the simplest cognitive level is remembering, and the most complex cognitive level is creating. As we look at each of the levels in turn, I'll try to put them into different real-world contexts to help you understand.

The first and simplest cognitive level in the taxonomy is the act of *remembering*. We have two types of memory. The first type is short-term memory, such as when you hear a name, a number or a **statistic** and remember it for just a short period of time. We have all been to a party where we've been introduced to someone whose name we can't remember half an hour later. We often use short-term memory to store information that isn't useful or that we're not sure will be useful. It would be quite different, for example, if we were being introduced to our new boss. It is partly a matter of attending, or paying attention, and the person's name in this last situation is more likely to go into long-term memory. Long-term memory is where we store information that is more useful to us or that is built up because we **encounter** certain ideas and details over and over again.

So, the first level of the taxonomy, *remembering*, is basically about *retrieving* knowledge from long-term memory: recognizing and recalling things that we have studied and consciously tried to remember. Other times, we try to remember things we didn't expect to have to remember but that we might have unconsciously remembered. On an exam, simple questions asking you to remember facts are often the most boring questions. In this case, you are asked to simply repeat something you have memorized, such as a list of dates or **chemical** formulae. It's important to remember, but it's not a particularly high level of cognition. Most people can remember Einstein's famous **formula**, $E=MC^2$, but very few people actually understand what it means.

The second level of the taxonomy is *understanding*. When we understand something, we can say we're constructing meaning from something that we've learned. Now, to contrast this with the first level of remembering, let me give you an example. I can teach you a phrase in Chinese or another language you don't know, and I could get you to remember it, but you would not have to understand it. For that reason, *understanding* is a higher cognitive level and allows us to **interpret**, clarify, paraphrase and translate ideas. When we understand something, we can find examples and classify new ideas. Understanding helps us to make predictions and draw conclusions. In an exam, you are asked to show your understanding of something when you see the word *explain* at the start of a question. To go back to the Einstein example, a simple explanation of $E=MC^2$ is that energy and matter are different forms of the same thing. Energy can be turned into matter, and matter into energy when matter travels at extremely high speeds. By using Einstein's formula—energy equals mass times the velocity of light times the velocity of light—the amount of energy can be calculated.

Once you understand something, you can move on to the third cognitive level, *applying*. Applying quite simply involves executing or carrying out a procedure of some kind. Again, we do this every day. We all spend a lot of time on our computers, and there are a lot of procedures we undertake without thinking. For example, I know all of you are good at opening and answering e-mails, downloading files and searching the Internet. I also know you think this is both natural and easy, but these are procedures that would likely mystify your great-grandparents or perhaps your grandparents. In the exam context, a typical *apply* question would be to use a formula to solve a math problem, like calculating the area of a triangle.

The fourth level of the cognitive taxonomy is *analyzing*. Analyzing is breaking information into parts and then deciding how these parts relate to each other as well as to an overall structure or purpose. Often this process of analyzing includes deciding what is important and what is not important. For example, if asked to analyze the causes of the first Gulf War, considering both of the opposing forces, you might decide that factors included the invasion of Kuwait, the protection of oil resources and the punishment of an unfriendly dictator on one side, and historical grievances and the desire to expand territory on the other. Among these, you would have to consider which were more or less important in the decision-making processes of those involved in starting the war. Given this process, you can see how analyzing is a higher-level skill; you need to *remember, understand* and be able to *apply* what you've learned.

The fifth level of the cognitive taxonomy is *evaluating*. Like the other cognitive levels, this is something we each do every day. When we evaluate, we're making judgments of some kind, often based on a **criterion** or set of standards that apply to a particular situation. For example, if you order a meal at a restaurant, you might evaluate the meal based on presentation, price, taste, quality and quantity of the ingredients and so on. In the exam situation, you would probably be asked to evaluate a product, a process or an event and either develop the criterion yourself or use a set of criteria you've already learned.

The sixth and most complex level of the cognitive taxonomy is *creating*. When we create, we are using most, if not all, of the previous levels—*remembering, understanding, applying, analyzing* and *evaluating*—together. We illustrate these other cognitive levels by producing something new and original. In fine arts, it might be a painting, a sculpture, a dance, a play or a video. Similarly, in engineering courses, you might be asked to create a robot or design a new car.

Let's take the example of the new car to see how you might put in place all the cognitive processes. First, you're going to *remember* what you know about cars ... different kinds of cars and machines that move. At the second level, you're going to *understand* what makes cars move—something that travels easily over a surface, such as wheels, and some kind of power source, like an electric or gas engine. You could go on to the third level of *applying* and show what you know by drawing some designs for a new car. Based on your drawings, you might *analyze* what makes cars work and go to the fifth stage of *evaluating*. As you *evaluate* your ideas and compare them to what has been done in previous cars, you're likely to have **insight** into how you can make a better car. All this prepares you for the final stage, *creating*. Here you bring together everything you know and produce something new. And then you've done it: you've created a new kind of car.

Going back to the example of Einstein's $E=MC^2$, the final cognitive level of creation was the invention of nuclear reactors for power and, less fortunately, nuclear weapons for war.

From everything I've said so far, you probably realize that we don't go through all these cognitive levels with every problem we're confronted with or even get to the stage of remembering information that is better left in short-term memory. It would be overwhelming to try to *remember, understand, apply, analyze* and *evaluate* everything we come into contact with, let alone go on to *create* something new. Yet, recognizing and understanding these cognitive levels are important: each time you learn something new, you should be questioning whether or not you understand it and whether or not it could apply to another concept or situation.

So, think about something that you know, or think you know, really well. It could be something you are studying or something you do for fun, such as a sport. Consider what level of cognition you're at and what you could do to learn about it at a deeper level.

LISTENING 2: Where Did I Put ... My Memory?

NARRATOR: These people are trying hard to remember: to squeeze every last memory out of their brains. They are world-champion memory experts, gathered here to defeat their arch enemy: forgetfulness. These memory masters are a **symbol** of us all, in the never-ending war between remembering and forgetting.

It's a battle that's becoming tougher as we live to an older age and are overwhelmed by the information age. We meet people we know but can't recall their names. We forget where we put our purses, our wallets and our keys. Sometimes, we can't remember the word for the **thingamajig** to wash the salad. And by the way, where did I park my car?

For North Americans, memory loss is the second greatest health concern after cancer, and we can't just forget about it because there's so much to forget. We live in an era of information overload, from PIN numbers to alarm codes to personal **security** passwords for our cappuccino makers. No wonder we sometimes forget that our missing glasses are nearer than we think.

WOMAN 1: Oh, I can't remember anyone's name. They could tell me five times, and I would have no idea.

WOMAN 2: My memory should be really good. I study memory, I should know how to make a memory, but I can't seem to always remember the memory.

WOMAN 3: We forget where we put our keys; we forget that we've seen a movie already until we're halfway through it. We forget things through our lifespan, but we pay more attention to the act of forgetting as we get older because it's **threatening**.

MAN 1: Memory is the greatest thing I have—**versus** money, versus any material good, versus cars, anything. I—I just don't want to lose my memory.

MAN 2: Just imagine that right now, I take out your memory. What would then happen? What would be left? Nothing!

NARRATOR: Are we all doomed to lose our minds, or are there ways to keep our memories—and even make them better? If you can lose your memory, can you find it? Let's take a trip down memory lane and find out how we can all remember more.

Humans have been forgetting things as long as they've been remembering them, and sometimes, that leads to disaster. Here on Newfoundland's rugged coast, forgetting where the rocks are can cost you your life, so sailors learned to **navigate** by memorizing songs that gave directions.

PAMELA MORGAN: "Then nor'-nor' west for thirty-three miles/Three leagues off shore lies Wadham's Isles."

NARRATOR: These songs were a kind of GPS for countless **generations**, says well-known local singer Pamela Morgan.

PM: The points of the compass that are described in this song are very **precise**. You couldn't miss not a word or a line of that, or you'd find yourself in trouble. So people had to remember that song word for word because it was a matter of life and death. "But unkind fortune unluck laid/A sunken rock right in the trade."

PROF. DANIEL LEVITIN: Ancient humans would sing songs like "Over here is the water well," or you know, whatever melodies and rhythms they had then, and, uh, "Eat this plant, don't eat that plant," "Don't drink from that well over there," you know, "So-and-so's uncle did, and the neighbouring tribe killed him." This kind of knowledge song, we see the vestiges of today even though we have writing. And we can write down these important things in encyclopedias or in cellphones. Every kid learns the alphabet through a song.

OTHERS: "A, b, c, d, e, f, g/H, i, j, k, l, m, n, o, p/Q, r, s, t, u, v—." After that I don't know. "W, x/Y and z/Now I know my ABCs, won't you come and sing with me." [Laughing]

WOMAN 4: So you remember that, but you forget your car keys, or you forget somebody's name that you knew all your life.

ALEX KAJITANI: "Just sit back, relax./Let out a little smile./ 'Cause the rapping mathematician is the hot new style."

NARRATOR: Music class has been cancelled in many schools, but in California, one teacher still thinks it's a formula for success. [Kajitani teaching: "What do we call this kind of fraction, where the numerator is bigger than the denominator?"] He's the rapping mathematician, Alex Kajitani. [Kajitani teaching: "... an improper fraction. It's very simple to remember because: If it's bigger on the topper, it must be improper. If it's bigger on the topper, it must be improper. The denominator's skinny, and the numerator's fat. Very nice."] This is a tough, low-income neighbourhood, where marks lag way behind the state average. But Kajitani has changed that tune with the memory power of music.

AK: They would not sit still in their seats, and they certainly couldn't remember a math rule that ... that I had taught them. But what I noticed is that a rap song would come out on Monday, and by Tuesday, they seemed to have every word memorized. One day, I had enough, so I wrote a song. [Kajitani teaching: "Come on! What's a crooked line? It's a **radical** sign. And when you see a perfect square? Just pull it out of there. Yeah!"] And at the end of the week, my test scores shot through the roof, so I've been math rappin' ever since.

STUDENT 1: It's, like, sometimes we're doing tests, and you can hear kids, like, singing the songs, you know. So it does help you a lot. I get better grades now.

STUDENT 2: Well, before I didn't like it as much. I thought it was kind of lame, but now I like it. It's cool. [Rapping: "... negative numbers, you've really got to know. And when you start at zero, to the left they go. And to the right are zero ..."]

NARRATOR: The students did so well he made a video that's become a YouTube sensation [Rapping: "... the number line dance, it starts at zero. And when you do this dance, you're the neighbourhood hero ..."]. It spread to schools all over the States, and Kajitani was named California Teacher of the Year

[Rapping: "... negative to the left, positive to the right. It's the number line dance and I can dance all night."]. Maybe this is still a good way to remember things. We all learn songs, rhymes and similar tricks in class that last a lifetime.

MAN 3: "I use my eyes, I use my ears, before I use my feet."

MAN 4: "Peter, Paul, Andrew, James, John, Philip, Bartholomew, Matthew, Simon, Thaddeus, Linus, Cletus, Clement, Sixtus, Cornelius, Cyprian, Lawrence, Chryosgonus, John, Paul, Cosmas and Damian, and all the Saints."

DL: "Neo-cortex, frontal lobe, brainstem, brainstem. Hippocampus, neural node, left hemisphere." If only I could sing where I set my keys, or where I parked my car, it would be a lot easier to remember.

NARRATOR: Can we find other techniques that work as well as **memorable** songs? What else can stir deep forgotten memories and help us memorize new ones?

[Dave Farrow speaking: "Hello, I'm Dave Farrow and welcome to Millionaire Memory!"]

Dave Farrow teaches memory courses to business people eager to recall the name of every client. [Farrow teaching: "By **visualizing** something unique and different involving ..."] And Dave's got lots of unusual techniques.

DAVE FARROW: The next time you have to remember someone's name, try to turn it into a picture. This could be weird at first, but say my name, for example: Dave. Think of a wave, like a wave knocking me over. You'll never forget it. Someone like Mike: imagine, like, a giant boom microphone here, and Mike's holding onto it. Mary: uh, think of her dressed up like the Virgin Mary. Well my last name is Farrow. It's spelled f-a-r-r-o-w, but it sounds similar to an Egyptian pharaoh.

NARRATOR: Dave also teaches students like this at his old high school in Kitchener, Canada, where he is today's **motivational** speaker. [Farrow speaking: "My dream is to triple the memory of everybody in North America and around the world. So I think you'll help me out with that, right?"] Dave knows what it is to have a poor memory. As a student here, he was **diagnosed** with two learning disabilities and almost dropped out of school.

DF: I had a horrible memory. I was at the bottom of most of my grades, I, uh, had a lot of difficulty reading because of my dyslexia, and I just got depressed. What am I going to do, I'm not—I don't have any choices in life, you know. If you don't have your brain, what are you, you know, what are you going to get by on, right?

NARRATOR: Dave spent two years privately studying anything he could about improving memory, from the latest brain science to ancient Roman **methods** for mastering the mind.

DF: And that's when I saw a huge **turnaround**. I was getting 99 percent on test after test. It was incredible. My big revelation was that memory is a skill. It's not some sprinkling of **fairy dust** on some people that other people don't get; it's something that can be taught. And when I knew that, then I wanted to be the best at it.

LISTENING 3: What's on Your Bucket List?

OSCAR: So, what's on your bucket list, Stella?

STELLA: Bucket list? What's that?

OSCAR: Oh, it's kind of a crude term ... Do you know the expression "Kick the bucket"? You know, when you don't want to say something unpleasant.

Stella: You mean a *euphemism*.

Oscar: Yes, a euphemism, for something you'd rather not say directly. So "kick the bucket" refers to dying.

Stella: And a bucket list?

Oscar: Oh, it's a list of things you want to do before you die.

Stella: Ah, well sure, I think everyone has a list of things they'd like to do. What sort of things are on your list?

Oscar: Well, you know I like to travel. But my travel list isn't a list at all; it's a map—a map of the world.

Stella: With places you want to go?

Oscar: And places I've already been. I use little **symbols**: red for places I'd like to go and green for places I've already visited.

Stella: Let me guess ... there are a lot more red symbols.

Oscar: Of course. I haven't travelled as much as I want to, and when I read about new places that interest me, I add a symbol to the map.

Stella: I've got a list of places I'd like to visit, but not countries or cities. They're monuments, like the pyramids of Egypt, Machu Picchu in Peru and the Great Wall of China. I also have a list of things I'd like to do.

Oscar: Like adventures?

Stella: Some are adventures. I'd like to try a really long wilderness walk, like hiking the West Coast Trail on the far side of Vancouver Island or a two-week rafting trip on the Korok River in Nunavik. But I'd also like a **mental** challenge, like reading *all* of a certain author's novels.

Oscar: The complete works of Jane Austen?

Stella: Already done that! After all, she wrote only six complete novels. But Charles Dickens ... ah, that's more of a challenge: twenty-two novels and fifteen other books of poetry, plays, speeches and travel writing. Actually, Dickens was a guy with a bucket list! When he was nine years old, he walked past a magnificent house and said to himself, "One day I will own that house!" Thirty-five years later, he did.

Oscar: Wow. I've got a book I'm trying to work through, but it's not a novel. It's a cookbook.

Stella: Really? You cook?

Oscar: Yes, I do. Surprisingly well! Someone once said, "The things you do every day, you should do well." We all have to eat—and I *love* to eat—so I decided I should learn to cook.

Stella: That's great. How far along are you?

Oscar: I've tried about forty or fifty recipes. Some were ... uh ... well, more successful than others. But there were at least a few basic **methods** that were easy and interesting.

Stella: I look forward to being your test subject! I guess this shows that you and I have different things on our bucket lists.

Oscar: Yeah, it's true. I've talked to a few people about this and sometimes I think, wow ... what a great idea—I should do that, too! Other times, I just have to shake my head and wonder how people could waste their time like that.

Stella: Really? Like what?

Oscar: Well, a lot of people have **precise** financial goals. They say things like "I want to make a million dollars by the time I'm twenty-five."

Stella: And you don't think that's a good ambition?

Oscar: Mm, nah, not really. I think they're missing the point. Making the money might be something you'd like to brag about, but it's not really an accomplishment in itself. If you said, for example, you wanted to make enough money so you could invest it and spend your life travelling: well, that would be better. Better still, if your ambition was to raise a million dollars to build a school or a hospital in a poor country ... now, that would be something to be proud of.

Stella: I see what you mean. And actually, I think for a lot of millionaires—especially inventors and other creative people—what they do is the **motivational** part and is more important than making money.

Oscar: Exactly. And some people say it's their ambition to retire early. But I think a lot of them don't really think about the next step. What are they going to do when they retire? That's what they should be thinking about.

Stella: I get it. If they retire, do they **visualize** themselves sitting around and watching TV all day?

Oscar: Probably not. But on the other hand, maybe the simple life is what some people want. Here's a story my uncle told me about being satisfied with what you have. One day, a businessman is sailing on a boat in the Caribbean and he sees the most beautiful island ever. He stops and walks ashore on a white sandy beach in front of a flower-filled jungle, with the scent of coconut in the air and the sounds of birds singing in the trees. The businessman **encounters** an old guy resting in a hammock and reading a book. "Excuse me," he says. "Is this your island?" "Yes," the man replies. "Well, I'm a businessman, and I'd like to tell you that this island would be the perfect place for a resort." The old man says nothing, so the businessman goes on. "You could build a resort over here and on the other side a golf course." Pointing out to the sea, he adds, "And then a marina with a big dock. You could make millions and millions of dollars." The old man interrupts him and asks, "Okay, but what would I do then?" The businessman is exasperated. "You would be rich! You could do *anything* you want!" "Well," says the old man, "The only thing I want to do is lie in my hammock on the beach and read a book. And I'm already doing that now."

Stella: [Laughs] Yeah, I get it. It's a good **insight** into ambition. You need to decide what you really want.

Oscar: That's right. A lot of people think working hard and making money is important, but there's a saying, "At the end of your life, you'll never wish you had spent more time at the office."

Stella: Mm ... family and friends first. But you said people had other ideas on their lists that you'd *like* to do. What are some of their goals?

Oscar: I guess you can divide them into several categories. Some people want recognition. If you're a scientist, you probably want a Nobel Prize, and if you're an athlete, you probably want an Olympic medal. But fame is a bit like money. We all want the recognition of our peers, but fame should be about having new opportunities to do something *really* exciting. Do you know Carl Wieman?

Stella: No, sorry, never heard of him.

Oscar: Well he's a perfect example. In 2001, he won a Nobel Prize in physics. In his field, we could say he's a rock star. In 2004, he was voted United States Professor of the Year, and he could have continued his work at almost any university or any research facility in any country in the world. But what did he choose to do instead? His real passion was to improve the teaching of science. When the University of British Columbia offered him a chance to do just that, he surprised the world by turning his back on jobs that would have given him a lot more prestige and paid him a lot more money. He wanted a chance to make a difference and get kids excited about science by emphasizing experiential learning—not just studying science in books.

STELLA: Wonderful. So recognition isn't everything. What other categories have people used on their bucket lists?

OSCAR: Well, travel is a big one—everyone has somewhere they want to go—but the really interesting and **complex** stories are from people who have plans about *how* they're going to do it.

STELLA: Like riding across Africa on a motorcycle?

OSCAR: Sure, and that's possible if you save enough money, but other people who want to go around the world, for example, might study how to teach English, which will help them pay their way.

STELLA: Yeah, I know what you mean. Someone I met wanted to be a flight attendant because he thought that that would make extensive travel part of his daily life.

OSCAR: Exactly. Another category is doing something creative, like writing a song or a book. The great thing about that is the Internet makes it easy to share what you do. You don't need to get a contract with a publisher or a record company. Others want to learn first-aid skills or languages, and many people want to create something with their hands, like building a house or a musical instrument.

STELLA: Sounds like a lot of work.

OSCAR: Not everything on your bucket list has to be. One of my ambitions is to see every movie that has ever won the Academy Award for Best Picture, starting from 1928. Do you feel like renting a video with me tonight?

STELLA: I'd love to, but I have a date ... with Charles Dickens.

CHAPTER 3
Selling Dreams

LISTENING 1: Stealth Social Marketing

NORA YOUNG: First up, advertising. McLuhan studied advertising as a key to the culture. His 1951 book *The Mechanical Bride* focused on it. But McLuhan's quips about ads, like "All advertising advertises advertising," were talking about mass **media** advertising. I wonder what he'd make of some of the dark corners of today's online **marketing**. Like, tell me if this ever happens to you.

You're online, logged into a **social networking** site, and seemingly out of nowhere, up pops a message or a friend request from a total stranger. "Wait a minute, who's Rick G.?" you think to yourself. "Is that the guy I met at Debbie's barbecue ... maybe?" You squint at the profile picture. "He looks kind of familiar." So you click through to see the stranger's profile. "Oh yeah, we live in the same city. And he has *Mad Men* listed as his favourite TV show. Oh, what the hey." And you click to approve the friend request.

Now sure, that total stranger could have been the *Mad Men*-loving guy you met at Debbie's barbecue last summer, but it's also possible that he doesn't exist at all. That he's a **mirage**, a fake account, a carefully crafted online persona created by a marketing company. It's a fairly common technique these days, and there are different names for it. Sometimes it's called "**stealth** marketing," sometimes it's called "sock puppeting," because the account is just one of many in an army of fake profiles, all controlled by an unseen hand. And there's a less devious-sounding name for it.

EMILY: Uh, I like to call it ... online **viral** marketing.

NY: That's Emily. Actually, her name's not really Emily, and we've changed her voice a little bit. Emily has worked as an online viral marketer.

EMILY: I did this job ... uh ... for a few different companies, and it's been on and off for about the past five years.

NY: Emily agreed to come into our studio and give us a rare behind-the-scenes look at how this kind of **subtle** online persuasion happens. We changed her name and voice because Emily still makes a living in the online world, and revealing her **identity** could affect her future employment. But really, it's her past jobs that we most wanted to talk to her about. Basically, on and off for five years, Emily's job was to create a bunch of fake online **profiles** and flesh them out so that they seemed like real people.

EMILY: Each of them would have, you know, dreams in life and things to talk about other than just the service or the product. If the account was that of a photographer, they would tell stories about their **pursuits** as a photographer, to sort of subtly ... throwing in different products and services to get the message out there.

NY: Over the years, Emily created a lot of fake profiles.

EMILY: Well, it added up over time, because ... uh ... for each new client, new accounts would be created in different cities around the world. In ... in the **scope** of between dozens and hundreds of different accounts across different social networks and bulletin boards. That's just from one company, which is not ... not the only company providing services like this.

NY: Emily and her colleagues would then assume these identities and try to befriend as many people as they could. The goal was to create as much **buzz** as possible about a band or an online video game without coming across as fake or spammy.

EMILY: To make a persona seem real, we would do things like deliberate typos. If we were in a certain region, we would look at what other people in that region were saying and talking about and what sorts of slang they would use, and we would just try to **emulate** that. We would talk about **mundane** things: craving chocolate bars and ... crushes on boys and whatever else normal people online complain about. Every day we would go out and find, you know new funny things online to post and make comments on other people's posts and just get involved in the online community.

NY: If you're anything like me, you're probably thinking, "That seems like an awful lot of work to promote a band or a web service or a video game." Employing teams of people to control hundreds of fake accounts just to get a few positive product mentions out there.

EMILY: Even in the midst of doing this work, it always seemed a little crazy to me. But there really is something to be said for receiving a message from what seems to be a real individual and not from what is considered a traditional source of advertising ... uh ... because it adds a certain **legitimacy** to the product that is very difficult to replicate otherwise.

NY: Now, many social networks have rules that explicitly forbid setting up fake accounts like this, and for viral marketers, that can be a challenge.

EMILY: For Facebook for sure, while it used to be really easy to befriend total strangers on Facebook ... now there are all sorts of warning messages: "Do you actually know this person?" If you don't know them and they report you and you try to do this to too many people, then your account gets shut down immediately. An example of something that could be done to overcome that is to say, "Oh, you know, this is my new account because I didn't want my grandma and parents to see my wild side, and so I'm looking for all new friends," and anything ... anything we can come up with to get around that. And ... I mean, the work ... the work involves a level of **deception** that, of course, one would feel conflicted about doing. At the same time, it's a relatively small level of deception, it's not ... you know, it's not on the same scale as Internet **predators**. And ... but in a way they are comparable ... uh ... just because it is a form of deception and trying to go out there and befriend strangers for **ulterior motives**. But, ...

NY: Emily told us about one campaign that she worked on that really highlights the strange **tension** that can happen when an online friendship is based on false premises.

EMILY: It was a campaign that was running in the fall, we had a Facebook account ... for somebody and ... you know, they lived in a certain city and had ... a certain history. And among their friends, one was having a group Thanksgiving dinner. And we received an invitation to somebody's ... American Thanksgiving dinner, very far away ... through Facebook. And in a way, that was sad because that was such a nice gesture to make to someone who they really didn't know, and they just wanted to make sure we had ... we had somewhere to spend Thanksgiving.

NY: It kind of makes you wonder which of the names on your contact list might not be real, doesn't it?

EMILY: Um ... I think maybe I'm over-**skeptical** ... I just assume that things are online marketing, even when perhaps they aren't ... but an example is one ... one client was a band who wanted their song to be well-known, and so one of the companies I was working for hired a girl to do ... a strip-tease ... on a video, and she ... there was no full nudity, she just went down to, like, a bikini, and she put on what she said was her favourite song to dance to, and it was of course the song from this band. And ... at the end of it ... people went out and tried to promote this video, and ... it got oh, lots and lots of views on YouTube ... and it's still up there somewhere, and ... although the promotion is long over.

So ... whenever I see a video that has, you know, clips of a band's music, I always wonder, you know, did ... did someone really choose this song, or is this ... is this just some advertising company? And it's really difficult online to know ... who's who and where ... the message you're reading is coming from. And even when it seems like it could be, you know ... an authentic source ... there really isn't a good way of determining because there are such clever and crafty means and lengths that people will go to, to mask ... their identities online.

LISTENING 2: Understanding Propaganda

Today, in this lecture, we will be examining an interesting **phenomenon** within the field of political science: propaganda. I would like to first give a general overview about what is meant by the term *propaganda*. Propaganda is the deliberate and systematic use of information to communicate a particular—often political—point of view. Propaganda is meant to shape public opinion, to influence and persuade, most often through emotional appeals and, frequently, by ignoring the truth, or at least the *whole* truth. A number of propaganda techniques have been identified. To help you understand the **concepts** involved, I'm going to further define propaganda by giving a few historical examples and by discussing how propaganda is used today. Please take notes, and if you have any questions, I will be happy to answer them at the end of the lecture.

As mentioned earlier, propaganda has as its main goal the shaping of public opinion toward a particular point of view. But sometimes, we might not be completely aware of what that point of view is or what purpose is being promoted. Take for example a propaganda campaign that comments on another country's human rights policies—that paints a picture of a people or ruler as being evil. Creating an impression of evil, or **demonizing**, might lead eventually to justification for a war, yet the purpose of justifying a war is not understood by the public at the outset of the propaganda campaign.

Propaganda, in this sense, is an old tactic, but the word *propaganda* has not always had a negative **connotation**. In some countries, it still doesn't. But this is the sense, the political and pejorative sense, that we will talk about today, rather than the more ameliorative sense of the word. Oh, sorry, I see a few blank faces. *Pejorative* means "negative," and *ameliorative* is the opposite ... Got it? Good, let's continue.

As I said, propaganda is not a new tactic. Among the ruins of the ancient Egyptians, archaeologists found detailed records praising each new pharaoh—the king of the ancient Egyptians. These records of accomplishments included lists of the pharaoh's great battles, even wars that had in fact been fought hundreds of years previously. In this case, the propaganda—lying about what the pharaoh had done—was used to increase the power and prestige of the next pharaoh. Ever since those times, many leaders, such as those of North Korea and some African countries, have used big and small lies to make themselves seem more important so they could exert tighter control over their people. Many have even claimed to have been chosen for leadership by one god or another. It is all part of a **cult** of *leadership*, a common propaganda technique.

Another technique was one used by the Roman soldier and senator Cato the Elder, who lived from 234 to 149 BCE. He was one of many who used his speeches as propaganda to encourage attacks on one of the Roman Empire's rivals, Carthage. It is said that Cato ended every speech with the Latin words *Carthago delenda est!* which means "Carthage must be destroyed!" This is what is called an *ad nauseum* technique: if something is repeated enough, it begins to sound true. As the German dictator Adolph Hitler said, "The most brilliant propagandist technique will yield no success unless one **fundamental** principle is borne in mind constantly; it must **confine** itself to a few points and repeat them over and over." It's worth noting that Hitler's followers also used the *cult of leadership* technique to make Hitler seem like a leader sent to save the German people.

As we will see in a moment, this sort of repetition of ideas is a key way in which propaganda is spread. In Cato's case, the Roman armies eventually attacked Carthage, killing 62,000; all the remaining Carthaginians—50,000 of them—were sold into slavery. Cato's **persistence** in working for an end to Carthage was heavily laden with propaganda, conveying an *appeal* to fear. In an appeal to fear, natural worries are developed in order to create support for an idea or act.

During World War II, Hitler's Minister of Propaganda, Dr. Joseph Goebbels, used an American book titled *Germany Must Perish* to **instill** fear in the German public and to rally the German troops. The book **advocated** serious measures, such as the sterilization of German men to stop them from producing children.

In turn, the Jewish people were blamed by Goebbels and others for many of Germany's problems, that is, they were made into scapegoats. Before and during World War II, the German Nazis, under Hitler and Goebbels, committed one of history's greatest acts of genocide by murdering more than six million European Jews. Much of this was possible because of another propaganda technique, an *appeal to prejudice*, which is linked to both demonization and scapegoating. Both the German public and soldiers were taught to think of Jews as being less than human in order to **justify** the horrors to which Jews were subjected. This was done through clever disinformation campaigns, such as the promotion of materials that purported to expose secret Jewish plots. A famous one was *The **Protocols** of the Elders of Zion*, a forgery that supposedly outlined an international Jewish conspiracy to do three things: control economics, control the media such as newspapers and radio, and destroy the lives of non-Jewish people. Even though the document was clearly shown to be **fraudulent**, *The Protocols of the Elders of Zion* was studied as if factual in German classrooms after Hitler came into power and was, in the opinion of some historians, Hitler's primary justification for **initiating** the Holocaust—the systematic murder of so many Jews.

Okay, so far we have examined the propaganda techniques of demonization, the cult of leadership, *ad nauseam* statements, scapegoating, appeals to fear and appeals to prejudice. Let's look at some other techniques.

Bandwagon as a propaganda technique is an appeal to follow the crowd: to join a group or activity because so many others have, and since so many others have, this must be the winning side. Humans naturally want to belong to groups, particularly winning groups. Pointing out that they can be part of a group, especially if that group is opposed to something that has been labelled evil, is a powerful technique. A bandwagon technique pressures those people who do not want to lose favour or be left out. For example, if we say, "Don't be a coward. Let's go to war with the Republic of Freedonia; it's a war we can win," people who don't want to be seen as lacking in bravery or who want to be seen as winners might be more **inclined** to support the idea.

Selective omission falls just short of lying. In selective omission, important facts that support the propagandist's point of view are given, while other important facts that would argue against it are not. For example, if the only fact you were given was that Canada spends more than twenty billion dollars a year on its armed forces, you might conclude that Canada is a warlike nation because this sounds like a lot. But Canada spends more than seventy

billion dollars on education. Moreover, to really understand what both of these figures meant, you would need to be able to compare them to other countries' spending, including the percentage of national income different countries spend on education versus armies.

Propaganda often makes use of a technique called *glittering generalities*. Glittering generalities are words linked to highly valued concepts such as democracy, honour, glory, love of country and freedom. You've probably heard these glittering generalities used in political campaigns, in slogans, in an effort to bestow the same positive feelings on a candidate or a political party. If a political party says something like "Choose a better tomorrow," it's hard to disagree. If the political party **links** the message to other things that are positive, through photographs and other images, it creates positive feelings. Advertisers know this, which is why they often associate young, healthy, happy people with the products they want you to buy.

The last technique we will examine is *transfer*. Transfer is the attempt to generalize from an individual or an individual *incident* to a larger group. For example, if we think that a leader is evil, we can use propaganda to transfer that feeling onto a wider group. This is why a wartime poster might feature pictures of the other country's leader, portraying him or her in a negative light, especially in cartoons.

Up to now, I have talked about different propaganda techniques. Now, I would like to talk about how we can consider propaganda in terms of *white, black* and *grey*. These three colour codes refer not to the propaganda itself, but rather to each one's **source**. *White* propaganda is plainly understood to be from the individual or group that stands to benefit from it. A nation at war, for example, might clearly put its name and flag on a propaganda poster attacking its enemies. *Black propaganda* is based on deception, which makes it look like something published by the enemy or another targeted group. *The Protocols of the Elders of Zion* is an example of black propaganda. Although it was written and first published years earlier in Russia, it was used extensively by the Nazis for black propaganda. *Grey propaganda* makes it unclear where the information came from. For example, a news station might receive an "unofficial" tip, or a political group might create a so-called research organization whose only goal is to produce documents that secretly support their **ideology**. Grey propaganda looks independent, so people are more likely to believe it.

As you can see, propaganda is a complex and interesting topic. We've reviewed demonization, the cult of leadership, ad nauseam statements, scapegoating, appeals to fear, appeals to prejudice, bandwagon, selective omission, glittering generalities and transfer. Furthermore, we can see that these can be **disseminated** in three ways, through white, black and grey propaganda channels. Now let's look at more specific examples of how each is used in politics.

LISTENING 3: A Mountain of Rice

OSCAR: Hey Stella, have you started your project on **viral marketing** yet?

STELLA: Viral marketing? No, Oscar. But we have another week, don't we?

OSCAR: [Laughing] Ah, my friend! You've been fooled by the calendar again!

STELLA: What do you mean?

OSCAR: It's not due in a week; it's due tomorrow!

STELLA: Why do you torture me like this?

OSCAR: Because it's true, and because when you need my help, you need to do nice things to pay me back.

STELLA: Okay, we'd better get started. Do you have time?

OSCAR: Sure. But you haven't asked what I want in return yet.

STELLA: Fine, tell me. What do you want in return?

OSCAR: I want some rice.

STELLA: Rice? Sorry, do you mean like rice for eating?

OSCAR: Yes, but to make it interesting, this is what I want you to do. Do you know how many squares there are on a chessboard?

STELLA: A chessboard? Uh, let's see … eight by eight squares. That would be … sixty-four squares.

OSCAR: That's right. So, imagine this: put a grain of rice on the first square and just double the number of grains on each square until you get to the sixty-fourth. Give me all the rice on that square.

STELLA: You want me to buy you a bag of rice? This is just weird.

OSCAR: No, it's not. It's actually part of a story and has a lot to do with viral marketing.

STELLA: Oh-oh. You're going to tell me another old story, aren't you?

OSCAR: You'll love it. Listen. An ancient Indian king was tired of fighting the neighbouring kingdoms, so he asked a philosopher how he could eliminate war. The philosopher nodded and went off. The king was curious and sent spies to see what the old philosopher was doing, and they reported that, each day, he just sat carving little figures. Finally, after much **persistence**, he returned with the first chess set and taught the king the game. The king was delighted to be able to play a game of strategy without soldiers being killed and asked the philosopher to name his price. The philosopher told him about the idea of grains of rice on each square of the chessboard. Everyone laughed. They thought the philosopher was an old fool for not asking for a bag of gold.

STELLA: Uh, I'm **skeptical** and guessing there's not a happy ending to this story.

OSCAR: No. Not for the king and not for you. The king asked for a bag of rice and had servants begin counting. They soon returned and said that the final square would have more rice on it than existed in all the kingdom.

STELLA: A lot of rice.

OSCAR: By the thirteenth square, you've passed a million grains. By the forty-first square, you've gone past the trillion mark. By the end, you've got a pile higher than Mount Everest.

STELLA: Okay, so this has *what* to do with viral marketing?

OSCAR: It's all about **social networking**. Think of the grains of rice as people on the chessboard. On the first square, someone has a great idea and tells two people. This doubles on the third square and by the fourth square, eight

people are sharing the idea and each telling two others. Again, if everyone told two people, in thirteen turns, you'd have shared your idea with more than a million people. That's a lot of **buzz**.

STELLA: Wow. So I guess there are some steps to making sure that happens. I mean, the idea has to be pretty powerful, right?

OSCAR: Right on both counts. You need to create a powerful message, and there are a few steps. The first step is that you need to give something away. Something for free.

STELLA: But wait a minute—isn't marketing all about getting people to pay for something?

OSCAR: Sure, but that comes later. To begin with, you have to have some kind of hook, and everyone loves something for free. Actually, people recognize that it's not *really* free, but it's not obviously **fraudulent**: there's just some catch that doesn't make it overly unattractive.

STELLA: Can you give me an example?

OSCAR: Sure, every time you turn on your computer and search for something, you're getting free information, but …

STELLA: … but I have to look at *advertising*. The advertising pays for the search engines.

OSCAR: Exactly. So let's get back to the viral marketing idea. What's an idea, a product or a service that you could create that other people would be interested in?

STELLA: Right, now we're back to the project. Mm … something that everyone would want?

OSCAR: Yes.

STELLA: Ah, here's one! My mom's secret recipe for chocolate chip cookies!

OSCAR: Oh, I can't believe you said that!

STELLA: Why?

OSCAR: Well, there's already a famous story about a cookie recipe. In the story, someone has a cookie in a restaurant and asks for the recipe. The waitress checks and says it costs two-fifty.

STELLA: You mean two dollars and fifty cents?

OSCAR: Well, that's the problem. It's a bit of a **deception**— expensive deception. The woman says she'll buy the recipe and later checks her credit card statement and finds she's been billed for two hundred and fifty dollars. So, to get revenge, she e-mails the recipe to everyone she knows for free, telling her story and encouraging everyone to share it. It's not true, but the story is great and ends up being **disseminated** in a viral way.

STELLA: Okay, so I see this has the "free" part, but you said there were some other steps.

OSCAR: Yes. The first step is to have something free. The second step is *making sure your message can travel easily*.

STELLA: How do you do that?

OSCAR: Well, in the cookie example, the story travels easily because it's short and memorable. You might not be able to remember the whole recipe, but you get the idea and will decide if you want to check the recipe and maybe make the cookies.

STELLA: Okay, what else?

OSCAR: The message, product or service should be able to *scale up*. That's the third step. This means that it should be able to go from a few people sharing to lots of people sharing. If you started a rumour of some kind in a school—something silly like the government is going to cancel all exams this year—it might travel around the classroom, but then, if it was a good rumour with some details that made it appear truthful, you might see it jump to other colleges and universities and eventually become a national **phenomenon**. But it would have to be something general enough for that to happen.

STELLA: I see ... free, can travel easy, scale up. What else?

OSCAR: A good product, service or message should consider human nature. Human nature is the fourth step.

STELLA: Oh, I think I know what you mean. In the cookie story, people spread the message because they think they are helping a poor woman who was cheated by restaurant staff with an **ulterior motive**.

OSCAR: Exactly, it's helping the little guy. It's also about vengeance, another strong human emotion. Other emotions might be pity or fear—like of a disease—or love.

STELLA: Free, can travel easy, scale up, emotional ... are there more?

OSCAR: Just two. The fifth step is that the viral message should use existing communication networks, and the sixth step is that it should take advantage of other people's resources.

STELLA: Okay, you're going to have to give me some examples. I think I understand the first one, though: using existing communication resources is like using e-mail to send the cookie recipe.

OSCAR: That's right. Nowadays, you could use Facebook or Twitter or other ways to share ideas, but you could also **confine** yourself to logos on T-shirts, bumper stickers on cars and so on.

STELLA: And taking advantage of other people's resources?

OSCAR: Well, let me give you an example. You know about the *Guinness Book of World Records*, don't you?

STELLA: Sure, it lists all sorts of odd things people do ... the biggest, longest, smallest, shortest, tallest, fastest ... that sort of thing.

OSCAR: That's right. And say you have a pizza restaurant and you make the world's biggest pizza.

STELLA: Your restaurant would get a **profile** in the book.

OSCAR: Not only that, but people would talk about you because you were in the book and would write stories about you in local newspapers. To find out more about the story, people would want to eat at your restaurant.

STELLA: Okay, so doing something that gets you in a book or in the news in some way—like a YouTube video of you doing something crazy—that will make you famous.

OSCAR: Yep. And you're doing it by using someone else's resources.

STELLA: Okay. I'm all set.

OSCAR: Not yet. First, you have to pay for all my advice.

STELLA: You want a million bags of rice?

OSCAR: Nah, I'll settle for a pizza. Let's go eat.

CHAPTER 4
Creating the "Me" Brand

LISTENING 1: Defining and Marketing Yourself

Today, in this lecture about business, we will be discussing marketing, but starting from an unusual point of view. That point of view is *you*. At some point in our life, each of us asks, "Who am I?" Even as I say the words, you probably have a **series** of images appearing in your mind about who you are. We define ourselves in many ways: by nationality, by profession, by the things we like to do, be it riding motorcycles, playing hockey or studying dance. What I would like to do during this lecture is explore these and other qualities in terms of a *business* model. Essentially, I want to explore **principles** of business that have to do with *branding* and will ask you to consider yourselves in terms of a "me" brand.

Before we go into the personal qualities that shape each of us and that play a part in creating what we can call our brands, let's discuss what a brand is. A brand is the idea or image that *defines* and *identifies* a specific product or service that **consumers** connect with the company or organization that owns and/or sells those products and services. Branding is when that idea or image is marketed so that it will be recognized by more and more people.

I'm sure you can quickly think of a number of different companies or organizations and how they are branded. You might be thinking about a **logo** or an image that defines the company, such as the swoosh symbol for Nike's athletic wear and sports products. The Nike checkmark-like logo is simple and subtle. It's similar in some ways to the golden arches logo of the McDonald's fast-food chain. Both these companies are also identified by **slogans**, such as Nike's "Just Do It!" Some companies, such as McDonald's, change their slogans over time: McDonald's has had at least twenty-three, including the more recent "I'm lovin' it." Other organizations have **abandoned** or **minimized** their slogans. The computer company IBM's slogan is the single word "Think!" but it's not used much anymore. Nor is one of Apple Computer's many slogans "Think different."

Brand **recognition** is tied up in many details beyond a logo, a slogan or a jingle. Jingles—short snippets of song to promote a product—were popular when most people got their news—and advertisements—from radio, but they are less popular today. However, brand recognition is based on many other details. If you think of a coffee shop like Starbucks, what features make it recognizable? When you go to a Starbucks, how many times do you see the logo on everything from cups to packages of coffee and other items, including uniforms? How are the colours of a Starbucks used to create a brand image? What kind of brand image is **projected**? How is it intended to make people feel? Can you think of another coffee shop—preferably a much older one that hasn't copied the Starbucks formula—and compare the two. Sometimes, what a new company does *differently* helps to define its brand.

So far we've been talking about brands and branding as they relate to companies and organizations. Let's return to what I called the "me" brand. In a 1997 article, Tom Peters, a business **consultant**, wrote about the ways in which an **individual** could distinguish himself or herself in the workplace. This he called the personal brand. Peters' idea was that if an individual applied the same principles of *differentiating* that businesses used to set themselves apart from their competitors, that individual would be in a better position to compete in the workplace.

It's an interesting idea and one that a lot of people have **embraced** over the past few years, particularly as social media have allowed people to "sell" themselves, so to speak, through online services like Facebook and LinkedIn, where you can create a profile of yourself through a formal or informal curriculum vitae, or resumé. For those of you who have already posted some kind of online profile, making sense of the next part of this lecture will be a bit easier.

Okay, now will be your chance to create a personal brand with a logo, a slogan or perhaps even a jingle. But before we do that, let's consider what factors influence personal branding. We can say that all individuals are shaped by, and take their identity from, several factors. These might include family and friends, relationships, work and hobbies, interests, **ethnicity**, personal appearance, gender, beliefs, values, choices, creations, possessions and education. Let's look at some of these factors.

First, let's address you at your most basic level. Your personal appearance conveys a lot of information about who you are. Usually, it takes only a quick glance—about three seconds—for someone to evaluate and make a decision about you. In this time, the person looking at you would become aware of your gender and reach a conclusion about your ethnicity, determining that you are, for example, Asian, without distinguishing your particular ethnic origin. They will get a general idea about your age and even your income level, if your clothing and overall appearance are an **indication**.

But few of these things are really important in branding yourself—unless they work to your advantage in some particular way. A large, strong man may appear more ready for physical labour than someone who is not, but it's only a suggestion. Billionaires often dress in casual clothes, so possessions or personal style are not always strong indicators of someone's wealth. The opposite can also be true: many people wear knock-off designer clothing and buy fake luxury items, like purses or watches.

I'm going to continue to frame these ideas in business contexts, so in this case, we can say that the personal impression that you give is like a packaging design on a box, or the cover of a book. You've often been told not to judge a book by its cover, but in the world of business, books are often judged by their covers and people often make snap judgments based on **initial** perceptions.

Regardless of what you look like and how others **perceive** you, aspects of your personal appearance can shape you, as does your personal history. The problems and successes you have over the years will **influence** who you are. Most of these begin with family and develop or change with friends and the relationships you have with them. Our beliefs and values are shaped when we are young. These can be religious beliefs, political beliefs or simply beliefs about how the world works. For example, you might have been raised in the belief that the world—and all the people in it—are either inherently *fair* or *unfair*. Related to such a belief are your values. If you think the world is fair, one of your values might be that you should be honest and work hard, believing such efforts will help you get ahead.

In a business context, for purposes of your personal brand, past relationships will have a lot to do with how you work with others. Do you get on well with people? Do you prefer to do things on your own or in a group? Are you good at organizing groups? Are you a better follower than a leader?

What are your beliefs and values? Where did these come from? In a business context, you are likely to have ideas about how the world of business works and what it takes to succeed.

Education and work experience can also shape your concept of your identity, that is, your personal brand. When you hear someone being described as having gone to a prestigious university or having worked at an important company, such descriptions become an important part of that person's image, and you might associate that with having a good work ethic: working as hard as possible to attend a good university or having an important position in a good organization.

At the same time, many people who have *not* graduated from university have gone on to create their own companies and have done well. Billionaire, and Harvard drop-out, Bill Gates is certainly one example. What Gates has created—companies such as Microsoft and Corbis, as well as a multi-billion-dollar aid foundation—has helped to define him. It's interesting to note that another thing that defines us, namely our hobbies and interests, is what led Gates to his success. In his case, it was a **fascination** with computers and writing code for them. Gates was certainly in the right place at the right time, but his passion for what he was doing was critical to his success.

We started off discussing the idea of the "me" brand. As an assignment, I want you to think about describing yourself in a few sentences. Then, reduce these to one sentence, as concise as possible. From this single concise sentence, write a slogan of a few words that **sums up** your brand. For a logo, think of a picture of yourself that sums up who you are. Perhaps you see yourself hitting a home run in baseball or simply enjoying something you love to do. See what you can come up with. As for a jingle, that little piece of song that summarizes you, don't worry about it for this assignment. [Laughs]

LISTENING 2: Self-Promotion for Introverts

CARMINE GALLO: Welcome to the Useful Commute on B-net. I'm your host, Carmine Gallo. In today's show, how to get noticed and get ahead, especially if you're an introvert.

Introverts tend to shy away from the limelight, and also, often, they get passed over for job offers and promotions while their more **extroverted** colleagues get all the attention. But our guest today says it doesn't have to be that way. Nancy Ancowitz, author of *Self-Promotion for Introverts*, is here to tell us how introverts can **leverage** what she calls their "quiet strengths." Nancy, nice to have you on the program.

NANCY ANCOWITZ: Thank you, Carmine.

CG: Nancy, you make a **distinction** between being an introvert and being shy. What's the difference between the two?

NA: Yes, if you're an introvert, you get your energy from your quiet time versus your social time—versus, let's say, working a room at a cocktail party. So there's nothing wrong with you if you're an introvert, and, in fact, 50 per-cent of the population is introverted. So being shy is something different; that's more social **anxiety**. And that can be addressed through **modalities** such as therapy. But if you're an introvert, there's nothing wrong with you; it's just a different way of being.

CG: OK, so for this topic, we're addressing that 50 percent of the population that sees themselves as introverts.

NA: Yes.

CG: What are—what are these "quiet strengths" that you say many introverts possess? How can we use those quiet strengths to get ahead?

NA: If you're an introvert, you tend to dive deeply into whatever you're working on—into whatever your **passions** are. So you spend a lot of time—you're probably good at writing, at reading, researching, listening—some of the quieter activities. And how can you use those to your advantage in the **workplace**? Well, get known as an expert in your area or areas of expertise—by writing about them for, let's say, trade publications, for the company newsletter and also through public speaking.

CG: Which would be a good way for introverts to get noticed? So let's talk about that: gaining **visibility** ... obviously a big **challenge** for introverts. You say, become known as an expert in a **particular** area. What are some quick tips, then, that you can offer us for taking that expertise, Nancy, and then making it more visible—helping us become more visible in the workplace?

NA: Sure. In the workplace, one thing is you want to be really clear about what your accomplishments are and get ready to be able to talk about them—one, two, three—just in a sentence or two. And you want to really make sure that your boss knows what you've done lately so that when it comes time for your review and it's time for a promotion, it's—it's not all hidden, all the great things that you've done. So getting that face time and getting—getting known for what you've done, taking credit for your own work. I think a lot of introverts are more likely to be behind the scenes and not known for what you're doing ... so, really important to take **credit** for your own work. Another thing is you want to have lunch with some people, so ask people to lunch from time to time. So we—as introverts we thrive more on one-on-one interactions rather than group. So—so decide who you'd like to—to have lunch with and get to know and to build your network, and for **mutual** benefit.

CG: So take credit for your work, uh, extend yourself, try to push yourself, to network and lunch with people. Those are some of the tips that you have for gaining visibility as an introvert.

NA: And another one is to chair **initiative**, so get your name **connected** with initiatives that are important at work. So—whether that means **chairing** meetings or taking on a special **committee**, or—it's just getting your name **associated** with things that are important to the organization and to you.

CG: These tips don't seem that hard to do, it—it's not like they have to change. It's not as though, Nancy, introverts have to change their personalities.

NA: No, no, absolutely not. I don't **recommend** changing your personality. It's taking the gems that you have and allowing them to shine.

CG: Nancy, in your book *Self-Promotion for Introverts*, I want to talk about one area that I found rather interesting. You talk about where to sit at business meetings. Tell us about that.

NA: Well I—I had the great fortune to speak with the Hearst Magazine president, Cathie Black, and she had a recommendation. She said introverts generally—in 98 percent of the time, women—sit in what she calls the "four dead zones." at the end of the table in each corner, as opposed to the end of the table, facing into the table. And she said that's the hardest place to hear anyone. So normally, she said, very strong people sit in the centre, and the bosses sit at the end. So, she said, sit one place away from the centre. And one of the things I'll add to that is, let's say you're in an interview setting—which so many people are right now. If you're an introvert, you tend to like private space. So if you're given a choice between, let's say, sitting on a couch or a solo chair, you might—you might want to think where you're more comfortable because it's really important to be comfortable on an interview.

CG: Well, Nancy, thank you for the tips on helping us crawl out of our shells. Uh, Nancy Ancowitz is the author of *Self-Promotion for Introverts*, her new book. Thank you, Nancy!

NA: Thank you.

CG: Thanks for listening to the Useful Commute. In our next show: how to turn your **entrepreneurial** dreams into a successful small business. Until then, for B-net, I'm Carmine Gallo.

LISTENING 3: Imagining Your Future

OSCAR: Stella, do you ever think about what you're going to do in the future?

STELLA: All the time, Oscar. What about you?

OSCAR: Well, to be honest, I spend most of my time thinking about what I'm going to eat for my next meal, but you know that assignment we have, to put together a flow chart about our future options? Well, I haven't quite done it yet.

STELLA: You haven't done it yet?

OSCAR: Oh, don't tell me you've done it already?

STELLA: I just finished. What have you done so far?

OSCAR: Done? Nothing. Nothing but questions, really. I know I have to start by **reviewing** my skill set.

STELLA: That's right. That's what I did. You have to write about what you can do and, more importantly, what you are good at and, most importantly, what you enjoy.

OSCAR: So, we're starting with a **series** of three questions? Okay, let's go with the first one. What I can do is my basic skill set.

STELLA: Yes, for example, what can you do on a computer? I know you can do quite a bit.

OSCAR: Well, I can do the basics: word processing, spreadsheets, databases and presentations.

STELLA: That's great. It's a lot more than I can do. But, more importantly, it gives you some **credit**, an edge, even if you're only a beginner.

OSCAR: What do you mean *beginner*?

STELLA: Let's start with word processing. How many words a minute can you type?

OSCAR: Uh …

STELLA: Do you even type with *more* than two fingers?

OSCAR: Sort of … I type eighty words a minute.

STELLA: Oh! I guess nobody does that with two fingers!

OSCAR: [Laughs] And I'm able to format documents, work on them collaboratively and use all the editing functions.

STELLA: Okay, then. You're an expert. But the important thing is that you should have some *evidence*—some examples of good work you've done in word processing and every other program you use the computer for.

OSCAR: I could hand in the PowerPoint slideshow I did. I can explain how I designed it and used it for a presentation.

STELLA: That's great! That shows **initiative**. It's exactly what you need to do. Nothing would be more embarrassing than going to an interview, showing some work and then not being able to explain how you did it. But what's **fascinating** about all different kinds of skills is how they open and close doors.

OSCAR: Open and close doors … What do you mean?

STELLA: When you're young, there are lots of things you do—or maybe your parents make you do—that open doors. For example, you studied music, didn't you?

OSCAR: Yes, ten years of piano.

STELLA: See, that opens up a door to music. You can read music and probably learn other instruments, play with other people and, if you choose to, perhaps even have a career in music. But for people in their twenties, starting a career in music from scratch is too big a **challenge**. Oscar, *you* have choices around music. I wish I hadn't **abandoned** my piano lessons.

OSCAR: But although I can read music and play piano for friends, I'm really not that good. I don't have a true **passion** for music.

STELLA: That's fine, but you're still ahead of the rest of the people who can't read music or play at all. And there are lots of careers in music that don't involve *playing* music.

OSCAR: It's true. Maybe I could **leverage** my musical skills to become a manager of a band or a writer who specializes in working with musicians … you know, like a music reviewer for magazines. Or maybe I could be a preschool teacher who occasionally teaches music to younger children.

STELLA: That's right. Like any other skill, music doesn't have to be the central focus, but it gives you an **initial** edge over someone who doesn't have a musical background.

OSCAR: I like the idea of combining music with other **entrepreneurial** skills, but I'm not really that interested in the jobs I just mentioned.

STELLA: Fine. And that's a good reason for moving on to the second point. What are some things that you are *really* good at?

OSCAR: *Really* good at? That's easy. I'm *really* good at mathematics. It's my best subject, and I'm one of the best students this year.

STELLA: And that's a *great* open door. Being good at math is second only to being able to read and write. It's an essential **workplace** skill for so many jobs from accountancy to finance to business to engineering … the list goes on and on. Do any of those interest you? Or, more importantly, can you combine any of your **individual** skills with your interests?

OSCAR: Mm … I had considered accountancy or business. Do you think I could combine those with music?

STELLA: Of course! You could be an accountant who specializes in working with musicians. I mean, it would probably be great for the musicians if they were able to work with someone who knew the difference between an ocarina and an oboe.

OSCAR: What's an oboe?

STELLA: It's a—

OSCAR: Just kidding!

STELLA: Mm … Unfortunately, humour isn't one of your *greater* skills. Let's move on.

OSCAR: Okay, so the third question is "What do I enjoy?"

STELLA: Yes, besides sleeping, eating and video games, what in **particular** do you enjoy?

OSCAR: Maybe this doesn't really count, but I … I enjoy travelling.

STELLA: Can you be more specific?

OSCAR: Sure. You know my parents both worked for the government, and when I was a child, we travelled a lot. We lived in five different countries, and last time I counted, I think I'd been to nineteen countries.

STELLA: Wow. That is interesting, and it's certainly something that **influenced** you, but what *skills* do you think travelling has given you?

OSCAR: You mean something besides being able to pack my own suitcase?

STELLA: Yes. For example, do you speak any other languages?

OSCAR: I speak bits of other languages, including Chinese and Arabic. And although I enjoyed learning them, I never really found time to continue.

STELLA: I **recommend** finding that time now. Learning a language is another fantastic way to open doors. It leads to so many opportunities. I wish I'd learned French.

OSCAR: I guess it's not too late for either of us. Did you ever think about taking some summer courses or studying overseas or getting a job in another country where they speak the language you want to learn? You could spend a summer working in a vineyard in France.

STELLA: Mm … Well, I'm certainly thinking about it now, but back to the assignment. Can you think of any other skills your time in other countries has given you?

OSCAR: Sure. I'm open to new ideas; also, I think I work well with other people from different cultures.

STELLA: This sounds good. And it sounds like it's an area where you have some experience. Maybe there's something around intercultural communications ...

OSCAR: Like working as a **consultant** for an NGO?

STELLA: An NGO? What's that?

OSCAR: It's a non-governmental organization. You know, groups like Doctors Without Borders and non-profit organizations that offer international aid in places like Southeast Asia and Africa. NGOs typically help people with the basics, to help them have a better life. Things like building houses, schools and hospitals, helping improve farming and working conditions, creating small businesses ...

STELLA: And you think you could help with that?

OSCAR: You know what? Yes, I do. I think I have the math smarts to help with businesses and the general smarts to talk to people about new ideas. Who knows, maybe I can even get someone started in the music business!

STELLA: [Laughs]

OSCAR: Anyway. I think those are things I might be interested in.

STELLA: It's a good start, and what you need to do is identify the rest of the doors that you might want to open.

OSCAR: Like learning another language.

STELLA: Sure, maybe a language that would be useful in those parts of the world where you would like to work.

OSCAR: I think I have a good idea about all of that ... but what about the closing doors thing? What did you mean by that?

STELLA: You can probably figure it out yourself. Can you guess the **principle** behind the expression?

OSCAR: I suppose it's *not* doing things like learning music or learning mathematics.

STELLA: Yes, not everyone is suited to activities like those or is going to be a major league hockey player. But there are lots of negative things you can do as well.

OSCAR: Like illegal things?

STELLA: Definitely. Think about it. Getting arrested for theft, vandalism or doing drugs could mark you for life, with a permanent police record.

OSCAR: That's certainly something to think about. I know that border officials in a lot of countries ask questions about whether you've ever broken the law. And if you have, they might not let you travel there. It's the same thing with a lot of jobs. If you have a criminal record, you just won't get the job. What other sorts of doors can you close?

STELLA: I guess it's different for different people. Sometimes your job choices can be a problem. For example, summer jobs working at a video game store year after year might not be great experience ... unless you end up working with video games or maybe owning a video game store yourself. But, generally, it would be better to get a range of work experiences that could earn you **recognition** as a good worker with different skills.

OSCAR: Yes, I get it: make the most of your opportunities.

STELLA: Exactly.

OSCAR: Thanks. Now, I need to draw a flow chart to map out the way this all works.

CHAPTER 5
Putting the Scientific Method to Work

LISTENING 1: Introduction to the Scientific Method

Hello, everyone. Welcome to this first **lecture** on the introduction to science. I want to start by asking how many of you are familiar with the scientific method. Hands up? Okay, several people. Good.

Let's rephrase the question to make it a little more difficult. How many of you can *name the steps* in the scientific method? Well, I still see a few hands up. Let's leave that question for a moment and consider an everyday situation.

You enter your home—let's say your front hallway—and it's *dark*. You try to turn on a light switch, but no light comes on. Not having any light in the hallway is a problem, so you consider a few things that might be causing it. You do a little research and see if other lights in your home work. They do. You then decide that the problem might be that the hallway light bulb has burned out. You find a new light bulb and change it. Okay! It works. You've **solved** the problem. Later, you run into a friend and casually mention that the light wasn't working but that you identified and solved the problem.

If the process I just described seems like something you would do, you are already aware of the six key steps in the scientific method. Let's go through them one at a time to see how they can be applied to countless scientific problems.

The first step is to identify a problem, a question or an **observation** that somehow excites your curiosity. It's something you want to find out about. In the example I gave, you made the observation that the light was not working and, naturally, you didn't want to live the rest of your life with a dark hallway in your home. It's a problem you wanted to solve. Sometimes, as I mentioned, the use of the scientific method begins not with a problem but with something you're simply curious about. Albert Einstein, for example, was curious as a child about several basic phenomena. One was a question many children ask: Why is the sky blue? As an adult, he was the first to overturn common thinking that it had to do with dust in the atmosphere and conclusively answer the question by precisely calculating how light scatters from molecules, causing us to see the colour blue. But back to the light bulb.

The second step in the scientific method is to do some research. For the light bulb problem, you checked whether lights were off in one or more other rooms in your house. Had they *all* been off, you might have suspected another problem, such as a more widespread power outage in your house or your neighbourhood. But at least one other light was on, so you decided that the light bulb *itself* was the problem.

Based on your research, in the third step, you formed a **hypothesis**—an educated guess about the cause of the problem. Your hypothesis was that the lack of light was caused by a burnt-out light bulb that needed to be replaced.

The fourth step was when you **conducted** an *experiment*. You tried replacing the light bulb. Now, in this case, the light bulb *was* the problem, so your experiment proved successful. However, your experiment could also have ended with the second light bulb not working either. Perhaps the second light bulb was faulty, or perhaps the electrical wiring in the hallway was the source of the problem. If your first experiment—changing the light bulb—didn't work, you might have developed one or more additional hypotheses and tested each of them in turn. For example, you might have tried both bulbs in another light socket.

However, as soon as you tried the light switch in the hallway and the light went on, you quickly moved on to the fifth step: you analyzed the data—the light bulb was working—and then drew the conclusion that your hypothesis of a faulty bulb was correct.

Finally, as a sixth step, you **published** your findings. You might not consider telling a friend a form of publication, but as the word suggests, you are making your findings *public*, and that's what's important. It's important because you can get **feedback** from people who examine your problem, your research, your hypothesis, your experiment, your data and your conclusions. These other people can verify or overturn your results with additional experiments. For example, your friend might ask to see the first light bulb and try it in another socket. Oh! Surprise! The light bulb works! In this case—if, in fact, the light bulb was *not* faulty—you'd have to reconsider your hypothesis, experiment and findings. Perhaps the problem was with the light switch: it contains a loose wire and works only **intermittently**.

As I said, all of this probably seems quite logical to you and matches the way you would solve most problems. What I want to turn to now is something you might find a bit surprising: it took scientists almost two thousand years to figure this method out.

We can start with the well-known philosopher many consider the first scientist: Aristotle. He was born in ancient Greece in 384 BCE and died at the age of sixty-two, leaving a legacy that was, by any measure, brilliant. He was a student of the philosopher Plato and, in turn, became the teacher of Alexander the Great. Now, Plato had another view of scientific **inquiry**. He—and many before and after him—thought that everything that was worth knowing could be arrived at through careful reasoning. Aristotle challenged this notion by **incorporating** measurement into his method. Although the ancient Greeks understood concepts of geometry, most thought that the idea of careful measurement was important only for people such as house builders. Aristotle was interested not just in measuring everything; he also thought understanding could be arrived at by careful observation. He used *inductive* methods to generalize from individual examples. And he studied a lot of examples: he made detailed notes on more than 500 species and used inductive reasoning to suggest what his observations meant.

Let me just stop here for a moment and define *inductive reasoning* and another method, *deductive reasoning*. In inductive reasoning, we go from one or more examples and try to generalize or make predictions. In deductive reasoning, we go from a large number of facts or details and try to make specific conclusions. Aristotle's approach to understanding the world involved inductive reasoning and featured three steps. First, he studied existing writings about a subject—we now call this a *literature review*. Second, he looked for general **consensus**, or agreement. Third, he conducted a systematic study, including extensive measurements.

Aristotle held sway over scientific thinking for a long time, but an Arab scientist, Ibn al Haytham (965–1040), who wrote a **revolutionary** book on optics, was among the first to add to Aristotle's method. In fact, his approach to problem-solving is much like the one we use today. He decided that it was necessary to first identify a problem, based on what you may have learned through observation and/or experimentation. From this you would next create a hypothesis and conduct an experiment to test it. His third step was to interpret the data and come to a conclusion, which, in a fourth step, should be published.

Other Arab scholars, working around the same time as Ibn al Haytham, added ideas such as the need to avoid, as much as possible, human observation as a form of measurement. After all, people easily make mistakes and what one person sees might be quite different from what another sees. Another Arab scientist, Ali al Rahwi (854–931), introduced the first *peer review*, in which results were first sent to other scientists for their comments before sharing them with a broader public. Other innovations included the increasing use of *deductive* methods to arrive at scientific truths.

Skipping ahead almost 500 years, the golden age of Arab innovations in science had faded away, but the ideas, available in translations, influenced the scientific thinkers of Europe, including one man from Pisa, in what is now Italy: Galileo Galilei. Galileo—we call him by his first name—was born in 1564 and died in 1642. He possessed one of the most important qualities of a scientist: the need to question everything. His most famous experiment challenged a notion most people had believed for 1,500 years: Aristotle's idea that heavier objects fell faster than lighter objects. On the surface, it made **obvious** sense, but Galileo's experiments showed that the objects fell at the same rate.

Galileo wasn't *always* right. He refused to believe, for example, that the moon had anything to do with the tides, but he generally applied scientific methods and rigorous measurement to every problem he encountered.

Throughout his life, Galileo went on to question many other commonly held beliefs, such as the Biblical idea that the sun revolved around the earth, and not the earth around the sun. His arguments supporting these ideas, first put forward by the scientist Copernicus, and many other of his beliefs conflicted with the teachings of the Catholic Church. The Church banned his writings and forced him to spend the last eleven years of his life under house arrest. Eventually, the Catholic Church admitted its errors and apologized—350 years after Galileo's death.

Perhaps Galileo's greatest contribution to the scientific method was to challenge widely held beliefs and hold them to scientific **scrutiny**. To really understand his and others' contributions to the scientific method, let's go back to our light bulb example and examine how the common man might have handled a similar problem a thousand years ago.

On entering his home and seeing that his fire had gone out or his candles would not burn, the man might have burst into tears and wondered why the gods were punishing him. He would have made hurried prayers, and when these had no effect, he would perhaps have called in a local priest to ask for advice. The priest would, in his own way, conduct some research and ask whether the man had done anything to **offend** the gods. The solution, or experiment, might involve sacrificing an animal or performing some other ceremony. Finally, if the prayers and sacrifices had no effect, the man might have decided his house was cursed and reluctantly moved away.

There are aspects to the scientific method in this story that some would say are simply part of human nature: when we have a problem, we try to find ways to solve it. In any case, I think you will all agree that contributions to our understanding of the scientific method have made life a lot better for most of us.

LISTENING 2: Fostering Innovation

NORA YOUNG: Well, Steven Johnson's been thinking a lot about that lately. Steven's the author of a number of books about science and **culture**, such as *The Ghost Map* and *Everything Bad Is Good for You*. His latest is *Where Good Ideas Come From: The Natural History of Innovation*.

STEVEN JOHNSON: *Where Good Ideas Come From* is a book about spaces in history and in biology that have been unusually **innovative** and the patterns that we see in all those spaces.

NY: The book starts out by exploring the speed of innovation. Steven says that for much of the twentieth century, innovation—especially technological innovation—happened at a very measured, very **predictable** speed. Technologies like colour TV or AM radio or the VCR took about two decades to go from the laboratory to the **mainstream**. But these days it seems like innovation is happening at a much quicker pace. It seems that more and more, our lives are defined by rapid technological change. So, I started by asking Steven: "Is innovation happening more quickly now than it used to?"

SJ: Well, particularly when you look at what's happened on the Web ... that's one of the kind of **case studies** that's ... that the book begins with, which is why the Web has kind of innovated as quickly as it has. Think about what the Web was like in 1995. It was basically text only, occasional little images, graphics, no video, kind of no audio, very hard to publish, certainly nothing resembling a social network, and ... and so on. And in just fifteen years, all these kind of **core** elements of the medium have changed and been created ..., in fifteen years. And in fact, if you think about how the **medium** has changed, it's a bigger leap from ... the Web of 1995 to the Web of today than it was from radio to television; there are more features that have been added to the Web in just fifteen years. And ... and so part of the question of the book is what is it about the Web that's **enabled** this you know kind of **quantum leap** in the **capacity** for innovation?

NY: Uh hum. And what is it about the Web that's ...

SJ: What is it about the Web? I'm not going to tell you, that's it. The ... it is in part because it's an environment where ... people are allowed to, you know, freely build on top of other people's ideas. So you have these platforms ... I mean the Web itself is a platform that was built on top of the Internet ... When Tim Berners-Lee was coming up with the idea for the World Wide Web, it was **crucial** that he didn't have to invent the Internet first.

NY: Right.

SJ: Um ... you know, if he had had to invent a whole system of routers and, you know information pipes and connect them all across the world, he would have never done it. But because the Internet itself was an open platform where he could come and build something on top of it, it was possible

for him to do that more or less on his own—I mean he **collaborated** with some people ... and that's really what the Web has been, it's kind of these layers of innovation that are collaborative in the sense that somebody comes up with one standard, and then you come along and build something on top of that standard, and then somebody comes along and builds something on top of that standard. And that enables ... basically it means there's all this knowledge and expertise and discovery that people don't have to do. They don't have to go through that because they can just work on the top level of the stack.

NY: Uh huh. And you're arguing that an idea isn't a single thing, that it's more like a network or a swarm, or this ... uh, kind of ... bricolage as you say, of ... you know, **adjacent** ideas. Can you give me some examples of how that works?

SJ: Well, I mean, you know, one great example is ... is Gutenberg. So Gutenberg ... had done amazing **cutting-edge** work with metallurgy and developing his movable type and he had done some important work with inks. But he actually ... he went through a period where he really didn't have a kind of an actual printing **mechanism** or press, as it were ... which was kind of important to what he was doing. And so, he ends up going up into the ... it's come wine-harvesting season and he goes up into the Rhineland hills, and he drinks a bunch of wine ... which is another way to innovate. And he's looking over, and he sees this very ancient technology of the screw press, which had been around for thousands of years, which is being used by these vintners to press grapes. And he looks at this, and he says: "Wait a second, that's what I'm missing." And so he borrows this, you know, very old technology designed for something completely different and combines it with his ... his technology which, you know, were kind of new innovations although they were also based on older technologies. And it's true that as you said, kind of bricolage, this mixing together of different ideas and different platforms that he ends up taking something designed to kind of press grapes and turns it into something that prints bibles.

NY: But yet as a culture, I mean, we are just in love with this idea of the **solitary** inventor, you know, alone ... somewhere, you know ... Newton and the apple, or Archimedes in the bath, this kind of thing. Why do you think we love this idea about the ... the sort of **spontaneous** good idea that comes to one person alone so much?

SJ: It, yeah, it's very interesting, and people seem to do it, you know. I mean I talk in the book about how Darwin has this kind of story about his own "Eureka!" moment that he had, and it turns out, well, he did have the idea in his head, it was a much slower process. It wasn't—if you look at his notebooks—it wasn't something that just popped into his head. It was a much more **evolutionary** process, the idea of coming up with the **theory** of evolution. And it seems like ... I mean on the one level it's, it is a simpler story, there's a kind of a lovely clarity to "he was walking down the street and *voilà*, there it was, it popped into his head." But the truth is ... you know it almost never happens that way ... there's much more kind of quiet collaboration that happens ... ideas normally—particularly big ideas— take much longer time frames to develop. And I think they're much more interesting because of that. I mean I think that's ... it's actually a much richer story, the stories are kind of cooler ... when you see these unusual ways they collaborate.

I mean ... and I got to this theory in some sense because I wrote this book *The Ghost Map* a couple of books ago about John Snow, who I had always heard of as this brilliant medical detective who solved the riddle of where cholera was coming from ... in the middle of this outbreak in London in the 1850s. And when I went and researched the story to write the book, it turned out that he actually had had this collaborator, who no one had ever talked about, named Henry Whitehead, who was a local vicar and wasn't even a scientist. And Whitehead had done a lot of the key research and had really made some crucial kind of advances to the story. And it's partially because—and this is another big theme—precisely because Whitehead and Snow had very different skills and they came from different fields. And what you see again and again in these stories of very innovative people is that they have connections, social connections, to people who have very different backgrounds.

NY: And how much does timing have to do with it? I mean, you can think of things like, you know, there were video-sharing sites long before YouTube showed up, sometimes ideas are just a little bit too ahead of their time. How does timing factor into—not necessarily good ideas—but good ideas ending up being adopted?

SJ: The ... one of the opening chapters ... is called "The Adjacent Possible," and this is a wonderful phrase from the scientist Stuart Kauffman that I first read about ten years ago. I've been trying to figure out a way to get into a book all this time, and I finally figured out a way to crowbar it in there. But it really sets the kind of ... the theory up, in a way, and the idea is that at any given time, both in the history of life and biology, and also in the history of human science and technology, at any given time there are a set of, kind of a finite set of new things that can happen ... that the system has set up. It's almost like a chessboard, and in any given set in a moment in a game, there's a set of moves that you can make, and then there's a much larger set of moves that you can't make. And life and technology is like that in the sense that you cannot invent a microwave oven in 1650; it just cannot be done. You know, you have to invent a series of other things; other platforms have to be built before you can do it. And so the general ... the most general way of describing what happens when people are innovative is that they explore, they open new doors in the adjacent possible at that particular moment in time. And every now and then you—it's very rare—but every now and then you have somebody who does manage to kind of leap ahead. And what often happens is just that the idea kind of fails in this funny way. So Charles Babbage, in ... a brilliant Victorian inventor, basically came up with the idea for the programmable computer in, you know, 1840. And he tried to build this thing, but he was trying to build, you know, a digital-age computer with industrial-age technology. And it never really worked. He built a very smart calculator ... that did influence people directly, but his programmable computer, the analytical engine, just died out. And almost all of his ideas had to be independently rediscovered, kind of sixty or seventy years later, when people actually started work on building real computers.

NY: Uh hum. Uh, Steven, in the book you outline these seven different patterns that ... can lead us to good ideas. I want to talk about one in particular, which is the **hunch**. So first of all, what are we talking about when we use this word *hunch*, or *slow hunch*?

SJ: Yeah, the slow hunch is this idea—and I mean there's been a lot written recently about kind of instant hunches, kind of gut impressions. That's the Malcom Gladwell kind of "blink" idea. And this is really the opposite of that, which is a gut impression or a fleeting sense of something being interesting that lasts for sometimes decades ... And it's the idea that big ideas ... big ideas are hard to think, right? They're challenging, and sometimes the first clue you get about them is just that it's a little clue, it's a sense: "Okay, there's a problem here that's interesting; I think I should try and pursue it."

Uh ... you know this is true of Tim Berners-Lee ... that's a great example with the birth of the World Wide Web. He started working on the Web in the early 1980s at this Swiss physics lab. It wasn't at all the, you know, a global medium, a hypertext medium, the way it turned into; it was just a private little project to organize information inside the lab. And he worked on it for eight years, as—really—as a hobby. He didn't even tell his bosses about it for many, many years. And then, and it was because he had an environment that allowed him to kind of keep this hunch kind of lingering in the margins of his mind and to tinker with it for so long that he eventually ... eventually kind of went to his bosses and said: "I think I may have invented a whole new medium." ... "Can this be part of my job?" But if he tried to do that right away, if he'd sat down and said, "Okay, I'm going to invent the most important communications platform of the late twentieth century," he would have failed. You know, it had to be this slower process.

LISTENING 3: Urban Legends

OSCAR: Stella, I have to tell you the most *unbelievable* thing!

STELLA: Unbelievable? Then why should I believe it?

OSCAR: Huh?

STELLA: This isn't another one of your urban legends, is it? You know, one of those stories that sounds too good—or too bad—to be true?

OSCAR: No! I mean, well ... maybe.

STELLA: Okay, go ahead.

OSCAR: Nancy told me that her friend's uncle works at the library and they have a *major* problem.

STELLA: And that is?

OSCAR: The library is sinking! It's sinking into the ground at an alarming **rate**. And here is the funny part: the *reason* for its sinking. When the architects and engineers were designing the building, they failed to think about the weight of the books. There are *hundreds of thousands* of books in there, and they have added so much weight that the whole library will probably have to be torn down and replaced.

STELLA: Ah, right. That, or we'll have an underground library.

OSCAR: You don't believe it?

STELLA: Not for a minute. It's an old urban legend—a story that, in this case, makes you feel smart because it makes someone else look stupid.

OSCAR: What do you mean?

STELLA: I mean that it's highly unlikely that the engineers and architects would have **conducted** thorough studies yet overlooked the weight of the books. In any case, I've heard this story before.

OSCAR: You have?

STELLA: For years. Not only that, but I've heard a few variations. Other versions have to do with a swimming pool that sinks because the engineers forgot a crucial fact: that the water in the pool would add so much extra weight. Another one is about apartment buildings sinking because those "**cutting-edge**" engineers didn't consider how much the people living there, along with their possessions, would weigh. But all these stories are the same.

OSCAR: The same? How?

STELLA: Like I said, they're humorous because they are really jokes about people who we think should know something **obvious**. These experts appear to make simple mistakes and end up looking foolish. Also, like all urban legends, the story usually has to do with a so-called friend of a friend. It's someone you don't know or can't track down easily to check on the truthfulness of the story. An urban legend might start as a **spontaneous** joke and be misunderstood by the person hearing it.

OSCAR: Well ... it *sounded* reasonable.

STELLA: And it's not a bad story—certainly it's not the *worst* kind of story. It doesn't make people think or do stupid things. Not like many of the more **predictable** urban legends.

OSCAR: You seem to know a lot about them.

STELLA: I have an aunt who e-mails me these kinds of stories all the time. She seems to think they're all true just because someone else has e-mailed them to her. There are really three types. The first one is something humorous that doesn't hurt anyone, like the one you told me—it simply tries to make someone seem silly. This first category includes scary stories, too—ghost stories, for example, that are given some appearance of truth. A common one is the ghost hitchhiker. Have you heard that one?

OSCAR: Sounds familiar, but ...

STELLA: It's not as believable, and there are a lot of variations, but it generally starts with someone saying, "I was driving home late last week when I noticed a **solitary** hitchhiker standing by the side of the road and picked him up (sometimes it's a "her"). I tried to talk to him, but he was not responsive. A little later, I turned to say something else and ... wait for it ... the hitchhiker had disappeared!"

OSCAR: Ooh ... creepy!

STELLA: Yeah, sure. Anyway, later on, the driver learns that a person matching the hitchhiker's description was killed in a terrible accident or an **unsolved** murder along the same road a week earlier ... or maybe a month, a year or even a hundred years earlier. The hitchhiker has been trying to get home ever since.

OSCAR: Well, I don't think I'd fall for that one.

STELLA: No! Really! It happened to my sister's friend! [Laughs] You see, the more details you throw in, the more likely it seems. And if you already believe in ghosts, you'll find it really easy to believe.

OSCAR: And the second type? What's the second type after harmless urban legends?

STELLA: The second type is the sort of thing that makes you think badly of other people for cultural or even racist reasons. These are stories that try to show how another nationality or **culture**—or even another sex—behaves badly or stupidly. Typical of these urban legends are stories about women who don't know how to do some kind of job that is more commonly done by men, like fixing a car. Or it might be a similar story about immigrants to a new country misunderstanding some concepts, like using a toilet to wash their feet. One of the really popular ones is an old story about a department store in Japan. In this one, the Japanese store decorators have mixed up Christmas and Easter, so at Christmas, they put up a crucifix, you know, how Jesus was nailed to a wooden cross. They put up this crucifix, but with Santa Claus on it.

OSCAR: Santa Claus instead of Jesus, really?

STELLA: Of course not! It's someone's idea of a bad joke. But in this case, it's a joke that has racist overtones: it's trying to show that Japanese people are too silly to understand Christmas. But people start it as a kind of story that sounds like it might be believable. Again, parts of the story will include so-called facts, such as, "Somebody's uncle's friend was visiting Tokyo and ...." It goes on from there. It's the sort of story that makes people think they are smarter than the Japanese. This kind of story is probably started by someone who feels insecure. The Japanese are successful in so many ways, so this kind of lie tries to suggest that, although the Japanese are very advanced in some areas, they are way behind in others. It's nonsense, and it's meant to **offend**.

OSCAR: You said there were four types. The first type was humorous; the second type seems to be racial. What's the third type?

STELLA: The third type is e-mails that make people feel good about doing nothing, or doing worse than nothing.

OSCAR: Feel good about doing nothing? I don't understand.

STELLA: It's okay. Have you ever heard of Amy Bruce?

OSCAR: Amy Bruce? No, I don't think I have.

STELLA: You will someday. Amy Bruce is the topic of a viral e-mail message. Just like the chain letters that were sent out before e-mail, it's a very popular kind of e-mail that asks you to send out copies of something, in this case, a poem written by a young girl dying of cancer. So, there is the sympathy trick ... of course you feel sorry for a young girl dying of cancer, who wants to share her poem. But it gets worse.

OSCAR: How?

STELLA: The e-mail promises something else: it tells you that for every e-mail you send, three cents will be sent to a hospital for cancer research.

OSCAR: Sounds like a great thing to do, but I'm guessing it's not true.

STELLA: It's certainly not true, and it's worse than not true. In this kind of e-mail, which you might send to a hundred people in your address book, you are wasting goodwill. You get the warm feeling that you're helping someone— helping poor cancer patient Amy Bruce—when really you're doing nothing.

OSCAR: But you said it was worse than doing nothing.

STELLA: Yes, that's right. Think about it. The next time someone representing an honest and good cause asks you for a donation, you might think: "No, why should I? I've already done my part and helped raise hundreds of dollars for cancer research!" You might feel you don't have to contribute anything else. So, it's a *false* sense of helping. And the common **consensus** is that it's really a shame.

OSCAR: That's terrible, but there's one more, something more terrible?

STELLA: There are lots of different kinds of e-mails, including ones that can trick you into giving details of your bank account and losing all your money, but I think the most terrible ones are those that give bad advice, particularly bad advice that affects people's health.

OSCAR: Can you give me an example?

STELLA: Sure. Have you ever heard about the lemon cure?

OSCAR: Lemon cure? No, a cure for what?

STELLA: It's another cancer one. Cancer is a serious disease, and people worry about it a lot. Anyway, the lemon cure e-mail says that scientists have discovered that eating lemons is more effective than chemotherapy in treating cancer. In this kind of story, there is an explanation of why you don't already know about this **revolutionary** development: so-called big pharmaceutical corporations are trying to keep it a secret because they want to extract the secret ingredients in lemons and sell these ingredients as expensive pills. Of course, the government has supposedly "**collaborated**" in the cover-up.

OSCAR: Not at all true?

STELLA: Well, lemons are good for you, but they don't, as the e-mails usually claim, cure twelve types of cancer. It's really sad because people who have cancer are often upset about having chemotherapy. Chemotherapy is an extremely painful process, and in countries where there is no national medical care plan, it can also be extremely expensive. Of course some people might jump at the chance to switch to a cheap and painless treatment like lemons from the grocery store.

OSCAR: But **sacrificing** proper medical treatment to eat lemons instead could kill them.

STELLA: Exactly. So, the next time you hear an unbelievable story, or read one in an e-mail, don't believe it until you check the facts for yourself.

CHAPTER 6
Saving the World, One Child at a Time

LISTENING 1: Eradication of Smallpox

VERONICA RIEMER: You're listening to the WHO podcast. My name is Veronica Riemer. In this episode we look at an **unprecedented** achievement in the history of the World Health Organization, the **eradication** of smallpox.

Smallpox is an acute **contagious** disease caused by the variola virus. Having originated over 3,000 years ago in India or Egypt, smallpox is one of the most **devastating** diseases known to mankind. For centuries, repeated epidemics swept across continents and **decimated** populations. The disease, for which there was no effective treatment, killed as many as 30 percent of those infected and left survivors blind, disfigured and **marginalized**.

In 1967 when the disease threatened 60 percent of the world's population, WHO launched an intensified plan to eradicate smallpox. Through the success of the global eradication campaign, smallpox was finally pushed back to the Horn of Africa with the last recorded case in Somalia in 1977. The World Health Assembly in 1980 declared smallpox eradicated from the face of the Earth.

Last month, a statue to commemorate the 30th anniversary of smallpox eradication was erected in the gardens of WHO. At the unveiling ceremony, WHO's Director General Dr. Margaret Chan applauded health workers from around the world whose dedicated work over fourteen years made this possible.

DR. MARGARET CHAN: Leadership at WHO was important, but an achievement of this scale ultimately depended on tens of thousands of dedicated workers who literally crisscrossed this entire globe, by jeep, donkey and fishing boats, on foot in jungle and desert journeys, from **nomadic** tribes in remote mountain areas to permanent dwellers in the scorching heat of Asia's slums.

The history of smallpox and its eradication has been written, and public health continues to benefit from the many lessons learned. Success has been **attributed** to a strong research **component**, an emphasis on **epidemiology** and surveillance, and the flexibility to adapt to new findings and change course when needed.

VR: Dr. D. A. Henderson was the Director of the WHO Smallpox Eradication Programme from 1966 to 1977. He spoke of the **daunting** challenges faced by health workers at that time.

DR. DONALD HENDERSON: I have often been asked whether I thought that the eradication of smallpox could have been accomplished in today's world with so much armed conflict in so many areas and with large populations **afflicted** by natural disasters such as in Chile, Indonesia and Haiti. But how soon we forget.

In the 1960s and 70s the programme was beset by major floods, famines, civil war, hundreds of thousands of refugees in various parts of Africa and Asia and we did not have then cellphones, we did not have e-mail, we did not have fax machines, we didn't have Facebook, we didn't have Twitter, telex was possible for ... on some occasions, but it was too expensive. And I think it is a **testimony** to the skill and creativity of the international advisers from some seventy different countries as well as the ministers and health programme staff who managed to overcome all of these and achieve what had been **deemed** impossible.

VR: Dr. Peter Carassco is a WHO Policy Adviser for **vaccine** security. During the eradication programme he was both a vaccinator and a field staff supervisor on three campaigns. The last one was in Somalia where he was responsible for tracking down and containing the last outbreak.

DR. PETER CARASSCO: The last phases in all the countries were basically the same. We used good surveillance, good surveillance, working with villagers, working with the health system to track down suspected cases and smallpox is one case that always has a rash and we had these little ID cards and we educated the population over years and we would get rumours. One thing that did help us at the end was a thousand dollar reward for a confirmed case of smallpox, and we got a lot of rumours from the last countries that had smallpox virus circulations. We were able to track down what we call the chains of **transmission**, shut them down with vaccination and that is how we got to eradication.

VR: The statue to commemorate this event which is placed in the WHO grounds depicts a vaccinator kneeling before a child ready to be vaccinated. In one hand he holds the unique two-pronged needle which was instrumental in the eradication of the disease. Behind the child is a mother from the Asian region flanked by a man from the African region, all lined up to be vaccinated. The statue tells a story of a global battle against an ancient scourge and reminds us that smallpox affected not only children—everybody had to be vaccinated.

Dr. Henderson tells us how this eradication success opened the doors for further WHO vaccination programmes.

DH: We salute this historic milestone as one of the most brilliant accomplishments in medical history. But smallpox eradication was not an end in itself and in 1974 the Assembly agreed to set in motion an expanded pro-gramme on **immunization** whose goal was to **ensure** that the world's children would also be protected against measles, polio, diphtheria, pertussis and tetanus. The goal was to reach 80 percent. UNICEF and Rotary International made this a priority as did a number of governments and a number of other agencies have participated. The 80 percent mark was reach in 1990, and with this, a new era has **emerged** for public health achievement through vaccination.

VR: If you would like more information about smallpox eradication there are links to photo galleries on the trans-cript page of this podcast episode. That's all for this episode of the WHO podcast. Thanks for listening. For the World Health Organization, this is Veronica Riemer in Geneva.

LISTENING 2: A Better Way to Beat Malaria

Welcome to the April 25, 2011, MSF Frontline Reports podcast. Doctors Without Borders/Médecins Sans Fron-tières, or MSF, is an independent medical **humanitarian** aid organization. I'm Kim Daley. This week: a better way to beat malaria.

The drug quinine, also pronounced *qui-neen*, has been used to treat malaria for centuries. It's been the main weapon in the battle against the disease, which is carried by mosqui-toes, and kills close to one million people every year.

The vast majority of the victims are children in Africa, and they die after the disease progresses to a **severe** form of malaria where their internal organs come under attack. At the moment, the treatment these children receive is quinine.

But now, there's a drug that has been proven in **clinical trials** to be a major improvement on quinine. It's called *artesunate*. And not only is it more effective, but the new medication is also far simpler and safer to **administer** than quinine, especially in the often remote places where malaria causes the greatest toll. Most importantly, artesu-nate could save 200,000 lives per year.

The World Health Organization has just revised its guide-lines calling for artesunate as the treatment of choice for children with severe malaria, and MSF is already starting to make the switch. But to make a revolutionary change and save hundreds of thousands of young lives across the

continent, the countries where the disease is **endemic** also need to make the move from quinine to artesunate in their national treatment guidelines. And that won't happen without the support of the international community.

Making the switch would be **transformative** for many communities across Africa and it comes with a small price tag of around thirty million U.S. dollars per year. So what is holding things up? Laura McCullagh reports.

LAURA MCCULLAGH: Colette is two years old and lives in North Kivu Province in the Democratic Republic of Congo, or DRC. Recently her mother and sisters rushed her to the local health centre because she was having **convulsions**, running a high fever and experiencing difficulties in breathing—all clear indications that Colette was seriously ill with severe malaria.

Health staff at the clinic set up a drip so that the little girl could be treated with the standard medicine for this illness in DRC, quinine.

It's a drug that's administered through an **infusion**—that's when the medicine is dissolved in a glucose solution and "dripped" into the body via a catheter and an intravenous or IV line—and as anyone who has ever experienced having a drip will know, this is not a comfortable procedure, especially for young children. As Anja Juncker, an MSF doctor in DRC, explains, it can be made even worse when less experienced health workers are the administrators.

ANJA JUNCKER: Giving an infusion to a small child can be very tricky and very difficult. You have to place the catheter in the right position in the vein to make sure that the infusion really goes into the body correctly, and especially in small children, this can be a huge problem. It is a challenge for the child because it means many times a lot of pain; you know you have to try to put in the IV line in different sites because many times it doesn't happen the first time.

LM: To deliver the correct dose of quinine, the infusions last four hours and are performed three times a day until the child is well enough to swallow tablets. That's a very demanding twenty-four-hour process for health staff to **monitor** and it's difficult for the young patient who's required to lie still throughout.

AJ: The child has to stay in bed, you have to keep him quiet, when the child is moving a lot around, sometimes the IV line doesn't drop in the same velocity as it's supposed to be. The child moves its arm, so the infusion stops. He opens his arm again and then sometimes the infusion goes much faster, and this can be very, very dangerous regarding the side effects of the medication.

LM: If the amount of the infusions entering the body aren't properly monitored, then patients can get too much of the medicine, or indeed too little. The side effects caused by an overdose of quinine include **vertigo**, nausea and vomiting, and some patients experience problems with their sight and hearing. Under dosing, however, means that the malarial **parasite** isn't knocked out by the medicine and the patient is just not getting treated.

Colette, who was looked after in an MSF-supported health centre, avoided these risks and went on to make a good recovery to the delight of her family. But there isn't always such a happy ending, particularly when those patients suffering from the disease live in remote and rural areas where the skills of local health staff may not be up to dealing with these complicated infusion procedures. Divin Barutwanayo works for MSF in Guinea, where teams are also treating patients with severe malaria. He explains how this has led to many people not getting treated.

DIVIN BARUTWANAYO: Today, all the complicated cases of severe malaria have to be referred to hospitals, and this creates real difficulties for people from the villages. There are no ambulances, very few vehicles around, and the roads are bad so if you're sent to hospital it's very hard to get food or for family members to come for support.

LM: But despite these drawbacks from the perspectives of both patient and caregiver, quinine has remained the standard treatment for malaria across the African continent and beyond for many, many years. A look around the shelves of any pharmacy in sub-Saharan Africa will show you just how widespread and familiar the medication is. This may now be about to change. Nathan Ford is the medical coordinator of MSF's Access Campaign.

NATHAN FORD: What we have seen recently is that over the last decade or two, evidence emerging from various trials conducted in Asia, and then in Africa have shown that, in fact, newer treatments, **alternative** treatments, are much more effective than quinine. So while mankind has relied on quinine for several hundreds of years for malaria, it seems today that we need to move on from quinine and start replacing the drug with the newer treatment, artesunate.

LM: Artesunate, which is derived from a Chinese plant whose **efficacy** against malaria was rediscovered in the 1980s, has proved itself in clinical trials. Not only does it save more lives because it's more effective and **potent** than quinine—overall, treating severe malaria with artesunate instead of quinine reduces the risk of death by 39 percent in adults and 24 percent in children—but also because it's proven to be a safer medicine without the damaging side effects that can be associated with quinine treatment.

But it's outside the lab, on the ground, where the clear advantages for patients and staff emerge. Artesunate is a drug that can be delivered by injection rather than through infusion, and this fact alone could radically simplify treatment. Dr. Anja Juncker again:

AJ: First of all we talk about a slow injection, meaning four minutes, versus having an infusion dripping into the body over four hours. The time of monitoring that medication is correctly administered is four minutes versus four hours. This is a huge difference for the staff taking care of that patient. And the second biggest advantage is for the patient, he gets his one injection and then it's done, the medication is *in*, versus needing this IV line kept open, which produces a lot of pain sometimes.

LM: The science and the experience to date are clear: artesunate is a faster, safer and overall more effective medication for children suffering from severe malaria. So why then hasn't it been adopted everywhere? Well, cost is one reason. The basic unit cost of artesunate is three and a half U.S. dollars, that's three times the basic unit cost of quinine. But Nathan Ford says those figures are misleading.

NF: Because quinine's more complicated to administer and because it results in more side effects and because death also has a cost, there have been cost effectiveness analyses in Asia and Africa which show that overall the difference in cost between quinine and artesunate is *neutral*, it's the same, you save costs using artesunate because you have less side effects to deal with, because health workers are less occupied having to administer a complicated drug like quinine.

LM: The way forward, he suggests, is an initial **subsidy** on the higher costs of artesunate from the international community to allow countries to make this lifesaving switch.

NF: There will be an initial **reluctance**, the cost savings will come over time, but that initial reluctance has to be overcome and it has to be subsidized by the international community. However, it's not going to be an expensive policy change: it's estimated that it will cost around thirty million dollars per year to save 200,000 lives, so what we need is a global plan to ensure that policy change happens rapidly. This means that the major international donors put their full weight behind supporting the policy shift, subsidizing the initially higher cost of switching from quinine to artesunate.

LM: Besides cost, there are other barriers stopping people from making the switch to artesunate. In Guinea, where MSF moved away from using quinine to treat the disease in December last year, there's still some difficulties in health staff and patients to accept the switch to a new treatment, as Divin Barutwanayo, the field coordinator there, explains:

DB: To start with, the health workers, some of the nurses, and the doctors were a little reluctant about using the new treatment, because quinine has been used for years, so it's not so easy to change overnight. And the patients too— everyone is familiar with infusions when a child has severe malaria, so when they received an injection instead, many at first thought they hadn't received proper treatment, and they wanted the infusions.

LM: That initial reluctance has now given way to greater acceptance as the information is broadcast in radio spots on local stations and local health workers take the new information into the communities. The message is getting through.

DB: We've started to see some positive changes—for example in January we only had six patients treated for severe malaria. With the new treatment in February we had twenty-seven, and in March we've gone up to forty-six cases, so people are beginning to accept it.

LM: Several other countries in Africa have voiced a strong interest in making the switch to artesunate. But that won't happen without leadership at the international level. Right now, the WHO is in the process of revising its guidelines so that artesunate becomes the treatment of choice for children with severe malaria. In order to make this switch a reality, there'll be a need, too, to go out and offer countries technical support and training in how to **implement** the new drug. Supply lines of the new drug also need to be improved and manufacturers of artestunate primed so that they can step up rapidly to increased demand once the switch is made.

It's a many-headed challenge, and while MSF also has its role to play by implementing the use of the new medicines in its own projects, Nathan Ford has the wider international community—the donors and the policy-makers—clearly in his sights.

NF: To my mind this is a very, very precise **intervention** with a massive reduction in **mortality**, it's simpler to use, there's less side effects and the cost is very, very affordable and well within reach of the international community, so for me this should be a very, very easy and winnable battle as long as there's a clear international weight put behind the policy change that needs to happen because right now today, almost every African country is still using quinine so they need a lot of assistance in the short term if the hundreds of thousands of lives that could be saved are saved as soon as possible.

LISTENING 3: Barriers to Solutions

OSCAR: Okay, I'm not waiting until the night before to prepare for our class debate. It's not quite a formal debate, but it's pretty close. Let's get this done.

STELLA: Remind me again, Oscar. What exactly is the topic?

OSCAR: Stella!

STELLA: Just kidding. I already have all my notes. We start with Bertrand Russell's quotation, "Every advance in civilization has been denounced as unnatural while it was recent." Basically, he's saying that new ideas and innovations have always been criticized. People criticized everything from cars to rock 'n' roll music.

OSCAR: That's right, and some people still do. In any case, we're on the supporting side, which means we need to make points that agree with the quotation.

STELLA: And do you?

OSCAR: Do I what?

STELLA: Do you agree with the quotation? Do you really think that every advance in civilization has been criticized?

OSCAR: Stella, in a debate, it doesn't matter what you think; you just have to support your side of the argument as best you can. The people who really have to decide are the people who will be listening to us: our teacher, classmates and the other people in the audience.

STELLA: Okay. Well, I think we have to **ensure** we have lots of examples to support our point of view.

OSCAR: Examples are good, and maybe we can start with **potent** examples, but we need to find principles as well.

STELLA: What do you mean by principles?

OSCAR: The quote basically says that every great new idea—ideas that make civilization advance or improve—has faced some opposition. We can give lots of examples of people's **reluctance**, but the other side will just give lots of counter-examples. You know, say the opposite.

STELLA: I see. Uh, actually, I don't see. Can we look at one of my examples?

OSCAR: Sure.

STELLA: Slavery. It's a bad thing, and everyone agrees that it's **devastating**, but when people first tried to get rid of it, there was a lot of opposition.

OSCAR: You know, the **eradication** of slavery is still going on around the world today. You have to be more specific. Talk about a place and time.

STELLA: Okay, before the American Civil War, that was 1861 to 1865, slavery was common throughout the United States, particularly in the South.

OSCAR: But why? And, more importantly, why did people want to keep slavery?

STELLA: It was a form of **subsidy** through cheap labour. Southern plantation owners needed lots of unpaid farm workers to keep crops like cotton and tobacco competitive.

OSCAR: Okay, so we can say that the opposition to abolishing slavery was rooted in greed. That's the principle: lots of people will ignore advances in civilization for reasons of self-interest.

STELLA: Yeah, I understand. By the way, do you know when slavery was outlawed in Canada?

OSCAR: No, but I'm sure you'll tell me.

STELLA: More than half a century earlier: slavery was abolished in part of Canada in 1793 and in the rest of Canada in 1803.

OSCAR: Interesting, but let's move on. We have one principle, the moral principle of greed, and an example, slavery. Here's another principle: *ignorance*.

STELLA: Ignorance? There are lots of examples for that, too. For instance, before people understood bacteria and viruses, they thought micro-organisms couldn't exist. If people couldn't see something, it was **unprecedented** to expect that they would understand or accept it.

OSCAR: Are you talking about van Leeuwenhoek?

STELLA: Yes. Antony van Leeuwenhoek lived from 1632 to 1723, and he found an **alternative** way to make microscopes so that they were powerful enough to let him see things that no one had ever seen before.

OSCAR: Okay, that's good, but where's the evidence for opposition to his ideas?

STELLA: Van Leeuwenhoek never wrote a book, but he sent a lot of letters to the Royal Society in England. It was actually called The Royal Society of London for Improving Natural Knowledge. The Royal Society investigated all sorts of scientific issues, and although they generally understood van Leeuwenhoek's descriptions of microscopic organisms, there was enough doubt about his assertions that they sent a group to Holland to check him out. The group included not just scientists but also lawyers and a priest. Eventually, what van Leeuwenhoek had seen was **deemed** the truth.

OSCAR: That's great. So, we have economic reasons and reasons of ignorance. What about *wilful* ignorance?

STELLA: By wilful ignorance, do you mean people lying?

OSCAR: Not just lying, but also being purposely *selective* with research. People who go out and search for studies and experts that support their point of view but ignore all other points of view.

STELLA: Yes. I have a great example for that: the Wi-Fi debate.

OSCAR: Wi-Fi? You mean like for wireless e-mail on your computer?

STELLA: Exactly. There are a lot of people who think it's too dangerous.

OSCAR: And they have a reason for their opinions?

STELLA: Well, they might cite some studies, but they pick the references that suit them and ignore everything else. The general ideas behind most of the objections are that we don't know enough about the issue, that the issue hasn't been studied enough, that it's reckless to expose people to unknown dangers and so on.

OSCAR: Well, I suppose you have to agree to some extent—unless there is different evidence on the other side.

STELLA: Well, there are government safety guidelines—after all, the government has to approve and **monitor** devices like computers that use Wi-Fi radiation.

Oscar: That all sounds quite vague. Do you have some facts that people would understand better?

Stella: Sure. Microwave radiation—the kind that opponents to Wi-Fi are concerned about—is far stronger from microwave ovens, radio, TV or mobile telephones than from machines using Wi-Fi. Twenty minutes on a mobile telephone is equivalent to a year's exposure to Wi-Fi. A trip on an airplane is equivalent to a lifetime's exposure. Of course, everyone agrees it would be better to avoid any unnecessary exposure to radiation, but we need to balance minimal—or non-existent—danger against the benefits of everything else in our lives. In any case, if you're opposed to Wi-Fi, are you really willing to give up microwave ovens, mobile phones, radio and TV?

Oscar: Not me.

Stella: Not many people. Even if you don't have Wi-Fi or even cordless telephones at home, you'll probably find that many of your neighbours' computers and Wi-Fi devices are operating in range of your home. Moreover, most businesses as well as libraries have wireless. We live in a wireless world.

Oscar: Okay, you've convinced me. I'm not going to throw out my computer and my phone.

Stella: So do you think we're ready for the debate yet?

Oscar: No, not at all. I mean, I'd say we're only halfway there.

Stella: What else do we need to do?

Oscar: We need to *frame* the argument, and we also need to find counter-examples and deal with them.

Stella: What do you mean, *frame the argument*?

Oscar: We can start with the quote, remember, "Every advance in civilization has been denounced as unnatural while it was recent."

Stella: Okay, but what then?

Oscar: Then we say, "This happens for several reasons, including self-interest, ignorance and wilful ignorance."

Stella: And then we give some examples?

Oscar: Yes … but it would be good if we had a single example that fit all three points.

Stella: I think that would be really hard to find.

Oscar: Then, lucky for you, I found one. In 1998, a British medical journal published a study that criticized common vaccines—you know, the shots that you get as a child to stop you from getting diseases like measles, mumps and rubella. This study linked the vaccines to autism. Autism is a mental condition with a range of symptoms. We see it in some children who have great difficulty communicating. These kids find it hard to form relationships and use language, and they also have trouble with some abstract concepts. Anyway, the main author of the study was a man named Dr. Andrew Wakefield. It was a big deal. At least in part because of what he wrote, experts believe that in Britain, use of childhood vaccines dropped to 80 percent; **intervention** also dropped in other countries, leading to outbreaks of some of the diseases the vaccines were meant to protect against. There was just one problem: the study was completely false. Of the twelve children in the study, three didn't even have autism. Others had been specifically picked for the study, which was

unethical and unscientific. Worst of all, Wakefield was working for a group preparing a lawsuit against manufacturers of the measles, mumps and rubella vaccines. They wanted to use Wakefield's research to sue the vaccine companies, so they paid him a lot of money, which created a conflict of interest. Yet for many people who know this, it still doesn't matter; they believe what they want to believe and they still refuse to give their children the vaccines they need to be healthy.

Stella: Wow, I see what you mean. It looks like Wakefield was putting his own self-interest before the lives of sick children. He was getting paid and didn't tell anyone. People believed him because his work was published in a medical journal, so they and the medical journal editors were ignorant. And people still believe him despite their discovery of the truth because they practise wilful ignorance. Great example!

Oscar: So you think we're ready?

Stella: Yes, I do. I think we're ready for the debate.

CHAPTER 7
Embracing Risk

LISTENING 1: Emily Carr: A Life Less Ordinary

Many of us long to live what we call *a life less ordinary*. The phrase *a life less ordinary* refers to someone who has made interesting choices about what to do in life. Usually, such people have avoided the safe and traditional path that most of us follow and set out to do something extraordinary, something far different from the expectations of those around them and, even, something shocking. We often call such people **rebels**.

Some rebels set out to be consciously and deliberately different, for example, by travelling to a far country and perhaps living with and learning from the local people. During the nineteenth century, there was a great deal of such exploration, with many travellers investigating life, customs, history, religion and other ideas in **remote** parts of Asia, Africa and the Middle East. Many of these explorers were women.

In other cases, a rebel does not set out to be so different, but in slow stages and through countless choices, achieves fame for doing great and different things. The Canadian painter and writer, Emily Carr is an example of the second type of rebel. Rather than pursue the traditional roles of her time, as a wife and mother, she travelled to remote areas under difficult conditions to pursue her love of painting and her interest in **First Nations** culture. Her paintings and written **accounts** of her travels have delighted and inspired others for generations.

Emily Carr was born in Victoria, British Columbia, in 1871, to English parents who had **immigrated** to Canada. Carr's father became a successful businessman and respected member of the community, and so Carr would have been raised with her parents' and society's expectations that she would follow a traditional path of learning how to behave politely, pursuing little or no post-secondary education, finding a husband and having a large family. But from her youngest days, Emily was the most rebellious of the four sisters in the family.

In the 1870s, Victoria, on British Columbia's Vancouver Island, was a rather wild place. Young Emily would have grown up with nature right at her doorstep. Bears, wolves and cougars would have been seen in and around town, and in the surrounding waters, she would have seen seals and killer whales, just as one does today. She would also have come into contact with local First Nations peoples.

Carr's life might well have been quite ordinary. Victoria was far from Canadian and international centres of culture, and there was no great artistic community in the city. But Carr had a talent for—and more importantly, a *love* of—drawing and sketching. As a very young girl, instead of spending her pocket money on candy as other children might, Carr saved and bought **plaster casts** of sculptures from the local tombstone maker. These casts were models the tombstone maker used to create carvings of angels and people for grave monuments. Carr used these plaster casts to draw from and to learn about **anatomy**. She also drew from nature, and her talent for noticing details in the world would have made her more keenly aware of her surroundings.

When both her parents died while she was still a teenager, she was placed in the care of guardians. At age eighteen, she convinced them that her talents in drawing were reason enough to send her eleven hundred kilometres south to San Francisco to study art at the somewhat **conservative** California School of Design. There she spent two and a half years and learned to paint in the traditional manner of the time, but the money her parents had left began to run out. When she returned to Victoria, she realized that she needed to put her skills to use in earning an **income** to support herself, so she began teaching art classes to children. Still, she wanted more, so she **embarked** on a study trip to England to learn more about European painting styles.

One of her first choices as a student was to turn down a traditional class in drawing from plaster models—she'd done too much of that already—and instead take life-drawing classes. At the time, drawing from nude models was scandalous, and she dared not tell her sisters or friends. Two years turned into a five-year stay when she became ill—too ill to travel. She returned to Victoria with little to show for her time in England other than a few bad habits, including a love of smoking.

After five more years in Victoria, Carr was beginning to become aware of the new European art movements. Using all the savings from her teaching, again she set off, this time for France, in the company of her sister Alice. They moved to Paris, and Carr took formal classes and studied with a private tutor. But Carr's biggest leap in education probably came from her exposure to new styles of painting, particularly impressionism and post-impressionism. In 1912, after two years in France, she returned once more to Victoria.

As I mentioned earlier, while growing up in Victoria, Carr would have had contact with First Nations peoples. Later, she also took an interest in visiting their settlements and learning about their culture. Carr was amazed at the **grandeur** of the totem poles and other structures she had visited on earlier trips. "We passed many Indian villages on our way down the coast," she wrote. "The Indian people and their art touched me deeply ... By the time I reached home my mind was made up. I was going to picture totem poles in their own village settings, as complete a collection of them as I could."

In 1912, she set off on a six-week summer trip by steame and canoe, exploring villages on the west coast of Vancouver Island, sketching and painting everywhere she went. It was at a time when many of the traditional villages were being abandoned, as First Nations peoples moved into cities. Carr realized that a great deal of First Nations culture was disappearing, and she wanted to create a record of it—a more emotional and, in some sense, *truer* record. Increasingly, she felt this, not just about First Nations settlements, but about the vast forests as well. Carr wanted to capture the very "spirit" of Canada. Speaking of the Canadian wilderness, she wrote, "More than ever was I convinced that the old way of seeing was **inadequate** to express this big country of ours, her depth, her height, her unbounded wideness: silences too strong to be broken. Nor could ten million cameras, through their mechanical boxes, ever show real Canada. It had to be sensed, passed through live minds, sensed and loved." Other trips followed, further north to First Nations settlements on the Queen Charlotte Islands. Carr spoke none of the First Nations languages, but she got by with **gestures** and her good nature. She loved to laugh and was given the name *Klee Wyck*, which means "the laughing one."

The paintings she created were exceptional and, today, may sell for more than a million dollars. But at the time, they were little **appreciated** and didn't sell. To make ends meet, Carr used the rest of her inheritance, some land, to build an apartment building with a studio for her and other rooms to rent that she hoped would generate enough income so that she could continue to paint. However, with the beginning of the First World War, the rental market **collapsed**: people were unwilling to pay high rents, and it became difficult for Carr to make ends meet, let alone find time to paint. Instead, she invented several **schemes** to make money, including growing produce to sell and making whimsical clay pots. She also bred dogs—more than 350 sheep dogs one year—and collected a menagerie of other animals, such as racoons and even a monkey that she tried to teach to sew. In 1927, her First Nations-inspired paintings, pottery and rugs were part of an exhibition at Canada's National Gallery. This exhibition brought her to the attention of the Group of Seven, then Canada's best-known group of painters. That exhibition and subsequent meetings with members of The Group of Seven inspired Carr to paint more. Eventually, ill health made it difficult for Carr to paint, and she turned her hand to writing and **documented** her time among the First Nations peoples. Her first book, *Klee Wyck*, won the Governor General's award for non-fiction. After so many years of being ignored, Carr became better known and appreciated for both her painting and her writing.

Today, with so many popular women artists, it's difficult for us to understand that, as a rebel, Emily Carr did something quite different. She was an artist when most famous artists were men. She painted the West Coast of Canada in all its wild glory, when European-trained painters were sketching **idealized** versions of Canada that looked more like the gentle landscapes of England. She wrote, "I am glad that I am showing these men that women can hold up their end. The men **resent** a woman getting any honour in what they consider is essentially their field. Men painters mostly despise women painters. So I have decided to stop squirming, to throw any honour in with Canada and women." Carr's **vision** of the First Nations peoples and the Canadian landscape helped to raise awareness of them both in Canada and around the world.

Carr died on March 2, 1945, at the age of seventy-three, having lived *a life less ordinary*, true to the rebel vision she embraced as a young woman.

LISTENING 2: Getting Comfortable Taking Innovation Risks

At some point, in the life of a **killer idea**, you're going to have to take a risk to see if the idea will become a killer innovation. How comfortable are you about taking risk?

This is the Killer Innovations podcast with Phil McKinney. Keep in mind that the information and opinions expressed in this podcast are Phil's, and Phil's alone, and they don't necessarily reflect those of his past, current or future employers. Now, here's Phil McKinney.

So, you've come up with that killer idea. To move it forward, you need to take a risk. Now, the range of risks can go from **investing** your entire retirement fund to quitting your job, to **convincing** others to take risk with you, where you're asking them to risk *their* retirement fund, *their* job security. But then you **hesitate**: the risk seems huge, and you start to second-guess the original idea. You ask yourself: "Is the potential value of what this killer idea is worth the risk?" And immediately, your **reaction** is to retreat back to the comfort of the safe option. Stay where you're at and do nothing. Before you give up, let's understand how our mind processes risk.

Back in 2005, a German researcher **surveyed** 20,000 people about their risk behaviour. Now, there's some interesting **outcomes** from this that may not seem logical. For instance, tall people are more prepared to take risks than short people. Women take fewer risks than men. And a willingness to take risks decreases **dramatically** with age. Now, the key influencers that came out of the entire survey were age, gender, height and parental education. How much education did the individuals' parents get? Now, people who were most confident with their lives—meaning they had good security where they were at, they'd had recognition, they'd had success **previously** in their lives—were more willing to take more risk.

So, if you're an older woman, are you **doomed** to realize your killer idea, meaning you're in this risk profile and therefore you should just give up? No. Half the battle is knowing your risk profile. The risk profiles—what I would refer to is that **comfort zone**: how much risk are you willing to take? If you're in one of the risk segments that's uncomfortable with taking significant risks, such as older women, then becoming aware of the tendency not to take risk is really the first step because you can change. It's understanding what makes you uncomfortable. Ask yourself why the potential for risk is so **unnerving** for you. Now, for older people, it could be the risk of losing money set aside for retirement. It could be the perception of losing face should the idea fail: you've worked so long and hard to have a successful career to have a big blow-out happen because you took this risk, and it didn't work out.

Sit down and write out in detail your concerns about taking the risk. Is it about money, is it about saving face, is about family, is it about something else? Whatever it is, list them all out. Then come up with ideas that **neutralize** each concern. For example, if you're concerned about losing your retirement money, then think about ideas where you can use moneys from others, whether it's raising venture capitalists, angel investors or something else. Or invest a little, set a goal. Try the idea out with a little bit of money. If the goal is achieved, then you invest a little bit more. You don't need to jump all in right from the beginning. Just as a gated funding model works in enterprises and in venture capitalists, you can apply that same model to your idea, as an individual.

The objective is to neutralize the feeling of risk. Risk doesn't go away. You haven't fundamentally changed the overall risk profile, but it's your feeling of risk, and by listing these all out and using your creativity to come up with ways to neutralize them, you can reduce the feeling of risk. This same approach works for your boss or your spouse, the difference being is that you need to identify their concerns on risk. What is their risk profile? What is the ... how does your boss going through and evaluating the risk of an idea that you're **pitching**? How do you convince your **spouse** to take a little bit of that money that's in the savings account and apply it to your idea? So again, the difference is that it's not about your risk profile, but if you're needing to get the idea over a hump, look at the risk profile for the key **decision-maker**—your boss, your spouse, somebody that you're trying to convince to join you.

Then apply the same level of creativity you used to come up with your idea to creatively address *their* fears about risk. All of us experience fear. Back in high school and college, I used to teach rock climbing. And the one thing I learned up on the face of the rock with students was is that everyone has a fear of heights. What's different is, is that everyone deals with it differently. Some people climbing rocks, that fear is an **adrenaline rush**, it gives them energy, it gets them focused. For others, that fear of heights is **paralyzing**: they get halfway up the face of the rock, they can't go up, they can't retreat and go down, they become totally stuck, they become paralyzed by their fear. The same when it comes to taking risk, whether it's investing in stocks versus investing in bonds. Quitting our job to pursue the killer idea or to stay in the same company and go for those—that twenty-five-year gold watch.

Everyone is not cut out for risk. But don't give up too early. If you're one of those people where risk and fear just paralyzes you, take a deep look at what is scaring you, what is causing that deep-seated fear and see if it's **warranted**. What is the real downside? Get a realistic **perspective** of what it is you are truly risking—what is it you would lose by taking this chance to go execute against your killer idea? See whether—if that risk is really—or that fear is really warranted and brainstorm at how to neutralize it. Use your creativity, the same level of creativity used in creating your idea, brainstorm ways to neutralize your fear. Neutralize that risk so that you can get comfortable with it. And then, take the plunge.

LISTENING 3: First Comes Failure

STELLA: Oscar, what do you have there?

OSCAR: It's a lottery ticket, Stella. I feel lucky, as though I'm finally going to win big.

STELLA: You *must* be joking. Do you known what people call lottery tickets?

OSCAR: Yeah, yeah ... a stupidity tax. That's an old one. But I'm a wild and crazy guy; I don't mind taking risks.

STELLA: Really? Spending two dollars on a lottery ticket **convinces** you that you're a major risk-taker?

OSCAR: Uh, well, maybe not.

STELLA: But it's an interesting question. How far would you go in taking risks?

OSCAR: Are you talking about buying more lottery tickets?

STELLA: No! Some people risk a great deal more than *two dollars*. Some risk their fortunes, some risk their lives, and some risk their futures and the futures of those close to them. How far would you go?

OSCAR: This sounds like a trick question.

STELLA: It's not, but it is part of our assignment this week. We have to find a famous person who has taken risks—and succeeded—and analyze the factors that made that person successful.

OSCAR: So, we should start with someone really successful?

STELLA: Not necessarily. Many people have become successful without taking risks. Think about people who have inherited their money or just started a little business with a **killer idea** that did well, or someone who happened to be at the right place at the right time but didn't do something **dramatically** different. None of these people necessarily took risks.

OSCAR: Instead, they've let other people take risks?

STELLA: Sometimes. If you look at a lot of the early computer software pioneers, they were just playing with things they enjoyed. They didn't **scheme** to become millionaires. The fact that the products they created became internationally successful and made them rich came as a bit of a surprise.

OSCAR: A nice surprise.

STELLA: But besides earning money, there are also many other ways to define success. You can look at people who have been successful in helping others.

OSCAR: But weren't you talking about risk?

STELLA: Yes. And why do young people take more risks than older people?

OSCAR: Because they're foolish?

STELLA: Mm ... sort of. Actually, doctors tell us that between the ages of thirteen and twenty-five, the human brain has not fully developed those parts that are necessary for assessing—or understanding—risk.

OSCAR: So it's natural for me to buy lottery tickets?

STELLA: Ah, no, I think that would be back to the foolish side of things.

OSCAR: Oh, too bad.

STELLA: People between the ages of thirteen and twenty-five are not only weaker at assessing risks—that is, balancing the risks against the benefits—they are also in greater need of stimulation—an **adrenaline rush**.

OSCAR: Oh, so that's why teenagers and people in their twenties like to do dangerous things?

STELLA: Exactly. It's a perfect combination: willingness to take risks and a desire to seek thrills. It also makes for fearless soldiers and pioneers, or at least *fairly* fearless ones. Young men and women may go into the armed forces excited about the risk; they see it as a challenge and don't think about war as being a threat to their lives, not in the sense that an older person would.

OSCAR: I guess fire fighters and police officers must feel the same way. Actually, a friend's brother was a fire fighter,

and my friend said they were beyond courageous ... you think they'd be hesitant about entering a burning building, but they're so well trained, they *charge* in. It's the adrenaline rush that drives them.

STELLA: Sure, adrenaline is really important for many people—that excitement you get from doing something dangerous. And there's a whole series of high-risk occupations for people who like that sort of thing.

OSCAR: Sure, but sometimes, of course, you have no choice. It's simply the best-paying local job you can get, depending on where you live. In most places, jobs in mining, forestry and fishing can be extremely dangerous. The workers deal with dangerous tools, unpredictable weather conditions and long distances from any medical aid. If you're seriously hurt, you might be **doomed** to die before you reach a hospital.

STELLA: Yes, and in some countries, the most dangerous job is being a journalist.

OSCAR: A journalist? Are you serious? You mean, reporting the news?

STELLA: That's right. Often journalists find themselves in dangerous situations, like covering a riot or a war, or sometimes find themselves investigating situations that organized criminals or even the government don't want investigated. Journalists can sometimes ... *disappear*.

OSCAR: I never thought of it that way—so much for becoming a journalist.

STELLA: Do you know who Winston Churchill was?

OSCAR: Uh, a British Prime Minister, wasn't he?

STELLA: Yes, but when he was young, he joined the army and also worked as a journalist; he was born to an aristocratic family and wanted the extra money to keep up his lifestyle. He asked to be sent to the worst war zones and, in 1899, set off to fight in the Boer War in South Africa. He was captured and imprisoned. He wanted to escape but was initially discouraged from doing so by the more experienced soldiers. Still, he succeeded in both breaking out of the prison camp and crossing almost 500 kilometres of enemy territory. It made him a national hero, yet he chose to go back immediately to fight. As British troops advanced, he and his cousin returned to the same prison camp where he'd been imprisoned, and the two of them convinced fifty-two Boer soldiers there to surrender.

OSCAR: So he took a lot of risks, but it seems they were **warranted**.

STELLA: And he faced a lot of failures. But he never gave up. He wrote, "Success is not final, failure is not fatal: it is the courage to continue that counts." He was a very inspiring speaker, and as leader of Britain during the Second World War, he combined his talents as a journalist and as a politician to write and deliver inspiring speeches. It was all the more amazing because, as a boy, he had had a speech impediment—a lisp.

OSCAR: So he took risks and had some failures *and* was successful. And it wasn't about increasing his **income**?

STELLA: That's one **perspective**, yes, he wanted money to support himself—who doesn't?—but his risk-taking went beyond that.

OSCAR: I suppose Terry Fox was a risk-taker.

STELLA: That's right. He was young, and he had a dream, to raise money to fight cancer, the disease that had cost him one of his legs. The idea of running across Canada was courageous; he must have known that it was a risk, that it would be hard on his health. But even though he never finished his task, dying before he reached his goal of running from the East Coast to the West Coast of Canada, he was, by every measure, a great success. Every year, hundreds of thousands of people run, following his example.

OSCAR: I guess someone else we could talk about would be Roberta Bondar, the first Canadian woman in space.

STELLA: Sure, I've heard of her.

OSCAR: As a child, Bondar was fascinated with science, and that interest never left her. Throughout school she was a great student and went on to become a great researcher, in neurology. In 1983, the National Research Council of Canada set up a Canadian space program and invited people to apply if they wanted to become astronauts. She applied immediately and went through months of interviews before becoming one of only six successful candidates—and the only woman—out of more than four thousand applicants. There was never any guarantee that she would actually get to go into space, yet for nine years, she put off having a family and devoted herself to her dream. It was a sacrifice *and* a risk, but her **vision** finally paid off: in 1992, her space shuttle took off, and she got to spend eight days in space, conducting experiments and taking photographs of the earth's surface.

STELLA: I'm impressed. How did you know all that?

OSCAR: I've already started my project. I'm talking about Bondar.

STELLA: Ah, good choice. So, what else are you going to say?

OSCAR: I'm going to talk about some other people who have taken risks, particularly some other people who have tried and failed. We're used to thinking about famous people as if they got it right immediately, that life was easy for them. But it often wasn't. The American president Abraham Lincoln lost the first election he ever ran in. He was a lawyer but actually gave up politics to start a general store. It failed, which by all **accounts** is probably why he decided to go back into politics. Steven Spielberg, the famous filmmaker, was a terrible student and applied to film school three times. Charles Darwin, the scientist who developed the theory of evolution, was told by his father that he would amount to *nothing* and would be a disgrace to himself and his family. The list goes on.

STELLA: I suppose many of these people took risks and accomplished great things partly to show the world that they could do better. Actually, Winston Churchill was also a terrible student but naturally **resented** getting caned—hit with a stick—by his teachers for misbehaviour. Once, as he was being punished, he shouted out to the teacher with the stick, "I will be a better man than you!" Of course, he was punished even more. But he was right, in the end.

OSCAR: When you're taking risks, there's a lot about not giving up. Did you ever hear about two Japanese guys called Masaru Ibuka and Akio Morita?

STELLA: No, never.

OSCAR: Actually you have—but not for their first invention. They started off making rice cookers. The rice cookers were completely **inadequate**; in fact, they tended to burn rice, and the two inventors sold only about a hundred of them. But they didn't give up. They kept working on other inventions and ended up starting a company called *Sony*.

STELLA: Wow. This fits in with something Mary Pickford said. Do you know who she was? She was one of the earliest movie stars, a Canadian actress who starred in the first silent movies. She said, "Supposing you have tried and failed again and again. You may have a fresh start any moment you choose, for this thing that we call *failure* is not the falling down, but the staying down."

CHAPTER 8
Slow Food, Please!

LISTENING 1: Slow Food—Now!

I imagine that most of you have had a fast-food meal this month, this week or maybe even today. The term *fast food* has been in popular use for more than sixty years although the concept of a quick bite prepared with more concern for speed and budget than for **nutrition** has been around for much longer. Today, I'd like to persuade you that you should seriously consider following the opposite trend, the Slow Food movement. After, I'd like to make sense of it with an example of one individual's journey from fast food to slow food.

The Slow Food movement began in Italy and was largely the initiative of one man, Carlo Petrini. Petrini, born in 1949, initially became known for his opposition to the opening of a McDonald's next to Rome's historic Spanish Steps.

His continuing opposition to fast food—or rather his celebration of the pleasures of traditional foods—became a movement in 1989, when he and others created a **manifesto** that laid out general principles about how food should be *good, clean* and *fair*. *Good* is defined as being part of a fresh and flavoursome seasonal diet that satisfies the senses and is part of the local culture. *Clean* refers to food production and **consumption** that do not harm the environment, animal **welfare** or our own health. *Fair* refers to **accessible** prices for consumers and fair conditions and pay for small-scale producers.

Let's look at each of these in turn. The idea of *good* focuses on local specialties. In most countries, food production has become standardized along the lines of a factory model. Often, the **economies of scale**—that is, the ability of large **corporations** to use their vast sales to drive down prices—mean that many traditional farmers cannot compete. Associated with this mass production is the loss of biodiversity as corporations look to save money by offering fewer choices. Take apples, for example. Between 1804 and 1904, 7,000 commercial varieties of apples existed. Now, that number has largely decreased in supermarkets to just *two* varieties, Red and Golden Delicious, and the sub-varieties of apples bred from them. Many small farmers are trying to bring back old apple varieties as well as a wide variety of other fruits, vegetables and **livestock**.

In terms of *clean*, the Slow Food preference is for food that is produced with few, if any, artificial pesticides or fertilizers. However, although **organic** is a preference, many Slow Food advocates favour locally produced foods that are *not* completely organic over organic foods that are imported over great distances, with the additional costs and **pollution** of shipping.

The third characteristic, *fair*, is also extremely important. Much of the food you eat may be produced in other countries, particularly if it is not fresh. The conditions for workers are often appalling—closer to **slavery**. The Slow Food movement recognizes that for local farming to be viable, the farmers need to be paid fair prices for their goods. These prices may be higher than those at the supermarket, but the difference in quality and taste makes buying local produce worthwhile.

At the beginning, I mentioned I would give you an extended example drawn from the experiences of one individual. I recently interviewed Michelle Pentz Glave, a Slow Food proponent who lives on Bowen Island, on Canada's West Coast.

The first thing I asked Michelle was whether she grew up eating what we now call slow food. She surprised me by saying no, quite the opposite. She said this was especially true when she was younger, living with her single mother. Her mother would pick Michelle up from the babysitter's after work, and they'd either buy packaged TV dinners or stop at a chain restaurant for a fast-food dinner.

Michelle, who keeps an extremely tidy and well-organized home, said they would toss all the wrappers into the back of the car, where the waste would remain, forgotten. Deep piles of **discarded** wrappers and boxes grew. While driving, a fast turn would send the wrappers and soda cans flying from one side of the car to the other. The mess was at least appreciated by Michelle's two dogs, who took advantage of car trips to forage for what she characterized as **petrified** fries and leftover portions of burgers still in their wrappers.

However, Michelle told me that her mother was something of a contradiction because, although they ate lots of fast food and had plenty of pancake mix and other convenience foods in the house, they also did summertime canning, made jam and often baked from scratch, creating meals from basic fresh ingredients. Michelle explains that her family eventually had a vegetable garden; she loved working in the garden with her mother, digging in the fragrant dirt. Michelle added that a special treat was their frequent stops for fresh fruit at roadside fruit stands; both cherries and apricots were popular local specialties.

On the other hand, her family was a standard middle-class family who used the microwave a lot, as many people still do. Once her mother remarried, they made a habit of cooking interesting meals and eating them together at the table almost every night. Her mother always set the table nicely, and they usually had candles. Michelle enjoyed dinnertime **bonding** as a family, which she explains is a "slow-food-ish" thing to do.

After graduating from Yale University, five years in Europe led Michelle to the conclusion that most North Americans are unable to **savour** the moment, really tasting food and making a meal more about people, conversation and flavours—and, most of all, not rushing it! The fast-food all-you-can-eat mentality is entrenched in North America. Too many people are so obsessed with **calories** or eating quickly that they've forgotten how to enjoy themselves when they are eating.

Michelle moved closer to the Slow Food movement when she got married and she and her husband bought their first house. Michelle worked for a newspaper, reporting on business, food and agriculture; she also wrote food reviews, which led to her **authoring** a guidebook for dining in Santa

Fe, New Mexico. During this time, she met an amazing farmer in Albuquerque, New Mexico, whom everyone called Farmer Monte. He had just **launched** a community support agriculture co-op.

Michelle first wrote about his work and then ended up joining his co-op. She was inspired by his passion and the joy he created around local eating. Michelle explains that his boxes of fresh produce were gorgeous and picking them up at his farm each week was a social highlight. She loved the way people gathered around the food and it became the glue of a little community of food lovers. Michelle says that she and the other members of the co-op were fascinated with Monte's struggles in the fields and adopted his worries and aspirations as their own. The more farmers she met and wrote about, the more passionate about local food and agriculture she became. Pretty soon she was hooked. Michelle started by trying to grow chili peppers in her own garden, and it all—uh, I guess we could say *blossomed*—from there. Soon she was making her own baby food, experimenting with cooking, shopping at farmers' markets and seeking out wine from local vineyards.

After moving to Bowen Island near Vancouver, Canada, with her husband and two kids, Michelle started a celebration called BowFeast, a play on the name of the island's annual festival, Bowfest. But rather than **positioning** slow food as a chore, she has tried to make it all about sharing the joy and excitement of growing food, eating local food, supporting local farmers and celebrating harvests. The event promotes local eating during one week of the year and includes a community farmers' market. It also involves local retailers and grocery stores and gets kids involved; it's all about having fun with food. A special challenge of BowFeast is to encourage the community to host do-it-yourself feasts, using as many local, or **regional**, ingredients as possible.

Michelle and her husband do so in their own home, traditionally organizing an outdoor meal in the garden for about twelve couples. Each couple brings a dish featuring as many local ingredients as possible. It's a magical evening with guests presenting their dishes to fanfare and applause. As a whimsical part of the celebration, a BowFeast King and Queen are chosen from among the guests and crowned with rosemary and lavender, acknowledging their support for local food over the past year.

This past year, Michelle connected with students on the island who have their own school garden. She invited them to participate in the farmers' market because, as she said, "It's important to get kids excited about growing and eating local food—and understanding why that matters.

Michelle also started a weekly harvest box program to get locally grown produce into the hands of her friends and neighbours. She goes out of her way whenever possible to connect local island farmers to customers who are happy to buy directly from them.

In keeping with the *fair* aim of the Slow Food movement, Michelle says that it is vital for the small local farmers on her island to be able to make a decent living. It's pretty much impossible at the moment, she says, but the more people who start buying from a grower down the street, instead of from a chain grocery store, the more realistic that goal will become. She'd like to work on this particular piece of the puzzle next—to figure out how to make it more attractive to become a farmer in the first place. She'd like to help the growers on Bowen Island boost their sales so that they can continue their important work. She says that her own experience growing food in her yard has given her huge respect for what the farmers do—the magic they work with seeds and soil. Michelle calls it a *miracle*.

I'm here today to tell you that you can each be part of this miracle. Sometime this week, take the time to enjoy a meal hand-made from local ingredients. Share this meal with friends and avoid distractions. Turn off your phones, computers and TVs. Celebrate the taste of real food, and perhaps think about growing even one vegetable, fruit or herb on your windowsill. Both your body and mind will thank you for it.

LISTENING 2: The 100-Mile Diet

DON GENOVA: About a year and a half ago, I met two brave **souls** named James MacKinnon and Alisa Smith. They were right in the **midst** of attempting to spend a whole year eating meals made with ingredients that were produced no more than 100 miles away from their home in downtown Vancouver.

ALISA SMITH: Um, well, here's the cupboards. This is what's left of what we **preserved** in the summer and fall. And we've got pickles here, uh, ketchup, although my first time making ketchup, it's very watery, I didn't boil it long enough. Tomatoes and these are plums from our tree up in northern British Columbia, our cabin in Doreen. And this is crabapple jelly, also from our trees up in Doreen. And strawberry preserves, we did a u-pick, probably in Delta.

DG: The contents of the cupboards sounded pretty good, but that was after living through the **bounty** of summer and fall. When they started their adventure on the first day of spring in 2005, it was a bit tougher.

JAMES MACKINNON: We **naively** thought that the first day of spring was when the first green shoots would **burst** from the earth, and within two weeks we'd be having spring green salads. And, uh, I don't know how many people remember the spring of 2005, but it was ... it wasn't ... and, uh, the winter just **lingered**, and the rain, and the cold, and, uh, that was a long, **lean** period for us.

AS: Yeah, that was when I **definitely** got sick of beets because beets were one of the few things we could buy in the store, and all kinds of **borscht** was had around here, and I normally like it a lot, but potatoes I can have in endless quantities, but **apparently** beets is not one of those things. And I have not had a beet for about eight months. [laughs]

JM: And even fish—there were no fish being caught in the spring, so we were really—for **protein**, we were running on ... on eggs, pretty much. We were having fritters, and cheese, and milk, and you know, dairy and eggs.

DG: A few months after I interviewed MacKinnon and Smith, I attended a food celebration in BC's Cowichan Valley. There I met Jenn Lamm, who was **inspired** by the couple to create a website encouraging a 100-mile diet for the people of her home base of Nanaimo, on Vancouver Island.

MAN: It seems to be a concept that people have really, kind of, cottoned on to. To say, "Hey, this sounds really neat, I want to try it."

JENN LAMM: And yet, it's so traditional. It's old-school, isn't it? It's so old, it's new again! But I think, especially for an island community, it's that much more important because we're dependent on, you know, very limited transport routes to get our food here, but also because we live in

such a **fertile** area, and we've forgotten how fertile it really is and what it can really produce, you know. And I always wondered, well why are we bringing in apples from New Zealand when we have such amazing apple orchards on this island? And for me, it comes down largely to a matter of food security. I want there to be, you know, apple orchards, and cheese **artisans**, and you know, locally grown vegetables, you know. For ... for the future. And to not be dependent on those transport systems who bring those in.

DG: In her first year of doing the 100-mile diet, Jenn Lamm was able to put together a pretty **respectable** resource list of foods for people to taste, including a very homegrown cranberry sauce.

JL: I've got cranberries, from Yellow Point, cranberries, out in Ladysmith. And it's basically cranberries, a little bit of blueberries from a local farm in Nanaimo, um, locally grown, um, locally, well locally produced honey, and unsweetened apple juice. It's all boiled down, it's alternative to that canned cranberry sauce you get for Thanksgiving, and I'm serving it on true-grain baguette.

DG: Now, tell me about this fruit here because this is something that you wouldn't think could be grown in Canada, but here it is.

JL: Here it is. It's a kiwi fruit. And Kiwi Cove Lodge is growing seven different varieties of kiwis. And they're growing ... what we have here is a grape kiwi fruit, and we're also growing the ... the typical fuzzies, both the green and the goldens.

DG: Jenn Lamm is just one of the people I've talked to over the past couple of years who have become **re-energized** by being able to discover the bounty that's right next door to their homes and the overall effect it can have on supporting a local economy of food producers who can really use the support. The excitement level **generated** by this diet has not started to **peak** by any means. In March, James MacKinnon and Alisa Smith published a book on their year-long experience called, appropriately enough, *The 100-Mile Diet: A Year of Local Eating*. It now sits at number twenty-five on the bestseller list at Amazon.ca, an **impressive** ranking considering how many books are released in Canada each week. The 100-mile diet was a nice, round figure Smith and MacKinnon thought would work as a title, with apologies to Canada's metric system. Somehow, the "160-kilometre diet" doesn't flow as well.

But next week, I'm going to take you to a place where people might think that foods coming from more than five miles away would be a stretch.

LISTENING 3: Food Security

OSCAR: Stella, what do you know about *food security*?

STELLA: Ugh, I hate that term. It sounds like the war on terror. It sounds like something to get people scared.

OSCAR: Maybe, but it's the topic of the debate we're going to have next week.

STELLA: A debate? I missed that. When did the teacher talk about a debate?

OSCAR: It must have been the day you were at the dentist.

STELLA: Mm ... Okay, tell me all the details about the debate. Let's start with the proposition.

OSCAR: Sure. The proposition in a debate is the statement put forth that one team argues *for* and one team argues *against*.

STELLA: And are we for or against?

OSCAR: We won't know until we get there, unfortunately. We might be on the affirmative—agreeing with the proposition—or on the negative—disagreeing with the proposition—but the teacher wants us to prepare for both sides of the debate. In other words, we have to be prepared to argue both for and against the proposition.

STELLA: I guess that's not a big problem. When you prepare for a debate, you should always look at the other point of view.

OSCAR: I agree. That way, you can answer the other side's arguments. You have to know everything about your topic but also anticipate what the other side will say and be prepared to respond to it.

STELLA: So, what's the proposition?

OSCAR: Uh, I have it right here. It's, uh, yeah, it says, "Resolved that food security is essential to world peace."

STELLA: Mm ... interesting.

OSCAR: Interesting *good* or interesting *bad*?

STELLA: It's good and bad because it really leaves it up to us to define what is meant by *essential* and what is meant by *world peace*.

OSCAR: Oh, I see ... uh, no, actually, I don't see. Give me a hint.

STELLA: "Food security is essential to world peace." Let's say we agree with that—that we are taking the affirmative side of the proposition.

OSCAR: Okay, we're for it. So our first job is to define food security and what is essential?

STELLA: That's right. I see you have some printouts and photocopies. What have you found so far?

OSCAR: Quite a bit, actually. For people to have food security, they need three things: *food availability, food access* and *food use*.

STELLA: Okay, can you break them down for me? What does each one mean?

OSCAR: The first one, food availability, means that there is enough food available—and consistently available. Basically, it means people can get food throughout the year without too much difficulty. If you think about someone who lives in the far north, you can imagine that they might be able to grow food during a short summer, but winter might be pretty grim.

STELLA: Right. What about food access? It sounds like the same thing. What's different about that?

OSCAR: Ah, food access means people have the *resources* to obtain appropriate foods for a healthy diet.

STELLA: Resources? Okay, so this is partly about having skills to grow food—

OSCAR: —or collect it, like people who fish or people who gather **regional** foods like seaweed on the beach or

mushrooms, berries and roots in the **midst** of the forest. Or maybe hunt animals in the wild.

STELLA: Right. But they have to be healthy foods that form part of a complete diet. I wouldn't want to try to get all my **calories** by eating only mushrooms 365 days a year.

OSCAR: That's right. And after food availability and food access, there's the third challenge: *food use*. This means that people use the food appropriately based on a good knowledge of nutrition and health. It's important that people know about water and basic sanitation, particularly where there is a lot of **pollution**. For example, in many countries, when they kill an animal, they will use every part of it for food ... they aren't as fussy as we are about what is and isn't edible.

STELLA: Ah, like chicken feet in Chinese restaurants. They don't waste anything.

OSCAR: Not only that, but, like chicken feet, these types of foods sometimes become delicacies. In the late 1800s, prisoners in the eastern United States complained if they were served lobster more than a few times a week; it was a cheap food then, but we **savour** it as a delicacy now.

STELLA: Good work, Oscar. I guess from here we can point out how many people around the world don't have food availability, food access and proper, definite ideas about food use. So that would be one of our arguments?

OSCAR: Mm ... sort of. Let's read that proposition again: "Resolved that food security is essential to world peace." The statement is referring to world peace, so we actually need to point out what a breakdown in food security would mean for world peace to be threatened.

STELLA: We can start with these problems now, but we need to talk about how these could get worse.

OSCAR: Okay. I've got some more information that covers that.

STELLA: Excellent! Let me have it.

OSCAR: There are already some strong arguments around the issues. I've found three. The first one is really interesting. It is that there *is* enough food in the world; the *real* problem is distribution—getting the food to the people who need it.

STELLA: Okay. I can see that on a couple of levels. If we're talking about fresh food, then even in Canada it's hard to get it to some rural communities if it has to be driven in trucks for hundreds of miles over bad roads. Do you know that if you shake whipping cream enough, it will turn into butter? I had friends living in the interior of British Columbia, and they said that by the time they got their delivery, the whipping cream had often turned to butter. Of course, that kind of trip isn't good for fresh vegetables or **livestock** either.

OSCAR: Yeah, and I guess that would make the cost of the food much higher. It's the cost of transportation, particularly when trucks aren't available.

STELLA: And, in some poorer countries, if the cost of international transportation is too high, that means they can't afford imported foods or even foods that have to be shipped a few hundred miles. In terms of world peace, I guess the argument is that people will fight, either to get **accessible** supply routes to food or to move to countries where there is food. What's the second issue?

OSCAR: The second issue is whether or not future food needs can be met by current levels of production. That is, do we have the necessary **fertile** land to produce enough food as the world's population grows?

STELLA: That's an interesting question. The population is definitely increasing. Even with wars and epidemics, it's always increasing.

OSCAR: We need to find out by how much the population is going to grow. We might try to predict how many more people there will be in twenty years' time and how that might affect the degree to which people might fight to control food production.

STELLA: Right. Having a few figures would be helpful, and I'm sure other people have done this research. We also need to have information on production: how much production is right now and how much it might increase in coming years.

OSCAR: It's tough to know. A lot of people get fish from fish farms now. That certainly wasn't so popular a hundred years ago. Maybe we'll be getting food in new ways.

STELLA: And maybe we'll be growing new high-**protein** foods that are cheap and nutritious. Mm, let's hope so. What's the third issue?

OSCAR: Okay, the third issue is all about globalization, you know, international trade. It doesn't make sense for farmers or fishermen to sell food to their neighbours if someone from a rich country in Europe or North America is willing to buy it for a lot more money, especially in lean years.

STELLA: I can see that. There's also the issue of foreign countries buying up large parts of Africa—thousands of square miles—to grow food for their own use. No one within Africa has any right to it.

OSCAR: Ah, well that doesn't seem right. And I suppose it also seems like a reason two countries might go to war ... one not wanting to supply food to another if they think they might need it for themselves.

STELLA: And in the case of a famine, if there was not enough food and lots of people were starving, it could lead to a war. Anyway, let's go back to the proposition. Remind me again?

OSCAR: "Resolved that food security is essential to world peace."

STELLA: Okay, we can start with that and say, "Food security challenges affect everyone, and in the absence of food security, individuals and nations could resort to fighting. For people to have food security, they need three things: food availability, food access and food use."

OSCAR: Okay, but so far, we're really just giving a definition. We need to add our three points, but let's keep them short. The first issue is distribution, the second issue is that food production can't keep up with demand, and the third issue is that globalization will make food more expensive.

STELLA: I think these are all easy to argue. And that's a problem.

OSCAR: Ah, do you mean the problem is that we need to argue *both* sides of the proposition?

STELLA: Exactly. So we have to find ways to say the opposite. We need to do that so we can also predict what the other side will say and then structure it with persuasive language.

OSCAR: By persuasive language I guess you mean that to persuade other people, we need to be *logical*. Our arguments need to make sense and the different ideas we put forward need to relate to each other in a convincing way.

STELLA: Yes, and our arguments also need to be *factual*. If we make an error in numbers, for example, our opponent might demolish our entire argument, and of course, we will feel foolish and lose the debate.

OSCAR: I agree, but I also think that our arguments should have some *emotional appeal*. You know the expression "A picture is worth a thousand words"? In a debate, an emotional argument doesn't replace facts, but it can help. *Logical, factual* and *emotional*. I think I have an idea that illustrates all three. You like tea, don't you?

STELLA: Sure.

OSCAR: In the class that you missed, the professor talked about growing tea in India. She started with *logic*. India has a large population and not that much land. It has faced problems growing enough food for its own population for centuries.

STELLA: Okay, so far I understand: too many people, not enough land to grow food. It's a logical example.

OSCAR: Good. Well, she took the India argument further. After the logical example, she offered some *factual* information. If a box of tea costs $3.20, how much does the person who picks the tea get paid?

STELLA: Uh, not sure.

OSCAR: Less than two cents. That's a fact and *factual* evidence is good. But it's not as persuasive as an emotional appeal.

STELLA: I don't know ... getting paid pennies sounds terrible.

OSCAR: But it's not *really* persuasive in an emotional way.

STELLA: So, something emotional is—

OSCAR: —exactly what she told us. A lot of the people who pick tea in India are children. India has fifteen million children working in different types of agriculture across the country.

STELLA: That's awful. And I agree: it's also emotional.

OSCAR: But to make it more personal, we can focus on the case of a single person. A lot of farm workers barely make enough to live. Many are born into debt and have to work to pay it off ... it's like **slavery**. An individual worker may be lucky and work for a particular farm, but most have to walk from their homes to distant fields, sometimes walking an hour or so just to find if there's a tea plantation that needs them that day. Now, imagine that worker is a young child.

STELLA: Mm ... Logical, factual and emotional. You persuaded me. Let's prepare the rest of the debate.

PHOTO CREDITS

NOTES

NOTES

NOTES

NOTES

NOTES

NOTES